KU-019-916

The Autonomy of Modern Scotland

LINDSAY PATERSON

EDINBURGH UNIVERSITY PRESS

HERTFORDSHIRE
LIBRARY SERVICE

No.
H31 300 756 6

Class
941·108

Supplier	Price	Date
BC	£12·95	2\95

© Lindsay Paterson, 1994

Edinburgh University Press Ltd
22 George Square, Edinburgh

Typeset in Linotronic Times
by Speedspools, Edinburgh, and
printed and bound in Great Britain by
The University Press, Cambridge

A CIP record for this book is available
from the British Library

ISBN 0 7486 0520 7 (cased)
ISBN 0 7486 0525 8 (paper)

Contents

Acknowledgements

I am particularly grateful to David McCrone, R. J. Morris and John Paterson for reading a draft of the book, and for making numerous insightful and helpful comments. Other valuable comments on the general ideas or on parts of the draft came from Malcolm Anderson, Alice Brown, John Cairns, Bernard Crick, David Garland, Christopher Harvie, Hamish Henderson, Alexandra Howson, James Kellas, Ian Levitt, Heikki Luostarinen, Neil MacCormick, Graeme Morton, N. T. Phillipson, David Seller, T. C. Smout and Bob Tait. The final version is my own responsibility.

References in the main text have been kept to a minimum, and are mainly confined to providing precise sources for quotations. A bibliographic essay and a bibliography are at the end.

1

Introduction

DOES SCOTLAND EXIST?

Unionist and nationalist rhetoric in the present debate about Scotland's future share an assumption that Scotland has not been independent since 1707, the moment when the last Scottish parliament voted to give up its sovereignty to the new parliament of Great Britain. The United Kingdom is a unitary state, the nationalists and unionists agree. The decisions that really matter are taken in London, even though they may be modified in minor ways before they have an impact on Scotland. For the unionist, this situation is a blessing: it has saved Scotland from internal division and from weakness in a dangerous international world. For the nationalist, it is a curse, subjecting the nation to economic decay, social dislocation and cultural dependency.

This book questions these assumptions. It starts from a more fundamental observation. Alongside the political debates, and sometimes permeating them, is the belief that Scotland is distinctively *ours,* to be defended against encroachments from outside. This sense extends right across the spectrum of politics. To take just one illustration more or less at random, here are some examples from the debate in the United Kingdom parliament about a recent controversial piece of legislation, the 1989 proposal to allow schools to leave the control of local education authorities. We find the leaders of both the Scottish Labour and the Scottish National Parties describing the bill as 'alien' to Scottish traditions. Labour MPs denounce it as 'anglicising', and threatening to 'Scotland's heritage' because it will 'destroy . . . what has been built up painstakingly over the past thirty years'. The leader of the Scottish Liberal Party objects that the English majority in the Westminster parliament know little about 'the long traditions of Scottish education'. And a dissident Conservative MP claims that Scotland has had 'a much more universal system of education than the rest of the UK'.

The obvious question for a student who had learnt that the UK policy process was unitary is why such a diversity of politicians can claim to be defending something that is distinctively Scottish – not just an ancient tradition, but one that has been constructed within the last generation. What would be even more remarkable for that student would be to find the same taken-for-granted assumptions in speeches by ministers of the Conservative government seeking to defend the proposals. The Secretary of State for Scotland invokes the 'traditional type of education in Scotland', based in the local community. And the Scottish Minister of Education can refer to the distinctive 'virtues of Scottish education'.

This kind of rhetoric appears at a moment when Scottish political nationalism is strong. As these quotations illustrate, it now embraces significant sections of the Labour and Liberal Parties, as well as the overtly nationalist Scottish National Party. Like all nationalisms, Scotland's is partly about defence of an existing culture and political tradition. It claims that the essence of the nation is about to be lost: words like 'destruction' and 'anglicisation' are common currency.

IS SCOTLAND DYING?

So the central problem of the book is a paradox: Scotland has, apparently, not existed politically for a very long time, and yet political rhetoric claims that its traditions are under uniquely serious threat. The paradox is made all the stranger by the recurrence of the rhetoric of loss throughout the entire period since 1707, and so the book unavoidably turns to history. This particular tradition started on the day when the Union document was signed, when the Earl of Seafield – a leading supporter of the move – referred to its being 'ane end of ane auld sang' (P. H. Scott, 1979, p. 65). If it did indeed end then, however, his political successors did not notice. In the middle of the eighteenth century we find Alexander Carlyle, Presbyterian minister and leading intellectual of the Enlightenment, claiming that if Scotland did not demand from London the right to organise its own people's militia, then the nation would have become 'a province and a conquered Kingdom' (Sher, 1985, p. 226). From the eighteenth century also, there are the now famous lines on the Union itself, written by Robert Burns in 1792:

> Fareweel to a' our Scottish fame,
> Fareweel our ancient glory!
> Fareweel ev'n to the Scottish name,
> Sae famed in martial story!

Again, though, if Scotland was departing, it took a long time about it, for the same sentiments occurred in the 1820s and 1830s. The novelist Walter Scott, objecting to a London proposal to abolish distinctive Scottish banknotes, wrote that

> I think I see my native country of Scotland, if it is yet to be called by
> a title so discriminative, falling so far as its national, or rather, perhaps,
> I ought to say its *provincial,* interests are concerned, daily into more
> absolute contempt. (M. Ash, 1980, p. 136; Scott's emphasis)

The convoluted syntax from a writer who knew very well how to write
perspicuous prose suggests a degree of confusion about what this thing
was – Scotland – that was disappearing. The confusion was shared by
Scott's opponents – the Whigs who promoted assimilation to England.
Henry Cockburn, for instance, lamented the end of 'the last truly Scotch
age' (Fry, 1987, p. 204).

But it lasted still for many decades yet, providing all manner of politicians
and intellectuals with a language of lament. The poet and nationalist
Edwin Muir wrote in the 1930s that 'Scotland is gradually being emptied
of its population, its spirit, its wealth, industry, art, intellect, and innate
character', and he explicitly associated this with the absence of a parliament
in Edinburgh – 'a handsome, empty capital of the past', notwithstanding
that most of the visible townscape and architecture of Edinburgh dated
from after 1707 (Muir, 1979, pp. 3–4). In the 1920s, a former Labour
Secretary for Scotland complained that the reform of Scottish local and
central government would 'remove from Scotland practically the last vestige
of independent Government and nationhood', again despite that system's
mostly dating only from the nineteenth century; indeed, despite the fact
that it was the inauguration of that system which occasioned the laments
of Scott and Cockburn (Hanham, 1970, p. 63).

Slightly later, the distinguished Tory politician Walter Elliot equated
the nationalising and centralising policies of the 1945 Labour government
with the 'denationalising' of Scotland. Although Tory nationalism of this
sort has declined, we still find it. The novelist Allan Massie, writing in
1984, quoted with approval a comment from Walter Scott: before the
growth of interfering government from the mid-nineteenth century, Scotland was left 'under the guardianship of her own institutions to win her
silent way to national wealth and consequence', a national golden age to
which the new right in 1984 were proposing to return.

At the same time, we have the growth of the oppositional rhetoric
shown in the quotations from the educational debate. A cultural polemicist
of the SNP claimed apocalyptically in 1989 that 'the pressures which now
face Scotland . . . threaten the survival of the national identity' (P. H.
Scott, 1989, p. 16).

The recurrence of this discourse of loss should give us pause, especially
since it usually asserts not loss but the imminent danger of loss if some
particular political programme is not adopted at once. As the historian R.
D. Anderson has observed, commenting on 'the use of the past as myth',
'the one constant [is] that whatever distinguishes Scotland from England

4

at any one time is regarded as traditional, even when the differences are quite recent' (R. D. Anderson, 1992a, p. 67). To be able to assert that something is being lost obviously requires that it be present in the first place. More strictly, it requires that it be felt to be present and, crucially, to have been created by the nation's own independent efforts.

This book is about these independent efforts. In effect, if not in constitutional theory or political rhetoric, Scotland has been autonomous for most of the three centuries since the Union – not a fully independent state, of course, but far more than a mere province. It has been at least as autonomous as other small European nations, for which the reality of politics has always been the negotiation of partial independence amid the rivalry of great powers. The forms of Scottish autonomy have changed as the state and society and the economy have changed, and what one generation might regard as autonomy might be felt by their successors to be dependency; we must be wary of that Whig aberration of judging the past by the standards of the present. Informal constitutional rules are important everywhere, but particularly in the United Kingdom, with its uniquely informal (and therefore impenetrable) constitution.

The process has not been easy, however, because it has depended also on recurrent nationalist protest. Ours is not the first generation to assert the right of Scotland to control its own affairs. Others have done so too – sometimes using the kinds of rhetoric I have been quoting – and have succeeded in securing Scottish autonomy, even though their achievements have not brought a Scottish parliament. The defenders of the constitutional status quo in the 1990s forget this – forget that the world we live in was created out of the tension between national assertion and the constraints of an interdependent world. Most of that assertion has not been secessionist, and so part of the process I will be describing has been the growth of an expectation in Scotland that reasonable requests will be responded to reasonably. Moreover, some of the nationalist assertion has even been for assimilation of Scotland to England – odd though this may sound to our ears today, when we are more used to hearing assimilation denounced as sell-out. What is distinctive about the phase of Scottish history that started in the 1960s is a feeling that the prospects for compromise may have declined – a feeling that merely asking for a parliament within the Union might no longer work, and that more extreme demands might be needed. Along with this has gone a cultural resistance to assimilation, creating a consensus of separatist nationalism right across Scottish intellectual culture, although not, or not yet, in politics.

As well as comparing Scotland with the past, the book also compares it with other places. The rationale for this is put well by R. L. Watts, writing about the Federal Republic of Germany:

Comparative analyses are useful because they give insights into, or draw attention to the significance of, certain features in a particular political system. The ways in which similar institutions operate differently, in which different institutions operate in similar ways, and in which unique institutions or traditions affect the political processes which predominate, can help us to understand a particular federal system more clearly. (Watts, 1991, p. 23)

Autonomy has taken many forms, and can operate in many different ways. A society can be almost wholly independent in one aspect of its existence (education, let us say) yet be almost wholly dependent in another (most usually defence policy). And that independence is perfectly consistent with freely chosen assimilation towards the norms of a larger neighbour.

The conclusion that will emerge from our comparative study of the eighteenth and nineteenth centuries is that Scotland's autonomy was closer to the partial independence of Norway, Finland or Hungary – places which did have parliaments for large parts of that time – than to the dependent condition of the Czech lands or Poland. For the twentieth century, the argument is different: it is that the nature of politics changed so much with the coming of the welfare state that formal independence mattered less, in practice, than control of the sometimes arcane rules by which bureaucracies operate. In this kind of politics, therefore, Scotland with its own branch of the bureaucratic state in the Scottish Office has had a similar degree of autonomy to the component parts of formal federations such as Germany, the USA or Canada.

The comparative examples are restricted to Europe and North America because these are the relevant ones, in the sense that they are societies that are broadly comparable in important ways with Scotland. I do not attempt to examine the situation of places that were colonised by the European powers in the nineteenth centuries, either their experience then or their constrained independence since the mid-twentieth century. I think that an adaptation of my arguments might be applicable, but that must await further study.

The plan of the book is shaped by these two dimensions of comparison – over time, and over space. First, though, in chapter 2 there is a discussion of ideas about the nature of the state and about nationalism. The state for which nationalist theoreticians have often claimed to be fighting is a much more complex thing than they acknowledge. Then chapter 3 traces the development of Scottish history in the eighteenth century, the key themes being the role of Calvinist Presbyterianism, of elite politics coupled with Enlightenment rationalism, and of a growing sense of Britishness. Chapter 4 does the same for the nineteenth century, the time when Scotland adapted its governing structures to capitalist industrialism. The context now was the British Empire, of which the Scots took advantage enthusiastically.

Scotland's own life continued to be governed locally, by a paternalistic ideology rooted in evangelical Christianity. This experience – of local autonomy within a wider multinational state – is not fundamentally different from that of some other small European nations, as is argued in chapter 5.

The key points about Scotland in the twentieth century, in chapter 6, are the growth of the welfare state, and with it a system of managed corporatism. This is true, also, of other places in Europe and North America (chapter 7), where the politics that mattered for the daily experience of the new mass electorates was the control of the allocation of resources within a consensus of social or Christian democracy. Whether we might be at the end of this process is discussed in chapter 8, which places the post-1960s controversy over Scottish self-government in a broad framework of debate about what has been called in the European Union 'the democratic deficit' – the problem of whether politics can indeed ever be permanently reduced to decisions about allocating resources efficiently, leaving untouched a dominant consensus about fundamental ends.

Part of my intention here, therefore, is to question some beliefs about Scotland's history. Thus the book is an intervention in a political debate, informed by an academic approach in the sense that it develops an argument from a theoretical position and cites evidence in support. It is not an academic history, either of Scotland or of the several other places that I use to illuminate the Scottish condition. The places I discuss are chosen as case studies of the circumstances which small nations have faced in trying to exercise autonomy. The book is an essay, and is therefore selective, partly through choice, partly through constraints of time, and partly – I have to admit – because my own linguistic limitations force me to rely on writings or translations in English. I am arguing that this way of looking at things is possible, not that it is the whole truth. Indeed, insofar as truth in politics emerges from the conflict of rival myths and theories, no one contribution could ever lay claim to being final: the claim to final truth is a legacy of the Scottish Enlightenment itself (although so also is the belief in the provisional nature of truth that informs what I write here).

A STORY OF SCOTLAND

So this is a personal position, not a claim for universality. The concerns of the argument, as well as some of the gaps, might be explicable, therefore, by an account of why I wrote it. Like the rest of my post-war generation in the UK, I grew up in a world shaped by the new welfare state. But, in Scotland, that also had an unmistakably Scottish dimension: the world of Dr Finlay, Miss Jean Brodie, Lord Reith, and – eternally – John Knox. This world was also, by the 1960s, imbued with debate about Scottish self-government; indeed, a crucial but easily overlooked feature of Scottish politics today is that anyone born in Scotland in or after the late 1940s will have no adult recollection of a time when self-government was not being taken for granted as a serious option, even if only to be rejected.

But it was not an option that made for serenity of spirit, because the history of the last twenty years of Scottish nationalism has not been one of political achievement. The key formative moment for Scottish politics in the 1980s and 1990s was the failure of the referendum in 1979 to produce an overwhelming vote for the setting up of a devolved Scottish assembly. A majority was achieved, no doubt; but those of us who were ardently active in support of devolution would be deluding ourselves if we forget that we all expected, as recently as 1977, an easy victory.

In a sense, that is the starting point for the questions asked in this book. Why – as the Conservative politician Malcolm Rifkind, a devolution-ist turned unionist, is fond of putting it – did one third of Scottish people vote against, and a further one third not care sufficiently to be bothered to vote at all? There seemed to be a contradiction in the simplistic nationalist response that all these people had been dupes of unionist propaganda: if nationalism is about asserting the rights of the Scottish people, then it should have more faith in the people than that. So, why these divisions?

More generally, as I came to read more about the history of the home-rule movements, in Scotland and elsewhere – first of all notably in the works of James Kellas, T. C. Smout and Tom Nairn – I started to ask why the Scots had accepted the Scottish Office for so long. Why was Labour – with its radical roots – so centralist (as it was in the 1960s and 1970s, and still is to some extent today)? In particular, why did most of the 1920s generation of Clydeside radicals not press for a Scottish parliament when they reached office in the first majority Labour government in 1945? The nationalist reply that they were politically schizophrenic about their Scottishness seemed simplistic and patronising; but so too did the stock socialist response that sensible people discard nationalism when they grow up.

Even among those who campaigned for devolution in the 1970s, there were splits. Some argued for a Scottish assembly on the rational but insipid grounds that the bureaucracy in the Scottish Office needed demo-cratic scrutiny. Others, in complete contrast, argued with inspiring passion but little reason that Scotland was a downtrodden nation that should get off its knees and throw out the English oppressor. What was to be made of these multiple strands?

I then found myself in the early 1980s inhabiting three worlds that seemed barely to connect with each other, but which were all undeniably Scottish. One was the Scottish theatre, where – as throughout Scottish culture at that time – there was a growing sense of Scottishness, tied to a vague internationalism and a millenarian socialism. This was rather more encouraging than the second world, the dejected activities of leftist politi-cians, where the key fact was the almost simultaneous debacle of the referendum and defeat of the Labour government. How did that pessimism fit with the growing optimism of the arts?

My third world was the most puzzling of all, however. This was policy-related academic research and teaching. There, the Scottish dimension was taken for granted in an almost wholly unproblematic way – certainly with none of the passionate angst that was to be found in the theatre. This policy world, in other words, was normal: the Scottish framework was simply there in the background, in almost exactly the same way as were the worlds of colleagues in England or the Netherlands or Australia or the USA or India. Indeed, so unproblematic were the Scottish reference points that they were taken for granted even by colleagues from these other places who had committed their lives to Scotland.

So the questions continued. If Scotland has not had autonomy, how can there be these unquestioned assumptions about a Scottish policy frame-work? If Scotland did indeed die three centuries ago, how could the cultural world be so passionately Scottish in the early 1980s? If the self-government movement had collapsed in 1979, maybe politics was actually irrelevant to culture?

But there was another strand to reflection at this time, which raised questions about what politics is. This was the thinking that is now loosely referred to as 1960s radicalism. From anarchists, feminists, social historians and many others, there was the compelling argument that political history had paid too much attention to 'high politics'. The most radical versions of this asserted that everything is political, most notably the personal relationships that constitute everyday life. If Scotland consists in these relationships, then it was certainly not possible to say that politics was irrelevant.

This 1960s type of debate was, at the time, conducted in a spirit of revolutionary iconoclasm. But as the visions died into the greyness of the 1970s and the triumph of the right in the 1980s, an odd thing happened: that intellectual tradition became associated with an acceptance of the immense complexity of politics and society. If politics really was grounded in everyday experience, then imposed revolutions of the type favoured historically by modernist socialism would not work. The writings of Antonio Gramsci and of Raymond Williams became popular among the Scottish left, as also did various critiques of social-democratic bureaucracy. From these came a feeling that Scottish self-government would change very little unless it started from a change in people's minds and sought to develop a type of democracy that was less paternalistic. And maybe people had failed to show enthusiasm in 1979 for a Scottish assembly because they were afraid of taking responsibility for their own lives.

So this book is my attempt to understand Scotland now, and more generally to understand the kinds of dilemmas which places like Scotland face. These places are other small nations and regions, but also – insofar as the debate is about the nature of democracy in modern society in general – the questions are faced by people in the big nations too.

Whether the understanding which I seek here can give us much of an indication of where Scotland might be going is more open to doubt. In conclusion, though, three things can be said with reasonable certainty. Whatever happens, Scotland's future will continue to be constrained by the outside world. Second, what will emerge in Scotland will be an evolution from the partial independence which Scotland has had, and which is described here. It will not be a revolution, unless the UK state actually collapses from its current economic malaise, and that still seems very unlikely. Neither will it be a mere maintenance of the existing order, however: evolution is quite different from stagnation.

The third unavoidable point is that, whatever happens, it is not predestined. The conclusion from the material which I discuss in this book is that there is scope for human agency except in the most extreme situations of absolute dictatorship. This is, indeed, a common theme uniting the libertarian left of the 1960s, the libertarian right of the 1980s, and the civic movements for democracy that have transformed Eastern and Central Europe in the last five years. If the collapse of the Soviet Union made these changes inevitable, it did not dictate the form they should take, as the evolving processes of negotiation and conflict since then make clear.

So there will continue to be in the Scotland of the late twentieth century a conflict between the safety of managed autonomy and the risky but exciting prospects of participation. We will not achieve utopia, any more than did reformers at each stage in the history of Scotland since the Union, or in the histories of other small nations. But, while pressing for utopia, they did achieve improvements, and did successfully defend their countries' autonomy. Perhaps 'realistic utopianism' is not too bad as an oxymoronic epigram for the stories which this book unfolds.

2

Forms of Autonomy

The overall argument of the book is in two parts, relating broadly to the nineteenth and to the twentieth centuries. This division corresponds to two theories of how the state has its impact on the domestic policies of the territories which it governs; I am concerned with foreign policy only to the extent that it impinges on domestic policy, although that is not an insignificant consideration. The first theory is a characterisation developed by the sociologist Gianfranco Poggi; its central proposition is that the nineteenth century was the era of the legal state, by which is meant a state which was subject to the rule of law, and therefore became an extension of the legal system. It is explained along with an account of sovereignty from the writings of F. H. Hinsley.

The second theory is summed up in the term 'technocracy', or rule by experts. In the emerging welfare states of the first part of the twentieth century, there grew the belief that political disagreements could be superseded by merely technical decisions: scientists, economists, planners and other professionals would allocate resources more fairly and more efficiently than factional politicians. They would thus achieve the central goal of these welfare states, the overcoming of social inequalities by state action. This concept of technocracy is explained here using ideas from Max Weber, Daniel Bell, Stuart Hall and several other writers, as well as some further ideas from Poggi.

The allocation of the two theories to the two centuries is for convenience only. There was rule by experts long before the twentieth century started, and the rule of law remained important after the nineteenth century closed; and, for some purposes, I follow the common practice of allowing the nineteenth century to run from 1789 to 1914, and the twentieth to start in the 1890s. These chronological terms are merely loose designations. The point of the theories is to provide useful organising devices for our thoughts: the legal state and technocracy are 'ideal types', broad abstractions from the empirical variations that are described in later chapters.

The sections of this chapter which follow the outline of the theories deal with the implications of social diversity. Nationalists have not usually had a very subtle conception of the state. But nationalism is inescapable in any attempt to understand how states have commanded legitimacy – that is, have had the authority to induce consent to their rule among their citizens. Indeed, nationalist politics in practice has usually recognised that the reality of the state is highly complex. Whether or not a state is organised as a formal federation is less important than whether the territories it governs are in fact federal – that is, plural and containing multiple partial sovereignties and autonomies. It is because of pluralism that constitutions change: no set of institutions can contain all social tensions for ever.

The particular late-twentieth-century version of these tensions concerns the problems of the welfare state. As the long economic expansion of the period after 1945 came to an end in the 1970s, conflict over resources became more acute. It no longer seemed possible to replace politics with technical decisions. The form of the welfare state was therefore questioned from both the left and the right of politics: experts no longer had the prestige they had acquired in the middle of the twentieth century, and so the legitimacy of the bureaucratic welfare state was undermined.

These issues – all of which touch on the Scottish experience – prepare the ground for a brief conclusion about the Scottish experience of the state in the period between the Union and the middle of the twentieth century, anticipating the main themes that are developed in more detail in chapters 3, 4 and 6.

THE LEGAL STATE AND SOVEREIGNTY

Poggi argues that there were six characteristics of the liberal state as it emerged between the Peace of Westphalia in 1648 and the mid-nineteenth century. It is, first, the only source of authority in the territory it governs. Second, that territory is unified. Third, there is a single currency, and, fourth, a unified fiscal system. There is, fifth, a single official language. And, sixth and most important, there is a unified legal system.

Being a theory – an ideal type – Poggi's account is a better characterisation of aspirations than of realities, and this is as true of the United Kingdom as of other states. Unity of authority and territory were achieved early on: indeed, that can be argued to have been the main concern of the English when they were negotiating for union in 1707, because their worry was to avoid Scotland's ever again becoming so disaffected that it could be a bridgehead for French invasion (chapter 3). But fiscal unity was never fully realised even in the nineteenth century, despite ardent attempts by business in Scotland to achieve a genuinely common market in the UK (see the discussion of commercial law in chapter 4). A single language was largely not in doubt – and, indeed, the Scottish literati of the eighteenth-century Enlightenment were to the fore in removing Scottish peculiarities (chapter 3). But they largely failed, and by the second half of the nineteenth century there was a vigorous revival of vernacular Scots culture (chapter 4).

Above all, however, there was not a unified legal system. The autonomy of Scots law was guaranteed by the Union (chapters 3 and 4). Scotland, moreover, was not as unique in this respect as is sometimes claimed, as we will see in chapter 5: the UK was not the only multinational state to contain more than one legal system.

So, if Poggi is correct about the importance of law, then Scotland must be regarded as having part of a 'state', because the society was regulated by the independent legal system. Professional legal knowledge became increasingly important for administrative authority as the nineteenth century progressed: we will see in chapters 3 and 4 that the legally qualified sheriff was the key person in Scottish government at that time, both locally and nationally. Society was allowed to develop in its own way: rulers governed public law, but social development depended on the private realm, and that was not interfered with in Scotland. The same is true in some other places (such as Finland), and nationalist rebellions were provoked in yet others when private law was threatened (for example Bohemia).

These legal reasons provide an explanation of why Scottish civil society remained distinct after the Union, and continued to develop in distinct ways. By civil society we usually mean nowadays those institutions that lie between the citizen and the state, and that is the meaning employed throughout this book. The concept which was developed by the Scottish social thinker Adam Ferguson in the eighteenth century was somewhat different, but is still relevant to this discussion. Ferguson believed that civil society – by which he meant society that was not still in a 'state of nature' – induced a loss of 'public spirit' because it transferred responsibility to state administration. This in turn threatened the very civilisation that had given rise to it, because it caused what we would now call apathy in the citizens. His resolution of the dilemma was to insist on the creation of institutions by citizens themselves – for example, the law courts (including lay juries) and citizens' militias. As we will see in chapter 3, these particular examples provoked campaigns by Scots to resist the encroachments of the central state in the eighteenth century.

Although the theory of civil society has changed – losing the normative judgments embodied in the term 'civilisation' – it still recognisably has its origins in these concerns of the Scottish Enlightenment. And the Enlightenment was of great practical political importance, permeating the thinking of influential Scots at that time. The autonomous local government, church and education system, the flourishing learned culture, and even the managed politics of Westminster were posited on the defence of a Scottish society that was insistent on not changing unless it chose to do so.

Thus, at the time when the liberal state was taking its shape in the UK, Scotland was defending and developing its distinct institutions. Some writers (Nairn for example) have argued that this remained permissible in the nineteenth century because the UK remained the only European state whose character had not been shaped by recent revolution. It could, therefore, tolerate significant power in the hands of 'estates' – in Scotland, local government, quasi-governmental national boards to supervise social policy, churches still with a significant social role, and the whole regulated by the independent legal system. Moreover, the Scots rightly prided themselves on having built this state, as well as having contributed to building the British Empire that governed foreign relations. The United Kingdom state was tolerated by its citizens for certain purposes of statecraft – mainly securing internal and external order – but was not an entity that would shape society.

The UK may have been peculiar in the extent of its pre-revolutionary inheritance, but, again, it was not unique: not-dissimilar structures of semi-independence based on civil society can be found elsewhere in Europe, as we will see in chapter 5. Everywhere in Western Europe, at least, the state developed on the basis of a division of powers between the public and private realms. The theory was that 'individuals entered into a "social contract" with the state in exchange for the defence of their rights and liberties' (Hall, 1984, p. 9); the liberties included (though mainly only for middle-class men) freedom of speech and of assembly, freedom of contract, and internal peace. Vajda argues that 'the really important feature of west European development from the Middle Ages onwards is the gradual separation of state and society' (1988, p. 341), which contrasts with the east European practice of congruence between state and society. Central Europe was always in tension between these two models, a point that is relevant to our discussion of places such as Bohemia in chapter 5. In particular, the main goal of liberal nationalists throughout Europe was to establish a polity which was based on that western model. Not only, they believed, would this allow trade and political liberty to flourish; it would also be the best guarantee of the development of the national culture, because that was conceived of as private. In Scotland, as we will see in chapters 3 and 4, there was no such tension, and cultural nationalism did not have to have a political programme at all.

We could stop here with the nineteenth-century theory; but it is worth pursuing the argument further, by asking whether Scotland had sovereignty. This will allow us also to understand why the UK state retained legitimacy in Scotland. Sovereignty is a notoriously awkward concept, and some political theorists have argued cogently that it should be dispensed with completely. They do have a point: what matters is the power to take decisions. Nevertheless, I do think that an analysis of mere power is not enough, because underlying power are a set of a normative symbols, expressing a society's beliefs about its own potential for power: 'at the political centre of any complexly organised society . . . there is both a governing elite and a set of symbolic forms expressing the fact that it is in truth governing' (Geertz, 1983, p. 124). The point for us is that Scotland never stopped seeing itself as a partner in union, having voluntarily surrendered some – but not all – sovereignty in exchange for the guarantees of the liberal freedoms we have been discussing.

Hinsley describes sovereignty as being not a fact but a concept. It arose in the struggles between society and the absolute state between the fifteenth and the seventeenth centuries, and was given its first recognisably modern expression by the English Tudors. They developed the idea of shared sovereignty between the monarch and the realm, and accepted that the king in parliament was superior to the king, parliament being the embodiment of independent society.

Over the following two centuries, there remained a conflict between two concepts of sovereignty – popular and state. The pole that gave it all to the state is represented by the theories of Hobbes, that which placed it wholly with the people by those of Rousseau. According to Hinsley, the eventual resolution which satisfied the nineteenth century came from Kant, in the idea of the 'notional state' (Hinsley, 1966, p. 156): sovereignty did not lie with the actual state (that is, the government of the day), but with a symbolic representation of the continuity of the state – for example, a constitution, or an abstract concept of 'the people' (not the real people). In practice, moreover, it was the law which came to embody the notional state.

There is an obvious link between this theory of sovereignty as the rule of law and Poggi's ideas of the legal state. The important conclusion for our discussion about Scotland is, again, that the Scottishness of the legal system embodied this sovereignty as Scottish. The Scottish High Courts were a symbolic centre of the type defined by Geertz; so also, in the ecclesiastical realm, were the governing bodies of the Presbyterian churches. Conflicts over these symbols occurred throughout the eighteenth and nineteenth centuries, as we will see in chapters 3 and 4, but these disputes took the importance of the symbols for granted: what was at issue was not whether Scotland did have the sovereignty they embodied, but rather over the political implications of that.

The power that these institutions exercised was not absolute, of course; but it was, at least, a sort of reserve sovereignty, sanctioning the ultimate right to secede. It was also a power in practice over those aspects of civil society that were felt to be essentially Scottish – education or Calvinist morality, for example. It was precisely the possession of sovereignty that allowed Scotland to believe that it was recurrently negotiating autonomy – choosing what powers to surrender in order to be more secure in the exercise of others. In a world where other small nations were frequently at the mercy of large empires, it is not surprising that Scottish nationalists should feel that this bargain was a good one, and – crucially – one in which Scotland continued to have some genuinely free choice.

That was also why the UK state retained legitimacy. Beetham (1991) argues that legitimacy has three aspects. It is, first of all, a matter of legal rules: what framework of law do people obey? The separate Scottish legal system legitimated the UK state in Scotland by making that state Scottish in its daily contact with Scottish citizens. Second, there must be frequent acts of consent to the rule of the state. These acts can be passive: there were very few challenges to the Union until the twentieth century, although there was questioning of its details. But, more positively, in the nineteenth century there were frequent celebrations of the achievements of Britain – its manufacturing, trade, liberties and empire. Third, Beetham argues that the rule of a legitimate state has to be justifiable in terms of the beliefs of a society. The shared Protestant religion of the British nations provided the justification in Scotland until well into the twentieth century. But so also did the shared belief in free trade: the legitimacy came partly from the essentially utilitarian idea that a system of government was justifiable if it helped to achieve the purposes which a society had set itself.

THE TECHNOCRATIC STATE

We still live in the world that was created by these nineteenth-century conflicts, and so the analysis of the legal state, sovereignty and legitimacy is still relevant to the twentieth century. But the nature of the state changed as the extent of its activity grew. In response to the emergence of mass democracy – the new enfranchisement of working-class men and all women – the state was expected to provide for the material well-being of most of the population it governed; out of this grew what we now know as the welfare state. To administer this efficiently, the bureaucracy had to become professional. It is this professional bureaucracy that is referred to here as technocracy – rule by experts, among whom are included not only scientists and technicians, but also economists, planners, doctors, educationalists, social workers and many others.

Thus authority became rational as well as legal: the purpose of bureaucratic activity was to develop the best means to agreed ends. As a contemporary commentator put it in a hymn to the new god, statistics, 'with the accumulation of sufficient data and the application of the calculus of probabilities, the state could be run by social mathematics – without debates' (quoted by Kumar, 1978, p. 26). Or, in the words of Daniel Bell writing in 1967, 'if the dominant figures of the past 100 years have been the entrepreneur, the businessman, and the industrial executive, the "new men" are the scientists, the mathematicians, the economists, and the engineers of the new computer technology' (Mosher, 1986, p. 74).

In this task, bureaucracy sought to minimise the power of parliament, especially by cooperating directly with interest groups and arbitrating between their competing claims. Local government was subject to much stricter central control than in the nineteenth century. There was more secrecy, as the bureaucracy arrogated to itself the sole rights to take decisions. The bureaucracy became self-perpetuating, not elective, even as it also became rigorously meritocratic.

So pervasive did bureaucracy become that bureaucratic rationality grew to be an end in itself, although originally thought of as a means: for example, the bureaucratic organisation of society for the more efficient production of goods – a means – created a consumer mentality; or the meritocratic organisation of education as a means to selecting the most academically able students created an education system that was dominated by examinations to a far greater extent than hitherto. Thus even the content of legislation was set by the technical experts in the civil service, in consultation with interest groups. What is more, argues Marquand, the legitimacy of a law depended not on its receiving a majority in parliament, but on an acceptance by all the social groups which it affected that their pressure group had been consulted. The legitimacy also came from the fundamental belief in science and planning: bureaucracies were believed to be the pre-eminent agencies by which these technical specialisms could be brought to bear on social problems. Politics, it was felt, was amateurish, and liable to obstruct good government by introducing unnecessary conflict. The bureaucrats controlled the pressure groups and the politicians. This was helped by the recruiting of civil servants – especially those in technical branches such as statistics or economics or criminology – from the same professional sources as the pressure groups themselves used.

But, if the pressure groups were partly controlled by the state, they also were genuinely autonomous, at least in liberal societies. Middlemas describes the interest groups as 'estates of the realm', engaging in 'multiple bargaining processes at all levels' (1979, p. 371). Corporatism, says Crouch, really has been about negotiation in liberal democracy, in contrast to the hierarchical control exercised by fascist or communist regimes. This is what T. Johnson called the 'mediative control' by professionals of their practices – not the full collegial control as in the nineteenth century, but a control exercised through their close association with state power.

For most of the states with which we will be concerned in chapters 6 and 7, this world of bureaucratic control emerged from the welfare democracy that came to dominate politics by the middle of the twentieth century. This was often inaugurated by social democratic or Christian democratic parties, but it was also true of communism, as we will see in the case of Poland, and of fascism in the 1930s. The earliest exponent of what we would now call the welfare state was Bismarck in late-nineteenth-century Germany. There were differences of emphasis among the versions of the welfare state – different balances of responsibility for individuals, collectivities and the state. But these were differences of degree, not of kind. All the versions were the inheritors of Saint-Simon's utopian vision of society's 'moving from the governing of men to the administration of things' (Kumar, 1978, p. 35). Even Gramsci – nowadays thought of as an apostle of a liberal communism – believed that the end of the state would be the dawn of the merely regulated society. It was possible for radical politicians to think in this way because they envisaged a social consensus over the fundamental goals of society: for example, complete agreement that the state should provide support for the weak, or should regulate the economy to maintain full employment, or should provide universal education. The decisions that were needed were, therefore, merely technical: how best to allocate resources to further these purposes.

As the quotations from Saint-Simon and others illustrate, moreover, the origins of the tehnocratic idea lie far back in the nineteenth century, and even in the Enlightenment. It was not difficult for rule by lawyers and doctors to become rule by civil servants and medical scientists. Technocracy was not a radical break, so much as a tendency which grew to reach its apogee in the mid-twentieth century.

All of this has application to Scotland, as is argued in detail in chapter 6. The bureaucracy was Scottish, through the Scottish Office, which has grown to embrace most domestic policy. The pressure groups were Scottish, also increasingly so. The middle-class professions were at least as Scottish as working-class ones: accountancy, medicine, education, law enforcement, local-government administration and many others had professional bodies that were either wholly Scottish or else had an autonomous Scottish component. All of this was like a system of estates – just as Middlemas says, and inheriting the estates of the nineteenth century. Scotland, indeed, came to be thought of as one large pressure group itself – an estate of the British realm – using its own bureaucracy to bargain for resources with London.

Moreover, the political origins of this new Scottish state were as firmly in social and Christian democracy as anywhere in Europe, the key figures being various centrist Labour and Tory Secretaries of State. The Scots were generally happy with what emerged because it delivered the material goods: they had exchanged any notion of a participatory self-government for a vast increase in what T. H. Marshall (1950) called social citizenship, but defined in emphatically Scottish terms. That is how the UK state retained legitimacy. In the words of the historian Christopher Harvie, 'from its foundation in 1885, [the Scottish Office] acted as a handbrake on the engine of [Westminster] parliamentary sovereignty, securing to successive groups of Scots a range of welfare rather than participatory rights' (Harvie, 1992, p. 250). There was nothing perverted or dependent about this: it was, as we will see in chapter 7, what happened to the welfare state throughout Europe and North America.

NATIONALISM

These theories of the state and of sovereignty can readily accommodate an important role for nationalism in shaping the modern world. For example, the role of the nineteenth-century middle class in agitating for liberal democracy and the rule of law became, in most Central European areas, inseparable from their claims for national freedom: the decrepit Austria-Hungary and the despotic Russian Empire would not tolerate liberalism, and therefore constitutional democracy for the Czech lands or for Poland had to be achieved by nationalist routes. The legal state which Poggi describes was, then, a universal aspiration. Similarly, the expressive role of sovereignty has an obvious potential for explaining why nationalist theory has placed so much emphasis on it.

For the twentieth century, too, nationalism has been crucial, often summed up in the phrase 'welfare-state nationalism'. In practice, the welfare state was a national project: the use of the state to extend welfare created a conception of the national interest which embraced the mass of the population for the first time. In some places – the Soviet Union notably – the building of the welfare state was inseparable from the process of building the state itself, and therefore helped to forge a new patriotism.

But we would miss important realities about what nationalist politicians did if we paid too much attention to the theories which nationalists have generated. These accounts pay insufficient attention to the complexities of political mobilisation and constitutional settlements. They fail to see that sovereignty, in practice, has been divided and partial, and that nationalist politicians have frequently settled for less than full independence, whatever their rhetorical claims might be.

In practice, claims for sovereignty did not require a separate state: 'the idea that nations can be free only if they possess their own sovereign state is neither necessary nor universal' (A. D. Smith, 1991, p. 74). Indeed, in the early nineteenth century, nationalist claims did not even require a political programme. If – as in Scotland – the essence of the nation resided in popular culture, which over and over again was interpreted as the family, then, in a world where states kept out of private matters, cultural nationalists could prefer to develop the culture autonomously by their own efforts. For example, Finnish nationalists in the nineteenth century showed strong patriotism for the Russian state, even while developing an independent Finnish culture. As we will see in chapter 5, Finnish nationalism became separatist only when the Russian empire became more centralist at the very end of the century. In Scotland we find likewise that, because cultural activity did not require political activity, and because specific political goals could be realised through the self-governing civil society, there was no serious agitation for a Scottish parliament until the 1890s.

Even nationalisms which were forced to demand a parliament because of the intransigence of the local great power came to outright separatism late on. The mainstream Irish nationalism until after the end of the nineteenth century was for self-government within the British Empire. The National Liberal party which dominated Czech politics in the second half of the nineteenth century advocated a federal Austria-Hungary, and happily worked within the imperial parliament for incremental expansion of Czech rights. Catalan nationalists paid almost as little attention as Scotland to securing a parliament: they settled for an influential role in the Spanish state, along with 'diplomacy, cunning, patience, manoeuvring, and appeasement' (Giner, 1980, p. 2).

There was also a strong strand of unifying nationalism in the nineteenth century, most notably in Germany and Italy, which it created as states. Scandinavian unification did not achieve state unity, but laid the basis for cultural and political cooperation: as we will see in chapters 5 and 7, this eventually yielded the most cohesive group of nominally independent states in Europe, despite the secession of Norway from Sweden in 1905.

None of this is to deny the symbolic importance of a goal of national independence for creating the nation: the 'imagined community', in Benedict Anderson's felicitous phrase, could cohere more readily around such a seemingly definite goal than around the more messy details of compromise. But there were other ways of achieving this coherence, as the case of Scotland illustrates. There were frequent assertions of Scotland's national integrity and ancient history; they were used to resist what were seen as English indifference (or, very rarely, deliberate encroachments). But they did not require any claim for independence. They were usually, in fact, firmly unionist: the argument was that, unless Scotland asserted its national rights, then the Union would cease to be a true Union and would become instead a subordination of Scotland to England. Nationalism also retained its assimilationist aspect from the eighteenth century, which led nationalists to advocate that Scottish institutions should be moved close to those of England (chapters 3 and 4). In this sense, these Scottish nationalists were pursuing a similar programme to their counterparts in, say, Norway: all of them would have argued that the nation could be truly itself only if it participated voluntarily in the political and commercial opportunities offered by a larger Union. The difference from Norway was that Scotland was already in that Union, and so was insisting on the voluntariness; Norway, in what was felt to be a dependent Union with Sweden, had to claim its independence in order to embrace a wider Scandinavian Union freely.

A similarly complex story is true of the welfare-state nationalism of the twentieth century. The state's Scottish image in Scotland created a sense of the Scottish national interest as potentially distinct from the British one, and therefore laid the basis for more separatist nationalism after the

1960s. Whatever may have happened since 1945, however, we must not forget that the welfare state was seen by many in Scotland – especially on the political left – as an outcome of Scottish campaigning, in other words as a Scottish national project.

FEDERAL SOCIETIES

Thus, if we still live in the world created by nineteenth-century nationalism, it is much more complex than a simple theory of homogeneous national states would imply. This complexity is because society is intrinsically federal, with multiple sources of power and multiple claims for rights. Thus, as Livingston argues, 'the essential nature of federalism is to be sought for, not in the shadings of legal and constitutional terminology, but in the forces – economic, social, political, cultural – that have made the outward forms of federalism necessary' (1952, p. 83). Federalism is a matter of practice not of theory: 'whether a constitutional structure may properly be called federal depends not so much on the arrangement of the institutions within it as it does on the manner in which these institutions are employed' (p.84).

Moreover, these outward constitutional forms are neither necessary nor sufficient for the true operation of federalism. '[A] society may possess institutions that are federal in appearance but it may operate them as though they were something else' (p. 84); we will see in chapter 7 that this accurately describes aspects of Germany after 1945. And 'what is more likely, [a society] may possess a unitary set of institutions and employ them as though they were federal in nature' (p. 84); to exemplify this, he cites the United Kingdom, 'whose constitution is most often cited as being typically unitary, [even though there are] many elements of British public life [that] are witness to the vitality of the federal principle' (p. 92).

Livingston was not the only writer to express such views on the type of state that emerged in the middle of the twentieth century. Similar accounts are given by Vile in his analysis of the structure of federalism in the USA, by Smiley's discussion of Canada, by Bulpitt writing about the UK, and by Duchacek in his exploration of the territorial dimension of politics in general. Faced with an autonomous civil society, no democratic state can do other than acknowledge that autonomy.

PROBLEMS OF TECHNOCRACY

Change takes place in the territorial aspects of constitutional arrangements precisely because of the federal nature of society and the nationalist and analogous pressures which this generates. No settlement can last for ever, because none can be satisfactorily attuned to all the conflicting territorial interests that are governed by a state, or by a group of states. The constitutional debate in Scotland since the 1960s is merely Scotland's most recent instance of this. It is not the nation waking up after about 300 years of abject slumber; it is the latest phase in a recurrent process of national mobilisation to readjust the bargain that emerged from the previous phase.

Underlying this latest stage, moreover, are some very general problems with twentieth-century technocracy, which in some respects have been present from the beginning. Poggi concludes his book on the state by asking what is wrong with a system of government that delivers material welfare efficiently and fairly (within its borders). Could it be true, he asks, that politics ought to be superseded by rule by experts? He rejects this conclusion on the grounds that democracy is morally superior to technocracy, however efficient that may be:

> Liberalism and democracy have the advantage over socialism of directly addressing some key problems arising from the necessity of rule, instead of down-grading such problems to the status of technical matters to be settled unproblematically after a resolution in the control over the means of production. (Poggi, 1978, p. 148)

Poggi forgets the tradition of libertarian socialism, but his main point is clear: it is an assertion of participatory rights over welfare rights. Part of the controversy in Scotland about self-government is whether greater participation has to be at the expense of maintaining the level of welfare which Scotland has enjoyed as part of what is still one of the materially richest states in the world.

The question is being asked, moreover, not really because of any rational critique of technocracy by intellectuals, but because of popular protest. The protest takes two forms, and in this respect Scotland is following a common European pattern. The one is a protest in the terms that the welfare state has claimed for its own – that the system is not, any longer, delivering the material goods that it once did. The other is a claim for participation, a defiance of technocratic rule by experts. But these two are closely linked: people want to participate – as we will see in chapter 8 – precisely because they feel that the system is not delivering the material welfare which they want first of all.

The problem for technocracy is that, in a world of unavoidably finite resources, there are always questions about ends, not only about means: in Bell's question, 'when [people] have different valuations, how does one choose? For this the technocratic view has no answer' (Bell, 1976, p. 358). There is therefore a crucial role for politics: 'no matter how technical the social processes may be, the crucial turning points in a society occur in a political form' (p. 360), the most recently relevant of which is the founding of the welfare state itself. We may think of the problems of providing a mass education system, for instance, as technical or professional; but we forget that we have such a system in Europe because of utopian campaigning by socialists and other radicals in the first few decades of the twentieth century. In a sense, it is a mark of the ultimate political success of these campaigners that the things they demanded are now so taken for granted that the problems of education have been redefined as technical – as means, not ends.

Weber predicted the problems of rule by technical experts right at the beginning of the process. Political conflict is inevitable because social conflict is too; the question is then one of political leadership sufficiently charismatic to control the overweening presumptions of the bureaucrats. Weber saw a parliament as a necessary forum for the emergence of such leadership, although he did not believe that charisma was bound to be found even there. Without a parliament, apathy was a recurrent problem, because – in an echo of Adam Ferguson's worries about the debilitating effect of all government – Weber believed that most people would be reconciled to bureaucracy if their material needs were met.

This critique can be found from writers across the political spectrum. The libertarian right's indictment of bureaucracy is perhaps most familiar, because it was popularised by Margaret Thatcher and Ronald Reagan. Their mentor, F. A. Hayek, argued that

> it is not the powers which democratic assemblies can effectively wield but the powers which they hand over to the administrators charged with the achievement of political goals that constitute the danger to individual freedom today. Having agreed that the majority should prescribe rules which we will obey in pursuit of our individual aims, we find ourselves more and more subjected to the orders and the arbitrary will of its agents. (Hayek, 1960, p. 116)

The same kind of critique came from the libertarian left, in the 1960s and later. After the Conservative party came to power in the UK in 1979, Sheila Rowbotham, Stuart Hall and others on the left argued that part of Margaret Thatcher's ideological success had been based on people's genuine and well-founded suspicions of the power of experts in the bureaucracy. They argued, again following Weber and Ferguson, that what could be readily characterised as the 'nanny state' sapped people's instincts to rebel.

Whatever the conclusions of the moral analysis may be, the important question for us is whether there are signs that the welfare state is actually becoming unstable. Bialar, for example, says that, so long as the state is considered legitimate by elite groups in a society, then almost no amount of popular disaffection will make any difference. He was writing well before the collapse of communism in Eastern and Central Europe under popular pressure, but his point may be more relevant to the far less oppressive states of the West.

In fact, a conclusion that we can draw from the histories surveyed in chapters 3 to 7 is that collapse or reform does indeed mostly require that elites want it to happen, but that also the elites themselves are often responding to popular pressure. The European professional classes, for example, did not invent the welfare state out of thin air: they were responding to real radical or even revolutionary protests and real voting for socialist or communist parties. Political pluralism has never been based on groups with equal power: the weaker groups know this through experience, and gain leverage by forming alliances with the more powerful to achieve social or constitutional change. In a pluralist society, moreover, the state itself becomes a site of conflict. This makes change easier to achieve than in totalitarian states, which lack that 'constantly critical scrutiny of social attitudes' (Vajda, 1988, p. 335). Insofar as the middle class is in any case the main consumer of critical debates (as of all cultural forms), the moral critique may be more effective than might at first appear.

This analysis of the problems of technocracy gives us a way of interpreting the recent self-government movement in Scotland without having to claim that it proceeds solely from unique causes: it is, at some level of generality, part of a widespread political phenomenon in Europe and North America, which only in some places is articulated as a claim for national self-government. The suspicion of bureaucracy is seen in the argument that a Scottish parliament could make the Scottish Office responsive to popular needs, and could make it conduct its business in a more open and pluralistic way. The need for political leadership – echoing Weber – is expressed as the insistence that only an indigenous parliament could achieve that: it is not enough to have committees of the Westminster parliament overseeing the bureaucracy, far less to have unenforceable documents called a citizen's charter. And the importance of elite groups is found in the key role played by the Scottish middle class, shifting from being the main beneficiaries of the welfare state to being self-conscious defenders of it against what was seen as Thatcher's attacks, to being now the leaders of a cultural nationalism, and increasingly also of a political one. These sociological currents are analysed in more detail in chapter 8; the simple point to be made here is that they are merely the Scottish middle class's local version of common middle-class experiences and reactions in many other places.

These changes might be undermining the legitimacy of the UK state in Scotland, but the process is inevitably slow: only under dictatorships can legitimacy collapse cataclysmically, and even there people's tolerance is remarkable. The rule of law decays at the edges: there is widespread non-payment of an unpopular tax, there is a refusal to cooperate in unpopular educational reforms, there are quite large demonstrations for self-government, but there is no concerted withdrawal of cooperation: Beetham's acts of consent continue, and the governing system is still broadly justifiable in terms of the liberal beliefs of Scottish society. But Scotland is not an exception in these respects; despite what some nationalists allege, there is

nothing craven about a society that takes its time over the political implications of profound social changes. That is how constitutional change happens: it is more subtle and more boring than the language of revolutionary
nationalism would allow.

SCOTLAND

Although I have been referring to Scottish examples throughout this chapter, it will clarify the later discussion if I bring the theory together in the
form of five conclusions for Scotland.

The first point is to distinguish between sovereignty and power. Scotland
has had quite a lot of power, at least in certain areas of social policy. We
cannot understand the nature of Scottish nationalism as always partly
defensive of Scottish practice unless we accept this: as we saw in the
examples of the educational debate in chapter 1, some of the traditions
that are being defended are no more than thirty years old.

The second point is that Scotland retained what Poggi calls a self-
regulating polity, even though this was never fully or openly democratic.
A useful distinction here is between two types of representation, 'trusteeship' and 'delegation' (McLennan, 1984, p. 242). A national parliament is
based on delegation in some form, and, on the whole, Scotland did not
have that. Scotland did have government by trustees, however – rulers
responsive to the electorate without being accountable to them. For Britain,
McLennan calls this the 'Tory ethic of responsible government' (p. 242).

Thus the third point is that Scottish nationalism is partly official nationalism, not only oppositionist (the terms are from Kellas (1991)). In other
words, not only did the UK state allow diversity, it actively encouraged it, in
the sense that the personnel in the state agencies in Scotland were self-
consciously Scottish. This is as true of the lawyers and other professionals
who staffed the nineteenth-century state as it is of the civil servants in the
Scottish welfare state of the mid-twentieth century. The Scottish governing
system as it exists in the 1990s was created by these groups and their political
allies. That is why even the supporters of the constitutional status quo can
use a rhetoric that is recognisably nationalist. It is not enough to attempt to
explain this as the state's having to adopt the language of nationalism in
order to placate nationalist critics: the writings, but more importantly the
practices, of politicians and civil servants in the Scottish Office show that
they have had a conception of the Scottish national interest in their minds as
they governed. The fight in Scotland is not over whether the nation exists –
as it is or has been in Brittany, Quebec, Catalonia, the Basque country and
Lombardy. Throughout the period since the Union, it has been over how
best to preserve and advance the nation's interests, and about how to define
these. If the national image has excluded large social groups – the working
class in the nineteenth century, say – that has been because the choices of
one group of Scots could prevail over the others.

The fourth point is that Scotland – and Britain – in the eighteenth century managed to create a depoliticised realm of cultural practices, in the sense that these cultural activities could be pursued free of interference from the state. After the Jacobite threat had vanished (by about 1760), the UK state almost never proscribed cultural activities in Britain for political reasons (although it certainly did so in Ireland). The state did interfere in culture – notably education. But – as we will see – that was largely for reasons intrinsic to cultural practices themselves, and, moreover, was nearly always at the invitation of the Scots, or of one Scottish faction using the power of the central state against another. This is in contrast to many other small nations, at least in nineteenth-century Europe, where activities that would have gone unnoticed by the political authorities in Scotland – such as publishing in a vernacular language – were proscribed, often violently.

This brings us to the final point, the importance of national beliefs. We could call them myths, as many writers have done for Scotland, in the sense that they are stories which people tell about themselves: in the words of Andrew McPherson, myths 'celebrate identity and values, and . . . describe and explain the world in which these are experienced or sought' (McPherson, 1983, p. 218). Thus when someone asserts that Scottish education is egalitarian, they are asserting a value which purports to be a description; and, if enough people assert that value often enough – especially if they are in positions of power – then it starts to become reality. But, although I will use these ideas, I prefer not to use the term 'myth': it retains an irreducibly pejorative tone, akin to the patronising implications of Marxist ideas of false consciousness. The self-confident Victorian bourgeoisie understood perfectly what they were doing when they built national monuments such as those to Walter Scott in Edinburgh or to William Wallace in Stirling: they were consciously constructing a nation through its symbols in a thoroughly modern and normal way. They were, in Geertz's terms, forcing the Scottish centre to become a concentrated locus of serious events. Their successors who transferred the Scottish Office to Edinburgh amid a great flowering of indigenous architecture in the 1930s were doing likewise. The same project is being advanced by the proponents of a Scottish parliament now in the 1990s: part of the justification for that, it is argued, is as a cultural focus. All these successive generations of nationalists have been engaged in a conscious process of symbolically constructing a community, in Anthony Cohen's phrase. None of these activities are reasonably describable as myth-making, in however subtly anthropological a way, if only because the protagonists knew what they were doing and were not at all cynical about it. And this book cannot avoid being part of that self-conscious process of constructing Scotland, insofar as it is offered as a discussion of the nature of Scottish power and identity. The same point could be made about the act of reading it.

That these nationalists – including the 1990s federalists in the Labour or Liberal parties – also had an allegiance to a British symbolic realm shows, not duplicity or even ambivalence, but merely a cultural subtlety to accompany the unavoidability of shared sovereignty. The Scottish National Party acknowledges a similar constraint in its policy of 'independence in Europe', exchanging the European Union for the UK as the external guarantor of liberty and security. For all the frequent myopia of nationalist political rhetoric, Scottish nationalists, like their counterparts in small nations throughout Europe, have often had a more intricate understanding of national identity than even the most insightful of the theorists I have been citing, although usually the theories are subtle enough to be readily adaptable to these multi-faceted experiences.

3

Eighteenth-Century Scotland
The Development of Managed Autonomy

Scotland's union with England in 1707 was a bargain. Scotland did surrender autonomy, but not abjectly: the bargain provided advantages to both parties. England gained peace on its northern border (more or less), and Scotland gained economic opportunities, political influence and the protection of most of its key institutions. As we will see in chapter 5, that was not bad going for a small and weak nation at the end of a century of almost continuous European warfare.

This chapter discusses the autonomy of the political system that emerged. The material is organised by themes, not chronologically. We start with an examination of the causes of the Union, because these remained continuing reasons for maintaining it as the century progressed. We look then at the system of political management that governed Scotland nationally and locally after 1707. This provided the liberating framework for the development of the Scottish economy from post-Union stagnation to the brink of the industrial revolution.

The system of government allowed a distinctive Scottish civil society not merely to survive but to flourish. Central to the ideology which underpinned this Scotland was the Protestantism of the dominant Presbyterian church. But the national beliefs also came from the two themes which unified Scottish Enlightenment thought – rationalism and Britishness, both providing peculiar opportunities for Scots to assert their rights as equals. In the final section, some provisional conclusions about the scope and strategy for autonomy of small nations are drawn out from the Scottish case.

WHY DID THE UNION COME ABOUT?

The debate about whether union was inevitable or, to the contrary, was imposed on Scotland by the English and their Scottish agents is intricate and endless. There is, certainly, clear evidence that the proponents of union invoked the real threat of economic or military retaliation from England. They may also have used bribery, although this common claim is not well documented and is probably exaggerated. It might even be the case that a majority of the population were opposed: there were fairly widespread riots in lowland areas against union – most notably in Edinburgh itself, where the Scottish parliament met – and numerous burghs, counties, presbyteries and parishes petitioned against it too (but only a minority of any of these categories sent in any petition).

But to concentrate on these events is to let the minutiae of politics blind us to history. This had not been the first attempt at union: the seventeenth and even the sixteenth century had seen such moves fairly regularly, and on only one occasion – the parliamentary union under Cromwell – had the Scots been coerced into accepting. Moreover, if the 1707 attempt had failed, it would almost certainly not have been the last: as we will see, the arguments which had encouraged all the earlier attempts continued to be persuasive in political debate for at least the next century and a half.

So, when we ask why the Union took place, the most interesting story is not the immediate political context. What is important is why union seemed a sensible compromise to many reasonable and patriotic Scots of that time, and for long after.

The first point is economic. Scotland was a poor country, suffering from intermittent war and famine throughout most of the seventeenth century. It had to search for new trading opportunities to replace those lost in Catholic France after the Reformation. In pursuit of commerce with England, Scottish distinctiveness was felt to be less important than securing markets. Thus whole segments of the economy were already financed by English capital in the late seventeenth century – gold-mining for example (although other areas were more indigenous) – and some successful companies would price their products in English, not Scottish, pounds. Flourishing businesses had influential shareholders based in London, and these were often Scots exiles aware that they had to move south if they wanted to have the best economic or political opportunities. Skilled English workers were imported when that was necessary to allow new technology to get started: an example was at the flourishing cloth manufactory at Newmills near Edinburgh. Even the Scottish government itself was not averse to following the logic of economics rather than rhetorical patriotism: at times it violated its own regulations against the importation of English cloth, and it did this because that was cheaper.

Thus, in their attitude to economic development, the Scots were already employing pragmatic arguments, not sentiment. Only at the very end of the seventeenth century did the Scottish government start to protect Scottish industry with tariffs, to which the English reacted in kind. The Scots, in turn, attempted to establish their own trading post in central America – at Darien – as a means of circumventing these new restrictions on trading with English colonies. When this collapsed, again under severe English pressure, many of its patriotic supporters turned to union as the only way to avoid recurrent bouts of protectionism which were bound to hurt Scotland more than England. But these people – for example, William Paterson, founder also of the Bank of England – accepted union only if it was satisfactory to Scotland on grounds of trade, industry and prices.

So, the economic motives for union can be described as instrumental. It can be argued that Scottish business elites were willing to use whatever tools came to hand for developing their economy. If possessing a separate parliament stood in the way of that goal, it could be dispensed with, provided that the ultimate protection which a parliament could offer to Scottish industry was available by other means. That the immediate economic effects of union were fairly dire does not invalidate this point. What matters is that people chose a constitutional means to an economic end. Moreover, as we will see below, there are good reasons to believe that the proponents of union were ultimately correct that exposing the Scottish economy to free competition would be to its benefit, even though that benefit took a lot longer to flow than they imagined.

Thus when we say that economic motives were one cause of the Union, we are not saying that they determined the way it happened at precisely the time that it happened. What we are saying is that the economic context shaped the whole drift of Scotland towards alliance with England over periods as long as a century or more.

A similar kind of point can be made about the second motive for union – military threat. Since England's aims were to prevent Scotland's invading – or being used as a route to invasion by more powerful states such as France or Spain – it is not surprising that English armies were being massed on the border. The English were concerned with excluding the Stuarts from succession: part of the dispute with the Scottish parliament was its refusal to promise to follow automatically the English choice of monarch. And the Scots, again being pragmatic, reacted in the intended way.

Was this military threat coercion? In one sense, it obviously was, just as the English tariffs were. But, in another, the armies and the tariffs were symbols of power. What mattered was not the actual armies, but that they represented the English capacity to thwart Scottish ambitions. The Scots concluded that it would be better to ally themselves with this power than risk its wrath. As Angus Calder has put it, the Union was in that sense 'a rational solution to a very dangerous economic and political situation' (Calder, 1985). Scots wanting confirmation of its rationality could readily have found it elsewhere in Europe at roughly the same time: in 1714, for instance, Catalonia was defeated by neighbouring great powers, and suffered – as we will see in chapter 5 – the almost total suppression of its autonomous institutional life. Scotland – like Catalonia – might have preferred if these external threats had not arisen; but there was not much that a small nation could do about that, short of turning to some other great power for protection, and for Scotland none suitable was available.

The main reason why no other state would come to Scotland's aid was religion – the third reason for union. Ever since the Reformation in the sixteenth century, Scottish Presbyterians had argued for British union as a way of safeguarding Protestantism against the continuing strength of Catholicism in France and Spain. As we will see below, and also repeatedly in later chapters, this association between Britishness and Protestantism remained a crucial underpinning of the Union for a very long time. What matters here is that it provided the ideological context for the pragmatic motives of developing the economy and avoiding war.

The Britishness of Protestantism was not an alternative to Scottishness, however, but rather a reinforcement of it. The Covenanters of the mid-seventeenth century were Scottish nationalists – protesting against the tyranny of Charles I, for example – precisely because they were Presbyterians: the most unbearable feature of that tyranny was its imposition of bishops on the self-governing presbyteries that ruled the church. With a nationalism thus defined by religion, English religious allies were felt to be allies also of Scotland itself. The Scots Presbyterians saw themselves as the British leaders in spiritual matters, but, during the war against Charles I, they also actively sought political and ecclesiastical union in order to defend their achievements. Far from this being a surrender to the English, it was in fact a mark of Scottish self-confidence: a people secure in its own identity and prospects could afford to choose its ally. Only when the English revolutionaries went further than the Scots wanted did the attractiveness of voluntary union wane. The execution of Charles I, for instance, of which the Scots disapproved, was followed by Cromwell's military defeat of the Scottish covenanting armies and the imposition of union.

Not all the Presbyterians resented even this, and in general the experience of Cromwell's rule did not permanently dull the religious appetites for union. The return of the Stuarts after 1660 revived the sense of a common British Presbyterian cause. This was reinforced in the 'time of Persecution' – military suppression of Presbyterianism. Charles II's attempts at parliamentary union in 1670 were resisted by the Scottish parliament only because no provision was made for the continuing independence of Scottish institutions. The possibility of a voluntary union based on religious freedom was opened up by the revolution of 1688–90. The new King William was felt to be a religious liberator for the whole of Britain, a guarantor of Scottish rights because he was a guarantor of Protestantism and – in Scotland – of Presbyterianism. It was widely believed that the Scottish church had won a great victory when it had secured its independence in 1690. It had done so, it was believed, by astutely allying itself with religious reformers in England. Defence of the religion was more important than defence of a secular parliament; if insisting on retaining the parliament risked invasion and the forcible suppression of the church's independence, then the parliament was dispensable.

That is not to say that secular concerns were unimportant, as our discussion of the economy has shown. The Convention of Royal Burghs, for example, was so central to the development of trade that the Reverend John MacQueen could write in 1694 that the fortunes of the nation as a whole were determined by those of the burghs (G. Marshall, 1992, p. 225). But secular politics involved the church too. It was the most important of the national governing bodies, more important than the parliament itself. Because it had not suffered any serious doctrinal split after 1560, it had become the most important source of social authority, judged by one recent historian to have been 'unequalled outside [John Calvin's] Geneva itself' (G. Marshall, 1992, p. 40). The parliament had played little role in the conflicts with the monarch before 1640, or after 1660: the role of national leadership had been taken by the church's general assembly, in contrast to England where parliament was central. In England (with memories of the time of Henry VIII), parliament became the key symbol of national independence and of the integrity of the nation against royal tyranny. That was not an obsession that the Scots could share. Surrendering their parliament in 1707 in return for safeguarding the church and the royal burghs could seem to be a good national bargain. In some views, indeed, institutions mattered hardly at all to the essence of the nation. The leader of the opponents of the union, Andrew Fletcher, ultimately was not a nationalist of a modern sort, believing that 'if a man were permitted to make all the ballads, he need not care who should make the laws of a nation' (Daiches, 1979, p. 108).

The Union which resulted was then a compromise. It contained safeguards for the continuing independence of Scots law, religion, education and local government, and offered to the merchants of the burghs some of the trading opportunities which they had long sought. The Scots knew they had struck a bargain, and this satisfaction – or indifference – extended beyond the elite groups who had done the negotiating. Although there were protests during the Union debates, the outcome was not nearly so controversial as the prospect of incorporation had been. For example, a Jacobite plot of 1708 failed before it got started, and there was no popular support in the Lowlands for the Jacobite rising of 1715.

POLITICAL MANAGEMENT

The system of Scottish national government that emerged from the Union settlement can be characterised as political management by a social elite whose values were moderation and rationalism. For most of the century, this elite had considerable freedom to govern and reform Scotland. The elite did face internal opposition, but these conflicts were contained within the Scottish realm: all parties took the political and cultural existence of Scotland for granted.

The greatest threats to that autonomous Scotland were in the first years after 1707. Most controversial of all was the London government's restoration of lay patronage in the church. The right of local congregations to select their minister was a cherished achievement of the 1690 revolution, and the 1712 ruling led to recurrent disputes throughout the eighteenth century over ministers chosen by the local landowners.

But too much should not be made of this undoubtedly important case of state interference with Scottish institutions in the eighteenth century. It was by no means simply an imposition from London: it can alternatively be interpreted as an astute move by the landlords, persuading London government that without some such concession they might flirt with Jacobitism. Patronage was approved of by the moderate elites that dominated Scottish government: opposition lay with the evangelicals in the church, which achieved a majority even there only sporadically until the eventual great schism over patronage in 1843. As is discussed further below, the disputes were within Scottish society between these two groups, not between a unified Scotland and London.

Similar comments can be made about the other important change in the government of Scottish affairs in the aftermath of 1707 – the abolition of the separate Scottish privy council (or body of aristocratic advisers to the monarch). This move was in fact instigated by Scots, in an attempt to undermine the power of people who had previously been influential at court. Again, it was not straightforwardly a matter of English imposition.

Whatever might be the interpretation of the events of these first years, however, they remained highly unusual as the century developed. The English politicians learned that it was safer to recruit allies in Scotland than to impose English policies and traditions: indeed, they were alerted to the danger of risking the Union by the Scottish attempt to repeal it in 1713. The response to this particular move was the appointment of the Scottish Earl of Seafield as Lord Chancellor, simultaneously a recognition of the importance of acknowledging Scottish autonomy and of the wide support for Union among Scottish moderate opinion. Seafield, the prime mover of the 1707 treaty, was not to be taken for granted; but neither could he or his Scottish allies forget the reasons why union had been attractive in the first place.

Thereafter, as Phillipson has said, 'successive ministries . . . walked more warily; for the rest of the century, there was very little legislation impinging on Scottish institutions, and what there was was initiated in Scotland', by which he means by Scottish lawyers and the Scottish moderate elite (Phillipson, 1970, p. 140).

The dominant personage in the system that emerged was the Scottish manager – the politician who coordinated the Scottish lobby in London, who was a source of advice on Scottish matters to the monarch and to English politicians, and who, above all, exercised enormous patronage in Scotland. The most notable managers were the Duke of Argyll (for about fifteen years after 1746) and, especially, Henry Dundas (from Argyll's fall until after the end of the century). These men effectively governed Scotland as a sort of subordinate monarch of the British crown. They were not wholly independent rulers, but neither were they mere territorial agents of London. Until the time of Dundas, Scottish business rarely came to the Cabinet in London. With Dundas emerged the insistence that Scotland was a partner, not a colony, and the expectation that it would be allowed to do what it wanted, provided always that it did not threaten the security of England. The unavoidable presence of England induced caution, but not a defensive one: as we will see below, moderate Scottish opinion adulated English culture as offering a positive programme for developing Scottish society. In any case, caution by local ruling elites was hardly unique in Europe, as will be discussed in chapter 5: the Finnish or Polish or Bohemian middle classes were continually looking over their shoulders at Russia or Austria or Prussia.

In the degree of constrained independence which he did exercise, the Scottish manager stands in contrast to the governor-general of Ireland, who was always British and always primarily an agent of central government. It is also a contrast with Scotland in the seventeenth century, not only under Cromwell. Then – even with its parliament – Scotland was regarded as a subject province; now, it was a partner, and this status had been recognised by the Union. But it was not caused by the Union: the political climate had changed because the English and the Scots now agreed with each other ideologically, so that the English could allow the Scots themselves to police any threats to English peace. For example, the Scottish manager could be trusted with pacification of the country after the Jacobite rising of 1745–6: there was no doubting the allegiance of the vast majority of the Lowland Scottish population to the Hanoverian succession. The defeat of the Jacobites was, indeed, a significant victory for the whole system of politics in post-Union Scotland, securing not just Scotland but Britain as a whole from what was felt to be the threat of continental despotism.

Argyll and Dundas governed through a range of institutions that contributed to making Edinburgh 'patently a centre of government' (Murdoch, 1980, p. 11). Even those parts of government in Scotland which did not answer directly to the manager were distinctive: for example, there were separate Scottish boards for collecting taxes. When the London government of the Duke of Newcastle tried after 1754 to appoint Englishmen to Scottish revenue posts, it met such resentment that it had to withdraw. The withdrawal and the resistance happened, though, for pragmatic reasons, not sentimental nationalism: Argyll persuaded Newcastle that appointing Englishmen would needlessly inflame Scottish passions, and – even better – that leaving the appointments to Argyll's own patronage would allow him to recruit numerous Scots to the government's side. Thus, whether through the manager directly, or through other distinctive Scottish agencies, the British state in the eighteenth century was always mediated through what Fry calls 'native Scottish surrogates' (Fry, 1987, p. 79).

The manager did not merely channel opinion from and to London, however: he initiated reform as well. Examples include legislation to allow the Convention of Royal Burghs to promote trade (1727), and the reform of the bankruptcy law in 1772 in a manner that made Scots law far more conducive to company formation than English law until well into the nineteenth century. In the main, though, the system allowed Scotland its autonomy through 'benign neglect' (Whetstone, 1981, p. x), in which social change happened at the pace chosen by Scottish civil society rather than by government. In particular, most economic and agricultural reform was carried out by enterprising landlords and merchants. As Murdoch puts it, 'central government largely limited itself to war and diplomacy, and raising revenue in support of its action' (Murdoch, 1980, p. 22). Fry argues that Scotland could choose which elements of its identity to retain (Fry, 1992, p. 14) – a circumstance highly favourable among small nations in Europe, as we will see in greater detail in chapter 5.

The whole was embedded in the regulatory framework of the Scottish legal system. The period has been described as the golden age of Scots law, when the system enjoyed almost complete freedom from legislative interference, and when, therefore, it could develop according to its own chosen logic (*The Laws of Scotland,* para. 630). This was because 'Scotland was one of the least "governed" countries in Europe' (para. 630): that is, having the fewest legislative interventions. The legal system remained independently Scottish: although appeals in civil cases were allowed to the House of Lords from 1711, that body is best thought of as Scottish, not English, when exercising these powers.

Moreover, this uniquely self-governing system performed the role which Poggi assigns it in his theory of the legal state. The national politicians were lawyers, and the tight Edinburgh legal circle was the place where they did their business. The same importance of the legal profession can be found in local politics. As we will see in the next section, the key figure in local government was the sheriff, who moreover acted as the liaison between the locality and the centre. From the time of Dundas onwards, the sheriffs had to be legally qualified.

LOCAL SOCIETY

It was at the local level that Scottish autonomy ultimately lay. Britain in the eighteenth century was learning how to hand over 'low politics' to what Keating calls 'trusted local collaborators' (Keating, 1988, p. 56). This was as true in England and Wales as in Scotland, but the previously existing Scottish civil society ensured that the resulting local autonomy would allow Scotland to develop on indigenous lines.

There were four important institutions locally – the sheriff, the commissioners of supply, the parish and the royal burghs. The most influential of these was the sheriff. After the Dundas reforms of 1747, he was the judicial and administrative representive of central government. He sat as the local judge, called jurors to service, organised elections, ensured that Crown duties were collected, and became the representative of central government in times of disturbance. The sheriff was appointed by the Lord Advocate, who, as head of the legal system, can be thought of as part of central government. But the appointment usually followed the recommendations of local magnates. What certainly did not happen was appointment by London ministers: this was an important contrast to the situation in other small nations within multinational states elsewhere in Europe, as we will see in chapter 5.

The sheriff also brought together the small band of electors into regular county meetings of the commissioners of supply, and forwarded their petitions to the government in Edinburgh or London. The commissioners of supply had originally been established in 1667 to collect the land tax, but they also acquired responsibility for other taxes, some of which they had to spend on maintaining roads, bridges and ferries (important tasks in Scotland's difficult terrain). They evolved into the body which expressed the views of the county landholders and of the towns contained in the county: most landholders were entitled to attend and vote at the meetings, the principle being that all the people who were taxed should have a say in how the taxes were levied. They sent delegates to national meetings in Edinburgh, which would propose as well as comment on legislation. All government correspondence to and from the county was directed through the convener of the commissioners, who was elected by them.

Overseeing the daily lives of the country was the parish. It was the basic administrative unit of the church, and was in charge of what would nowadays be called social policy – poor relief and education, for example, some of these activities being done in conjunction with the councils of the larger towns. In accordance with Presbyterian principles, the parish was governed by the kirk session of elders, who were at least nominally elected by the male members of the congregation. The national forum of the kirk sessions was the annual general assembly of the church.

The royal burghs stood outside this structure somewhat, being, in theory, wholly self-governing. Thus, in these larger towns, the burgh councils exercised the powers which in the rural areas lay with the parish, the commissioners of supply or the sheriff. The franchise for the governing councils of the burghs was highly restricted, and most were in effect self-selecting. This led to conflicts with the urban kirk sessions, which were much more open: the Edinburgh general sessions (grouping all the parishes within the town) has been described as being 'as close to a truly representative institution as we are likely to find anywhere in the early modern period' (Sher, 1982, p. 182). Again, though, these conflicts were contained within a Scottish polity: they were among Scottish factions or social classes, not between Scotland and the British state.

These institutions were the ones that affected the ordinary life of Scotland – its education, morality, health, births, marriages and deaths. None of them was interfered with by London government, and all had their origins before the Union. They were autonomous within the very wide range of duties assigned to them. Tensions inevitably arose, for example between evangelicals and moderates, or between kirk sessions and heritors (the property owners from whom the bulk of church resources came, who were also commissioners of supply). And there were always in the background the tensions between a ruling elite and the mass of the population who were not enfranchised. But all these tensions were indigenous. In that sense, Scotland was similar to any European society. Where there was central regulation, it was imposed from Edinburgh, not London, and was largely mediated through the Scottish legal system in the form of the Lord Advocate and the sheriff. In short, it is difficult to imagine that Scottish local government in the eighteenth century – including the conflicts within it – would have looked much different had the Union never taken place. The same can be said, therefore, for the daily lives of the vast majority of Scottish people.

ECONOMIC DEVELOPMENT

Within this framework of new but also traditional government, the Scottish economy flourished as never before. That is not to say that its health was necessarily due to the Union: that causal question is too simplistic to be answerable definitively one way or the other. What can be said, however, is that Scots exploited the opportunities offered by Union in a way that they were unable to do in the seventeenth century.

The Scottish economy suffered from free trade in the years immediately after 1707. The manufacturing sector that had benefited from the artificial conditions of protection at the end of the seventeenth century faced sharp competition not only from England but from the Netherlands too. Much of it collapsed.

But protection could not have been a permanent policy in any case for a small economy that depended on trade. It was, as we noted, a short-term defence against English competition to which the Union itself was meant to be a lasting antidote. Campbell (1985) argues that the Union therefore pushed Scotland in the direction of complementary development, for example when the linen industry was promoted by the Board of

Trustees for Fisheries and Manufactures that was founded in 1727 deliberately to build up Scottish industry.

The Union was therefore permissive, not developmental. The Board was founded by government certainly, but not by London: it emanated from the patriotically Scottish government that we have been looking at. The Convention of Royal Burghs, similarly, acquired a new autonomy and importance for encouraging economic development after the Union, precisely because the parliament had gone. Insofar as the burghs were closer than the parliament had ever been to the sources of economic growth, this was a net gain for the autonomy of Scottish civil society.

In the wider British framework, there was no specific encouragement to Scottish goods, but there was free trade. In this context of more or less free competition, scope was created for the exercise of native Scottish industry and invention. That is why the economic growth that occurred from about 1740 onwards can be said to be due both to the broadly free-trade framework of the Union and to indigenous resources that dated back to the seventeenth century. It was also, from about 1760 onwards, due to wider growth in world markets, something which the newly strong British economy helped to stimulate but for which it was certainly not solely responsible.

Scotland was much less of a satellite economy by 1780 than it had been a century earlier when it was nominally independent. It no longer depended on imported capital, and this was, in the classic free-market way, a self-reinforcing process: the more Scotland could provide local opportunities for investing its own capital, the more scope it had for generating profits and hence yet more funds for investment. It now exported a wide range of manufactured goods, not only a few raw materials. This stimulated indigenous technology, inspired also by the flourishing scientific culture of the Enlightenment. Intellectual self-confidence allowed technology also to be borrowed from England as an equal. English merchants, in turn – in contrast sometimes to their politicians – respected Scottish industrialists, and had no wish to take them over as they had wanted to do in the American colonies or Ireland.

The Irish economy, in fact, provides an instructive contrast. It had been more developed than the Scottish one at the end of the seventeenth century, but fell behind in the eighteenth. Whatley has suggested that this was because Ireland did not have the self-confidently independent civil society that Scotland enjoyed. The Irish economy stagnated, because the British state was, if anything, even less interested in deliberately developing it than the Scottish one. For Ireland, free trade was destructive, in the absence of the local institutional resources to exploit it.

THE CHURCH

Alongside all the secular governing structures was the church – the body whose independence had been the cherished Scottish success of the Union negotiations. It was more than just a place of worship: as we have seen, it governed, it regulated, it policed behaviour, and it provided an occasion for popular participation of a sometimes semi-democratic sort. It also maintained, like the legal system, a pervasive link between the centre and the locality, and – far more than the rather arcane world of sheriffs and lawyers – was a way by which ordinary people, men and women, felt some involvement in the affairs of the nation.

The general assembly of the church was Scotland's parliament for domestic matters in the eighteenth century. It was much more democratic than the parliament at Westminster, or than the episcopalian Church in England. The general assembly consisted of ministers, elders, and representatives of the burghs, the universities and other bodies. In theory, the ministers and elders were elected by all the male members of local congregations, and at the very least they were more closely in touch with local opinion than the members of parliament or than any of the other personnel of the state. In theory also, these representatives had equal voices in the assembly, although in practice the Edinburgh-based academics and others were able to exercise undue influence. They exercised it, however, in the same kind of way as the political manager did – to protect Scotland's rights against other 'great men' in London. They were left free to do this by the political state because they were all moderates: this was conclusively demonstrated by their successive defeats of the evangelicals from the 1750s onwards.

The moderates governed the church within the framework of a rationalist ideology of Britishness (explained more fully below). Insofar as Protestantism was at the centre of this, it served both to cement Scotland into Britain – the Union being the best guarantee of religious liberty – and to emphasise Scotland's distinctiveness within this Protestant realm: Scotland's form of Protestantism was determinedly different. Far from Scotland's political character being at odds with a British identity, these were rather felt to be thoroughly reliant on each other. We will see in chapter 4 that this sense of mutually dependent dual patriotisms became deeper and more pervasive in the nineteenth century.

The local parish was not greatly affected by the controversies between evangelicals and moderates that shook the general assembly. If there was enthusiasm for Presbyterianism, it was not based straightforwardly on theological or even constitutional principles, but on patriotism: at the local level, bishops were opposed above all because they were felt to be culturally alien, to be English or – even worse – foreign and Catholic. There would have been wide agreement with the words of Mr Balwhidder in John Galt's *Annals of the Parish* (written in 1821): 'I never could abide that the plain auld Kirk of Scotland, with her sober presbyterian simplicity, should borrow, either in word or in deed, from the language of the prelatic hierarchy of England'.

After 1712, the kirk session had only limited legal power, but nevertheless it was socially important in the sense that it formed the moral tone through which education and poor relief were conducted. The role of the established church became administrative rather than legal: 'the church's role [locally] was defined not by "membership", but by its civil status', as Brown puts it; 'the parish church and the parish state were virtually one and the same' (C. G. Brown, 1989, p. 145). In some urban areas, the session and the town council overlapped, the secular authorities using the church to symbolise social cohesion. The landowners in rural areas did the same, in their combined role as heritors in the church and as commissioners of supply at the county meetings.

Thus the recurrent disputes over patronage, of which much has been made recently as having been a protest against the British state, were not simply nationalist. They were about maintaining the doctrine of 'twa kingdoms' – secular and divine – and so were expressing conflicts within Scottish society, not between it and London government. Overt civil power having been largely and uncontroversially transferred to secular agencies – all of them, like the sheriff, thoroughly embedded in Scottish civil society – the disputes were about the right of the church to continue to regulate morality. If this was a nationalist conflict, it was only so in an indirect way, and most of the evangelical upholders of church independence in theological matters would not have been willing to carry their protests into a secular challenge to the Union. They felt themselves to be fighting landowners and moderate town councils, not the British state. They were fighting the state only in the sense that their opponents were on the whole better able to call on the resources of the state to exercise their power. But, for precisely that reason, the state which was causing the evangelicals problems was Scottish, captured as it had been by the moderates, who would no more than their opponents have been willing to surrender the autonomy of either church or state to England.

In any case, the evangelicals sometimes won significant battles. For example, they persuaded the state to accept evangelical ministers in over two out of five parishes where the crown had the right of appointment. A notable instance was in Edinburgh in the 1760s, where the eventually successful popular opposition to the imposition of a moderate minister has been judged by Sher to be 'a critical step in the development of a "modern" democratic consciousness among the "people" of Scotland' (Sher, 1982, p. 202). He distances us from these terms 'people' and 'modern' to indicate that our conception of popular participation through elections in a system of universal adult franchise is not the only criterion by which to judge the effectiveness of popular political action.

That there probably was a widespread sense of popular ownership of the key institutions of civil society is seen in these agitations against moderate patronage. When ordinary people – women almost as much as men – demonstrated forcibly against lay patronage, they were implicitly acknowledging the importance of the church to them, even though they had little influence on its day-to-day management by the moderate elite, and even though the women did not even have a formal say in the election of the minister. In that form of participation, the Scots were no worse off than their counterparts elsewhere in Europe; and insofar as they frequently got what they wanted through their demonstrations, the political influence of the Scottish people can be judged to have been somewhat greater than most. And, to the extent that they achieved this because of the relative political tolerance which the moderate and unionist management exercised, the Union can be said to have indeed furthered Scottish liberties.

BRITISHNESS AND ENLIGHTENMENT RATIONALISM

The ideological theme running through this system of constrained independence was moderate rationalism. It was this which allowed elite Scots to believe that they were continually choosing to be in a Union. Social improvement was to come about through the application of reason; and reason told them that the best available model was English. No doubt we could argue that they were merely making a virtue out of necessity by this definition of 'reason'; but to judge that that was all there was to it would be to consign to self-deluding dependency such towering figures of the Enlightenment as David Hume, Adam Smith, Adam Ferguson and William Robertson. The nature of constrained free choice in general was something they thought a lot about; they, and their thousands of peers and students, were not dupes.

The desire for cultural assimilation to England had one origin well back into the seventeenth century, in the alliance of Scottish Presbyterians with English puritans. It was part of the tendency which saw the Union as a unique guarantee of religious liberty. But the origins were more complex than that. Politeness and rationality were European-wide movements of thought. Thus one of the gathering places of the rationalist elite, the Royal Society of Edinburgh founded in 1783, was modelled on the many European academies devoted to the cultivation of all forms of polite learning, not merely on the more narrowly scientific Royal Society of London.

The central political component of the moderate beliefs was liberty. This related primarily to trade, thought and religion. Thus the figures of the Edinburgh Enlightenment supported Catholic emancipation, the right to enter freely into contracts, and freedom of speech. Liberty was the goal to which all other considerations were subordinate. In particular, there was none of the later European equating of liberty with a national parliament, or with any special representative structures. The British parliament was acceptable precisely because it did not interfere, and therefore guaranteed liberty; only if it had ceased to do so would the issue of separating from it have arisen (as analogous questions did arise later in, for example, Bohemia). This explains why these same Enlightenment figures could oppose American independence: most of them argued that true freedom for the colonies could be achieved only under the auspices of the uniquely freedom-loving British state. State structures were a means to the end of liberty, not goals in themselves.

The belief in liberty was why the moderates were so opposed to Jacobitism, which seemed to threaten Britain with the reimposition of an autocratic regime. The full incorporation of the Highlands into the Scottish polity after 1746 ensured that the same values of Protestantism and moderatism would gradually spread throughout the country. Thus the defeat of the Jacobites by the forces of British moderation allowed the political unity of the Scottish nation to be asserted for the first time since at least the Reformation. That effect of the British Union may seem ironic, but the irony is an invention of later generations which have equated Jacobitism with a failed Scottish nationalism.

One way of avoiding such anachronism is to realise that 'Britain' to these eighteenth-century moderates had a similar rhetorical force to the use of 'European' in political debate in the late twentieth century. As Sher puts it, a 'Briton' in Scotland was synonymous with a Scot who wanted civil and religious liberty (Sher, 1985, p. 53). Something similar was true also in England and Wales, as Colley notes: 'being a [British] patriot was a way of claiming the right to participate in British political life, and ultimately a means of demanding a much broader access to citizenship' (Colley, 1992, p. 5). This sense was helped in Scotland by the growing feeling that the Union had made the Scots and the English into one political realm, at the heart of which was the defence of liberty.

At the same time, the moderate literati were defenders of Scotland: 'for much of the eighteenth century, assimilation [to England] was regarded not so much as a threat to Scottish life as a stimulus to it' (Phillipson, 1970, p. 144). This was partly for pragmatic reasons of trade, as it was before 1707: for example, the county of Moray in 1770 measured its corn in Winchester bushels because that would help sales in the south of England. Thus the Duke of Argyll's attempts to create a closer Union by administrative means were seen as splendidly patriotic.

Assimilation was not only pragmatic, but also a chosen cultural project. Far from English insensitivities to Scotland requiring the end of the Union, they were taken to demonstrate that the Union should be made more complete. The poets Robert Burns and Robert Fergusson, for instance, resented that the Union had not in fact created one realm; and they expressed their resentment in Scottish nationalist terms. The whole point of the Union was to remove the oppressions of politics on the Scottish character. Government, it was felt, should have nothing to do with moulding the character of a people; on the contrary, as Adam Ferguson argued, the nature of a government should be derived from the pre-existing culture that it was supposed to serve. If there was a public institution which was indeed believed to shape the private life of the country, it was law, and the Scots prided themselves on having avoided the fate that they had suffered under Cromwell, and that similar small nations were suffering elsewhere – of having their laws interfered with by a remote government. Thus Robert Burns or Robert Fergusson wanted a more complete Union in order to remove any political obstacles to Scots' following their own special ways of living and feeling. In this respect, they were carrying forward a view of the nation's essence which we saw from Andrew Fletcher at the time of the Union: ballads mattered more than laws. The successful assertion of this principle allowed the Scots to keep politics out of culture, and therefore in a sense to depoliticise nationality.

Three incidents illustrate this strand of assimilationist nationalism, one military, one cultural, and one, the most revealing of all, legal. The first is the campaign by the Scots literati for a Scottish militia at the same time as the English and Welsh were allowed to have one in the 1750s. This was precisely one of these issues that did make the London government edgy, because it did threaten peace: arming the Scots so soon after the defeat of the Jacobites was believed to be too risky. But to the Edinburgh literati, this was an affront to Scottish manly pride; and the failure of the Scots in general to rise in demand of a militia was believed to show that they were not fit for Union, but only for the slavishness of a colony. Thus nationalism here meant asserting the right to be equal with England by having, as far as possible, exactly the same institutions as England.

The second incident was over the fabricated poem Ossian, which James Macpherson tried to present to the world as a genuinely ancient epic in the early 1760s. This attempt was in itself an interesting reflection of the successful political integration of the Highlands into the rest of Scotland: thereafter, their Gaelic culture became available either for safely non-political celebration, or for thoroughly national projects that would contribute to defining Scottish culture as a whole. The London critics were sceptical about the poem's authenticity, and in Edinbugh this was felt to be a national slight on Scotland (though not by everyone: David Hume was sceptical too). The campaign in defence of Macpherson was a collective effort to have Scottish culture recognised as the equal of English – or of any in Europe, where epics were being discovered or invented in the first stirrings of romanticism. Macpherson's effort failed, but the cultural principle was triumphantly vindicated somewhat later by Walter Scott, whose novels established Scottish history as a worthy subject of study for the whole of Europe. Scott also explicitly separated the now acceptable culture of the Highlands from the previously threatening politics of Jacobitism.

The third example is a particularly vivid clarification of the complex balance between chosen anglicisation and defence of Scotland. It is the controversies over the reform of the Scottish High Courts. The dispute started with a proposal by Dundas to reduce the number of judges in the Court of Session (the highest civil court below the House of Lords) from fifteen to ten, largely to allow each of them to be paid a higher salary. He was forced to abandon the measure by strong opposition, which claimed that it was contrary to the Treaty of Union. It was argued that such a change required the consent of the people of Scotland, by which was meant the county meetings, and they opposed it overwhelmingly. Some of the rhetoric in the debate saw the move as prefiguring a general loss of Scottish rights, and thus was an early instance of that tendency noted in chapter 1 to interpret change in the way in which Scotland was governed as a catastrophic threat to the very existence of the nation. The agitation thus appears to be unambiguously nationalist, in a way that is still recognisable today.

But this same nationalist opposition also produced its own proposals for reform, and what is astonishing to a modern understanding of Scottish nationalism is that these proposals were deliberately anglicising. They suggested that juries should be introduced in the Court of Session, as the first step in an eventual complete assimilation of Scottish civil courts to those of England. The arguments come directly from the general themes of Scottish rationalist thought: England had established that juries were defenders of individual liberty, and so juries were an icon of those freedoms that Scots sought from the Union. There was even a Scottish nationalist mythology to go along with this proposal: James Boswell (in 1785) and others claimed that Scotland had once had popular judicial institutions of this type, but that they had been usurped in 1532 when a Catholic monarch had imported the Court of Session from despotic France.

Again, any apparent self-contradictions here are in our twentieth-century eyes only. The Scottish elites knew that the legal system was crucial to the autonomy of Scottish government, just as Poggi says. But the autonomy would allow them to choose how to reform the system, even if reason pointed them in the direction of anglicisation. The conclusion is that the Scots were self-confident in their dual identity, Scottish and British. The prospect of adopting English or British norms was not, in Phillipson's words, 'a juggernaut besieging Scotland from without, but . . . something to be sought from within, by an energetic and public-spirited ruling class'. Moreover, this was 'a process with which parliament ought to have little if anything to do' (Phillipson, 1969, p. 176).

Scottishness was for everyday occasions, Britishness for special ones. The new middle class, learning how to eschew Scotticisms in their speech, were actually much more linguistically versatile than their modern reputation for cravenness would allow. They chose when to be Scottish and when British, just as they defended their Scottishness while at the same time demanding equal opportunities in British politics and the British common market, usually successfully as we have seen. Britain was about war – especially against that same despotic France – and about empire. But that it also penetrated everyday lives is seen in the militia controversy, and in the pervasive importance of Protestantism. In a rhetoric that is still with us today, this dual cultural and political allegiance was expressed as the national right of Scots to be treated as equals within the Union. They wanted to trade as equals, to safeguard that trade by fighting alongside the English in defence of liberty, and to have their culture accepted as worthy of English attention. To have described this at the time as a betrayal of Scotland would have been like claiming today (or indeed then) that a feminist arguing for equal opportunities was betraying women.

CONCLUSIONS

Scotland in the eighteenth century, then, can be understood as an instance of a small nation choosing its fate in a constrained context. The Union itself was a compromise, which means that some things were gained or preserved, even while others were given away. To protect those gains required that the Scots be cautious, which could, no doubt, be interpreted as being timid if Scottish politics is compared inappropriately with that of the country's powerful southern neighbour. But the caution which Scotland exercised can be seen alternatively as simply a sensible strategy for any small nation trying to preserve some autonomy in a dangerous world. Indeed, Scotland's situation was fairly enviable by, for instance, Central European standards. Placating the English was quite easy because all that they were worried about was that Scotland might be the occasion for a military threat. The Scots demonstrated their loyalty by moderation in politics and by channelling the demands they made on London through dominant political figures who could be trusted by both sides (even though at times also hated by both as well). On the few occasions when England's military fears did seem to be justified – during the Jacobite invasions – the vast majority of Scots took England's side. And the outcome of these incidents was a firmer unity in Scotland behind the national project of modernisation.

There is a second reason apart from sensible *realpolitik* why the Scots' demeanour should not be seen as dependent: England's cause was theirs too. The Scots felt themselves to be privileged to be participating as equals in the construction of Britain and in the first steps in building an empire. And they could continue to have a conception of themselves as Scots precisely because the context was a Union, not a takeover: they had ensured that England would, on the whole, respect Scotland as the partner it wanted to be.

We must remember also that neither Scotland nor England was homogeneous. Scots factions would ally themselves with English ones – for example, Presbyterians with Puritans. Some Scottish groups would fight their internal Scottish battles by calling on the aid of stronger allies in the south. That Scottish minorities sometimes therefore won battles because they had used the state against Scottish majorities is indeed a sign of the constraints on Scottish independence. But it does not make eighteenth-century Scotland unusual in Scottish history: there are plenty of examples from before the Union where Scottish groups invoked English friends in aid, the main difference after the Union being that the aid was less often military. Neither does it make Scotland unique in Europe: for example, as we will see in chapter 5, the emerging middle classes throughout the industrialising world took as instrumental a view of constitutions and of alliances as the Scots did.

Therefore the politics that affected the daily lives of people in Scotland remained thoroughly Scottish because emphatically local. The significant conflicts were within Scotland, not against England. Civil society was autonomous from the state, in Scotland as throughout Britain. Its Scottish character derived from its roots well before the Union, and above all from the legal system and the Presbyterian Church. When civil society was regulated at all, that happened from a Scottish centre which, in these functions, retained much of the symbolic significance of sovereignty and majesty that it had always had. In having retained their church and legal system, the Scots showed a wise appreciation that there are multiple sources of social authority, and that the existence of the nation does not depend on any single one of them. A successful defence of an autonomous civil society was a real achievement, especially towards the end of the century when much of the rest of Europe was succumbing to despotism in reaction to the revolution in France. The preservation of multiple sources of social power was also astute at a time when centralisation threatened the actual autonomy of many small peoples.

The point of an independent civil society, however, was not as a national expression in itself, but as a means to that expression. The Scots could believe that they had won a great bargain because their culture could flourish and their economy could grow. This was their conception of liberty. It is not ours, nor that of nationalism: there was no mass franchise, nor even the nineteenth-century icon, a national parliament. But that does not mean that there was no national independence, nor even that people in general did not endorse the constitutional situation. By European standards, as we will see in chapter 5, Scottish autonomy was at worst normal, at best actually quite privileged.

4

Scotland in the Nineteenth Century
Building the Modern Nation

The dominant theme of nineteenth-century Scottish politics is successful nationalism. To assert this may seem perverse. In a Europe where nationalism was about attaining national independence, surely – some people have argued – Scotland is the oddity. It was an ancient nation that did not seem to care whether it had a separate parliament, far less independent statehood. Did this signal a lack of self-confidence, what has been called a cultural 'cringe' in the face of fashionable and dominant England? In chapter 5 we will find reasons to question whether seeking statehood really was the common goal of European nationalism. The present chapter examines why Scots could continue to believe that they were exercising real national autonomy even though mostly not demanding a parliament.

This chapter – like the previous – is organised by themes. These are similar to those in chapter 3, although the form of Scottish autonomy changed as the franchise was slowly opened up to wider social groups, and as the role of government steadily grew. First, we examine the nature of Scottish central government and national politics, particularly in its legal aspects and in its supervision of the nascent system of social welfare. The Scottish economy burgeoned in this framework. We then look at local government, the further development of institutions which were already in existence in the eighteenth century. As in that century, moreover, Protestantism – now of an increasingly evangelical sort – provided ideological cohesion along with Scotland's overwhelming support for liberalism. The philanthropy which this encouraged also gave middle-class women a role in social welfare, even though they did not yet have the vote in elections for the United Kingdom parliament: for the first time, therefore, a significant female group was drawn into the system of informal autonomy that Scotland had in its domestic politics.

A common chronology underlines these themes, however, hinging around four key turning points. The first is the widening of the franchise in 1832–3 to give real power to the new middle class of the industrial revolution. The second came in the 1840s, which can be taken as the start of significant state involvement in social policy: notably, the poor law was reformed, and the first school inspectors started work. These changes were partly a consequence of the split in 1843 in the Church of Scotland. The decade was also the period of the Chartists, the movement which agitated for much more radical parliamentary reform. The third phase started in the 1860s, when another significant extension of state activity took place. The final turning point was in the last two decades of the century. Local government was reformed to take the shape that it had until the 1920s (and that in some respects it retained until the 1960s). And the Scottish Office was established in response to nationalist complaints that the growing involvement of London government in social policy threatened to leave Scotland disadvantaged because it did not have an administration of its own. As we will see in chapter 6, the Scottish Office has grown subsequently to be the main agency of the welfare state in Scotland.

Under the aegis of semi-independent government, popular culture flourished, reinventing Scotland at the beginning of the age of mass democracy. It was partly a radical culture, for liberalism was strong even in social groups that did not have the vote. But it was also an enthusiastic imperialism. The idea that Scotland might have been considered a colony of England – as some recent political rhetoric maintains – would have been regarded not only as absurd but also as insulting. Scotland shared the attitudes of England towards subject nations. Scottish nationalism was self-confident because it had won: it celebrated the good fortune of being a partner in empire.

The penultimate section of the chapter traces the theme of successful national assertion through three episodes in the reform of education. These show Scotland deliberately choosing its own fate even while recognising the constraints that it could not avoid facing. As in chapter 3, the final section clarifies the lessons which can be learnt from the Scottish case for the general discussion of constrained autonomy.

CENTRAL GOVERNMENT AND EMPIRE

The Scottish political system was under as much pressure for reform in the 1830s as that in the rest of the United Kingdom. The old order had been ruled by the church and the gentry; both were becoming irritants to the rising middle class. The gentry was Tory, whereas the new classes were Liberal; thus the system of political management bequeathed by Henry Dundas to his son Robert was atrophying. The official church, too, was Tory because it was dominated by the lay patronage of these same gentry. More practically urgent, it was increasingly unable to cope financially or organisationally with the emergencies of growing urban poverty and social dislocation.

As in England, agitation for reform extended far beyond the middle-class men who eventually benefited directly. The conclusion came in 1832, accompanied by complaints from Tories such as Walter Scott that it marked the end of Scotland. The parliamentary and burgh franchise was vastly extended (although still embracing less than two per cent of the male population), leading to immediate Liberal dominance of Scottish politics. Thus the reform was welcomed by Liberals: it was believed, in the words of the Solicitor General, Henry Cockburn, to have given Scotland a consti-tution for the first time (Lenman, 1981, p. 162). The victory of liberalism, he said, was the 'liberation of Scotland', providing opportunities for patri-otic expression where previously there had been nothing but abuses and national frustration (Cockburn, 1988, pp. 446, 470). Not for the first, or last, time did one Scottish faction proclaim as a national victory what their opponents lamented as the final death of the true national spirit.

The Tories failed thereafter to capture the middle class, unlike in Eng-land, because Liberalism became the Scottish national ideology, firmly grounded in a cautious evangelical radicalism. When the church split in two in 1843 (on which more below), corresponding factions emerged to fight over the true allegiance of Liberal politics. But so dominant was the Liberal party that for most of the century it could afford these internal disputes and still soundly beat the Tories electorally.

Liberalism, in other words, became as much a national crusade as a matter of politics – a belief in free trade, free speech and religious rectitude. The political effects of this ideology were felt in practical good works, not in any campaigning for national rights of the sort that liberals did undertake elsewhere in Europe. The point is that the Scots did not have to do this because, after 1832, they believed themselves already to be in possession of those rights to a uniquely privileged degree. They prided themselves on being partners with England in the Empire, a continuation of that self-image which had been created initially by Henry Dundas. They continued to maintain this sense of union by asserting their national identity, as we will see later, but – because that assertion usually won them what they wanted – they felt no need to push further for fundamentally new national institutions.

In this they were helped by the English, who, as before, continued to let Scotland do as it wanted. England was aware of Scotland (and Ireland) as separate countries: when the prime minister, Robert Peel, was trying to woo the Scots bourgeoisie for the Tories in 1837, he referred to 'the three countries' of the UK, with their three religious traditions (Fry, 1987, p. 36). But for most of the time the English ignored Scotland. The Scots complained about English indifference – as they still do today – but were happy with the freedom that it gave them.

Real control of Scottish government lay with the Lord Advocate, who was nominally only adviser to the British Home Secretary, but who in practice could exercise substantial autonomy over affairs which did not

affect England's security. This extended to control of Scottish law enforcement – regulating the police force, and recommending to the Home Secretary when the army should be used to quell civil unrest. Even in emergencies,
London did not interfere directly, for example in the 1880s when Highland
crofters were protesting against landlords. So much did the Home Secretary
keep out of the politics of those bodies for which he was theoretically
responsible that they had to remind him what they were for whenever
they had occasion to make contact with him. This remoteness of Westminster government came about because of that growing tendency which we
noted in chapter 2 for the UK state to try to divest itself of local matters.
The purpose of the central state was to run the Empire; within the UK
(and indeed within the Empire more widely) the government functioned
by a system that was, in effect, federal.

In particular, parliament in London was rarely interested in intervening
in Scottish matters, unless Scottish factions invited it to do so. There was
a growing tendency for Scottish MPs to settle Scottish business outside
parliament, submitting the results for largely formal ratification to the full
house. Thus the Scots functioned as an informal domestic parliament
within the imperial legislature. For example, as we will see in detail later,
the English Lord Chancellor was willing to extend proposed commercial
legislation to Scotland only if the Scots could first reach a consensus that
this was desirable. The Scottish sub-parliament was especially important
for private bills, which were far more common and influential than they
are today (and had been so since before 1832). They were the means
whereby the governing councils of cities, towns, universities or various
other public agencies would extend their powers; they also provided the
legal framework for the development of railways, docks and other large
public works. A Scottish private bill would be proposed by a Scottish MP
and debated by other Scottish MPs. Usually, these Scottish votes would
determine the bill's fate.

In the building of the Scottish consensus, the continuing independence
of civil society was crucial and was what made that process genuinely
autonomous. Thus we find that the Scottish Board of Supervision, which
took charge of the poor law and related matters after 1845 (see below),
consulted with its local agents on the need for legislation, and then presented
the conclusions to the Lord Advocate; he in turn agreed to draft legislation.
Nearly always, this mechanism led to the legislation which the consultation
had proposed.

If the Lord Advocate was central, so also was the legal profession in
general. We will see later that the sheriff played an even more important
local role than in the eighteenth century. Lawyers took a prominent part
in Scottish national government – for example, staffing the new boards
that oversaw social welfare. Nationally, by the middle of the century, the
profession had gained a new self-confidence that they were a key estate in

the nation. They campaigned for Scottish lawyers to be given fair recognition as partners in the Empire, they commented on any significant legislation that might affect Scotland, and they instigated legislation when that seemed appropriate and urgent, often using private bills. Frequently this process was supplemented by Royal Commissions, which were ad-hoc bodies appointed to investigate the need for legal reform by examining expert witnesses. The use of Commissions grew as the century progressed, from about one per year in the early part to an average of seven in the middle, reaching a maximum of thirteen in 1859. The Faculty of Advocates also successfully resisted encroachments by the English courts on Scottish jurisdiction. The continued importance of common law meant that much of the daily regulation of Scottish society lay in the hands, not of parliament, but of the courts, responding to the urgings of lawyers.

For most men of the middle class, the national purpose to which any government was subservient was the pursuit of business. The Scottish economy did indeed grow massively in the nineteenth century, aided by the free-trade policies and by the expansion of the Empire. It was a self-financing economy, too, run by tightly interlocking networks of local entrepreneurs whose capital, education and culture were emphatically Scottish. The Scottish legal framework had been particularly favourable to business expansion ever since the reforms introduced by Henry Dundas in 1772. England did not catch up until 1856. Far from Scotland's being a colony of England, it actually had a fully-fledged national economy of its own. And for anyone who could not prosper at home, there was always the option of emigration to England or the wider empire. In all this, the Scottish bourgeoisie experienced more favourable conditions – sometimes much more so – than many of their counterparts elsewhere in Europe, for example in Bohemia or Poland. Liberalism often had to turn to political nationalism in these places simply to free an industrialising economy from the frustrations of an outdated empire (chapter 5). The Scots had no such problems, and therefore no such nationalist needs.

As before, of course, none of this would have been possible if the Scots had threatened English security. But there was no prospect of that, because there were no deep ideological divisions between the two countries. Scottish Liberalism and English Toryism may have detested each other in the way that is common between political parties; but on the fundamentals, especially of policies for foreign affairs and the Empire, they agreed.

The Empire, indeed, was something of which the Scots were immensely proud. It was theirs as much as England's: by the time of the high point of British imperialism in the last quarter of the century, the Empire allowed the Scots to believe that the special destiny that had given Scotland the lead in British Protestantism was now being extended throughout the globe. As Thomas Carlyle put it in his *Portrait of John Knox* in 1875:

Scottish Puritanism, well considered, seems to me distinctly the noblest and completest form that the grand sixteenth-century Reformation anywhere assumed. We may say also that it has been by far the most widely fruitful form; for, in the next century, it had produced English Cromwellian Puritanism with open Bible in one hand, drawn sword in the other . . . So that now we look for the effects of it, not in Scotland only, or in our small British Islands only, but over wide seas, huge American continents, and growing British Nations in every zone of the earth. (Carlyle, 1899, pp. 359–60)

A chosen people indeed.

Through this association with Protestantism, the Empire penetrated to everyday life. It provided the opportunity to emigrate, not only to missionaries but also to engineers, doctors and administrators. It also opened up vast markets, to which – after the middle of the century – were exported the products of Scotland's heavy engineering, and from which came the raw materials for the textile and tobacco industries. And, as we will see later, it also allowed Scotland to import and export culture, of which Protestantism was a central component.

Ruling over the Empire was the increasingly popular monarchy. Having ignored Scotland for more than a century and a half until George IV's visit to Edinburgh in 1822, the monarchy acquired a distinctively Scottish face under Queen Victoria from 1837. She and her consort, Prince Albert, fell in love with the romantic idea of Scotland, and their annual holiday at Balmoral Castle on Deeside advertised a journey to the Highlands as a fashionable tourist trail for the wealthy middle class throughout the United Kingdom and beyond. Victoria became a symbol of the unity of Britain and the success of the Empire, but her chosen identification with Scotland ensured that she became also a sign of the distinctive Scottish contribution to the entire successful enterprise.

SOCIAL POLICY

As in the first century of the Union, the political debates that did take place were not systematically between Scotland and England, but rather within the governing bodies of Scotland. Scottish social policy was governed by the system of supervisory boards that grew from the 1840s onwards – local and national committees of lawyers, other professionals, and aristocrats who were put in charge of administering all the subsequent social legislation that parliament produced in the nineteenth century. They ran the poor law, the rudimentary system of public health, and the lunatic asylums. They managed the prisons and the industrial schools for young offenders. They were in charge of registering births, marriages and deaths; and they oversaw the provision of burial grounds. Later they took charge of elementary schools, agriculture and the development of the Highlands.

They supervised several aspects of local government – for example, valuation of property (the basis of local taxes) and housing regulations.

The national and local boards which oversaw the poor law after 1845 provided such a successful model that it was repeatedly copied, either by giving more and more powers to these boards themselves, or by creating new ones on similar lines. Thus new intermediate institutions between the people and the state were all thoroughly Scottish. As a result, Scottish social administration was more centralised by the middle of the century than the English system, as the national boards acquired more directive powers over local practices. The key piece of legislation in this respect was the Public Health Act of 1867, which gave the Board of Supervision powers to direct local boards to take measures to promote public health. Nevertheless, even with this centralisation, the local state remained powerful, because the central boards had to work through a network of local inspectors who had considerable local autonomy. The inspectors were lawyers or other professionals, such as doctors, architects or surveyors; they were therefore embedded in wider Scottish civil society, through Scottish professional associations and, in some cases, the Scottish universities.

The reason for the change to the poor law in 1845 was a social-policy counterpart to the decay of the representative system before 1832. When the Church of Scotland split in 1843, the previous system of poor relief by the parish finally collapsed, although it had been insecure for some time. The 1845 Act established two tiers of government – new secular parish boards (of which more later) and the national Board of Supervision. This latter was intended to be representative, though not elected: for example, by statute it had to include the sheriffs of three named counties, which were widely separated geographically, the Lords Provost of Edinburgh and Glasgow, and two professional officers. Thus it is a graphic instance of the practice of representation by trusteeship rather than delegation which we cited from McLennan in chapter 2 – 'Scots, but not quite of the new Scotland', in the words of Levitt (1988, p. xl).

The board was left to itself by the United Kingdom state: it was very rarely mentioned in parliament. Indeed, there is no evidence that even the Cabinet took any interest in the Scottish poor law at any time between 1845 and 1921. The legislation which governed the board was permissive, and within that framework it had considerable autonomy. Similar points can be made about the other boards. The constitution of the Board of Supervision remained largely unchanged until 1894, when it became the Local Government Board with new responsibilities for overseeing the new county councils.

Thus a fair summary is that Scottish domestic government consisted of the national and local boards, and the councils of the large burghs and the cities. All were staffed by the new service professions such as law, accountancy, medicine and surveying. They were the other estate, to complement the lawyers and the churches. It is no surprise that the Scottish middle class – especially the professionals – could feel that, in social policy at least, they had created their own state, of a type which they much preferred to what they saw as the windy and ineffective rhetoric of parliament. These people wanted to do things, not to debate. The point is put well by W. L. MacKenzie (1862–1935), who was the statutory medical member of the Local Government Board from 1904 to 1919. His career could be taken as paradigmatic of Scottish middle-class philanthropy: of modest though not poor origins near Tain in Ross and Cromarty, he studied at Aberdeen and Edinburgh universities, worked as local medical officer of health in Kirkcudbright, Leith and Edinburgh, compiled several reports on the health of Scottish children, and instituted reform of Scottish housing. He wrote in 1914:

> Usually we think of the State as an organisation compelling as from above, not as an organisation created by ourselves from below . . . [but] the State is simply the name for all the institutions and mechanisms necessary to enable the citizen to realise the life of the family. If we keep steadily to that view, the State can never become an opponent of the family; it will become rather the higher plane of organisation on which the inner purposes of the family can alone be realised. (Levitt, 1988, p. xl)

That last point reminds us also that Liberalism continued to maintain the eighteenth-century separation between politics and the inner purposes of the people, believing that the purpose of statecraft was to free the nation from political interference; we return to this in our discussion of culture and nationalism later.

MacKenzie wrote these words when the system was in decline. The ideas of social welfare sponsored by the state had come to dominate the Liberal Party, partly in response to the extension of the franchise to much larger groups of working-class men. These ideas began to be implemented from 1906 onwards. Scottish government, too, was changing: the boards were being reorganised under the Scottish Office. And some people had resisted this change as threatening the end of Scottish autonomy (for example, James Moncrieff, who was Lord Advocate in the middle of the century). This debate and these changes belong to chapter 6, for they form the basis of discussion of Scottish government in the twentieth century. The point here is that a system of national government that had seemed to Walter Scott in 1832 to be a threat to Scottish autonomy had become, within eighty years, that autonomy's very essence.

LOCAL GOVERNMENT

The operation of the national boards depended on self-governing local politics. Most importantly, revenues for spending on social policy were overwhelmingly local in origin. The local professional officers of the boards were not the only arm of the local state; there was the sheriff, but real political power also lay with the burghs and the counties, run by the local middle-class elite – 'landowners, farmers, ministers, schoolmasters, businessmen, rentiers, shopkeepers' (Harvie, 1981, p. 8). Only the details of this differed from England, because Britain was then one of the most decentralised states in Europe. But – as in the eighteenth century – the prior existence of Scottish civil society ensured that local autonomy in Scotland meant that Scottish autonomy as a whole was preserved.

The local agent of the state – outside the cities and large burghs – continued to be the sheriff, whose powers grew. This happened mainly because most new legislation from central government placed initial jurisdiction with the sheriff courts – for example, in matters of health, factory acts, nuisances and building regulations. The local boards to oversee the poor law and other matters of social policy always included the sheriff. He was thus involved in virtually every aspect of social affairs. Another reason for the expansion in the sheriff's role was a popular preference for settling disputes in the sheriff courts rather than in the courts of the justices of the peace. The sheriff courts were even preferred to the central Court of Session and House of Lords, which had become congested. In particular, the sheriff court of Lanarkshire (based in Glasgow) became, in effect, the main commercial court of Scotland.

One response to these extended powers was appointing more sheriffs substitute (that is, deputies), prohibiting them from taking any other office, and requiring them to be qualified advocates. This professionalisation of local administration cemented the sheriffs even more firmly into the culture of the national Scottish legal system. Their national character was aided by the fact that the sheriff and sheriffs substitute were chosen by the Lord Advocate, on the advice of the local elites. This is an important difference from local officials within other multinational states in Europe: the prefects and similar personnel in Austria-Hungary, Spain and France were appointed by the imperial centre, not by, say, Bohemia, Catalonia or Corsica. An equally important difference is that the sheriff never had any power to dismiss elected local councillors or their staff. The Lord Advocate, working through the legal system, thus turns out once again to be a key figure in Scottish autonomy, but even his powers were limited by local self-government.

The forum for that local autonomy in rural areas continued to be the commissioners of supply until 1889, when they were transformed into county councils on a more firmly democratic basis. As before, the commissioners were the voice of the county, and the avenue through which central government would communicate with it.

In the urban areas – which were growing in size and importance – local democracy was transformed in 1833. Burgh reform had been at least as important as parliamentary reform (and, indeed, the one entailed the other, because before that time the burgh councils had elected some of the MPs). Their franchise expanded throughout the century, broadly in parallel with the reforms for parliament. The scope for independent action by the towns was increased in 1862, when the Burgh Police Act allowed for new police burghs to be set up. This was in response to a pessimistic belief that the ancient town councils were so mired in undemocratic corruption that reform was not enough. The elected police authorities were empowered to take over the running of local affairs. Whether this should happen, and the extent of the transfer of powers to the police commissioners, was to be decided by the town's significant property holders. The main impact of the Police Act was in the newly industrialised towns which had not previously had a council at all, and which had expanded rapidly. But even in other places the police authorities became parallel administrations to the old councils. Only at the end of the century was the parallel system ended.

Thus there were strong electoral incentives for burghs to develop efficient local administration. Moreover, whether governed by new police authorities, or by reformed versions of the old councils, the burghs were jealously independent. Being elected from the urban middle class, rather than appointed from the rural landowners, the burgh authorities were dominated more by the Liberal Party than was the Board of Supervision. The larger of the burghs could prevent the board from having any say at all within their boundaries. More constructively, the burghs used private bills in parliament to initiate programmes of social welfare aimed at tackling the same problems of social dislocation as had led to the setting up of the board. They also acted as local agents for some aspects of central government legislation, such as the health and safety aspects of the Factory Acts.

The burghs were like a fourth estate after the law, the churches and the boards. The Convention of Royal Burghs rivalled the churches' general assemblies as a national body, and lobbied for legislation throughout the century in much the same way as the Faculty of Advocates did. Its most successful national campaign was for the setting up of the Scottish Office under a Scottish Secretary in 1885 (on which more below), and in that campaign it did function like the diets of Central European nations. It carried the symbolism of national sovereignty, even though its demands were for limited reform.

THE CHURCH AND PHILANTHROPIC ORGANISATIONS

If Scottish politics was an internal affair, then the most burning issue was religion. The Church of Scotland broke in half in 1843, and lost as a result a great deal of its political influence. This Disruption has been judged to be the single most important event in nineteenth-century Scottish politics, a 'national revolution' (Fry, 1987, p. 59). Such an interpretation has been followed enthusiastically by some recent nationalist works, claiming the event as Scotland's version of the nationalist rebellions that were to appear throughout Europe over the following eighty years.

Certainly the event was important in terms purely of church politics. Two out of every five ministers resigned office, taking with them about half the members. With amazing fortitude, these people – men and women – then set about creating a new Free Church from scratch. That they soon ran into financial difficulties should not detract from their achievements – building churches in over 700 of the roughly 950 parishes, and schools in over 500 of them.

Undoubtedly, also, the issue of the Disruption was constitutional – a protest against the right of lay patrons to appoint ministers. Since this right had been reintroduced in 1712 by the London parliament, and since that parliament refused to accept the Claim of Right protesting against patronage in 1842, there is a case to be made that the break was, in part, a form of national assertion. The members of the Free Church understandably regarded their demonstration and subsequent achievements as a great victory for Scottish Presbyterianism over the secular state.

However, the main reason why Fry is right in his assessment of the importance of this event is that it marked the end of a particular sort of church influence on politics, not a nationalist revolution. Even the most ardent champions of the Claim of Right pulled back in horror from anything more than a rhetorical challenge to the Union. No church could any longer claim to be the state, or even the local state. In fact, this decline had been true before 1843 too, for about one quarter of all adherents of Presbyterianism at that time were already members of various small churches that had broken away earlier. These groups came together into the United Presbyterian Church in 1847. Equally importantly, as we have seen, the established church was increasingly incapable of responding adequately to social problems as industrialisation grew.

Even more dismaying for the Presbyterians, both the continuing Church of Scotland and the new Free Church claimed to be the true national established church. The United Presbyterians were voluntarists, opposed to establishment in principle. When the Church of Scotland did not simply collapse in the face of the 1843 schism, the political stage was thus set for endless warfare, as each of the three factions recruited allies in the Liberal party. Fry judges that the ultimate political effect of the Disruption was therefore pernicious: 'petty and malicious impotence precluded any serious search for solutions in accord with [Scotland's] traditions' (Fry, 1987, p. 52). An extended example of how these jealousies could delay much-needed reform is given later, in the discussion of education.

Nevertheless, the extent of state interference with the church can be exaggerated, and it diminished as the century progressed. Lay patronage was abolished in the Church of Scotland in 1874. The government respected the churches as sources of social advice, the Lord Advocate for example consulting them over educational reform. By 1885, the prime minister, Gladstone, was willing to accept the essence of the Claim of Right: church affairs, he said (referring now to the question of disestablishment) are 'a Scotch question, and ought to be decided by the people of Scotland – that is, Parliament ought to accept their sense' (Hanham, 1969a, p. 437). He was doing no more than articulating what had in practice been the case for some time.

Thus church politics had the same characteristics as Scottish politics as a whole: the key divisions were within Scotland, not between it and London. The disputes over lay patronage were between congregations and the Court of Session, not London. It was Scottish judges in that Court and the House of Lords who invented the concept of the absolute sovereignty of parliament to justify their defence of patrons' rights, and they justified this in turn as a defence of the traditional national role of the Church of Scotland. As the historian S. J. Brown has written, 'the Scottish Reformation was sufficiently muddy territory to enable both sides to claim historical justification' (S. J. Brown and Fry, 1993, p. 13). The UK parliament was thus dragged into the disputes by Scottish invitation.

In any case, the churches retained great moral influence, especially locally where their strength lay (as it had always done). Scotland remained overwhelmingly Protestant, and the disputatiousness of the theologians did not prevent members of the three churches from working together amicably in secular forums such as local poor-law boards. The Scottish middle class was too mundanely practical to allow ideological disputes to stand in the way of getting things done; and, in any case, the schisms in the national church were by no means unique in Europe.

Indeed, various apparently secular reforms had among their greatest effects a transformation in the nature of Protestantism, and a strengthening of its influence on social policy. The reason why the evangelicals won control of the general assembly in 1834 – and therefore were able later to issue the Claim of Right – was the reform of the burghs: their somewhat democratised governing councils sent more evangelicals than before. The heritors remained the most substantial figures in the community, retaining moral power even though the formal governing role of the church might have declined.

Formal power was not the only way in which the church could govern.

The various state takeovers of traditional church functions in the second part of the century, although ostensibly secularising, were, in fact, victories for religious evangelicals, skilfully using the opportunities of state authority and finance to further their projects. As C. G. Brown argues, 'between the 1870s and the 1920s, the churches had played a significant part in creating and controlling local civil government'. New institutions had been set up 'in large part at the behest of Presbyterian dissenters seeking the break-up of the established church's monopoly control of civil institutions' (C. G. Brown, 1992, p. 65). The local poor-law boards were dominated by ministers and elders, and so became surrogate kirk sessions, as did the school boards after 1872 and the parish councils after 1896. In some parishes, the kirk session of the Church of Scotland was still policing morals as late as the end of the nineteenth century, even for people who adhered to other churches.

More informal still were the burgeoning philanthropic organisations. This also gave middle-class women a role in social policy that was substantial without challenging male dominance of the more formal structures. For example, there was the crusading zeal of the women who made up the National Vigilance Association to save children from prostitution (Cree, 1993). This enthusiasm stemmed from religious principles, but these were not only Presbyterian: the Scottish Episcopal Church had its base in the wealthy middle class, who preferred its moderation to the evangelical fire of the Presbyterians. That church, although allied to the Church of England, was emphatically Scottish, conscious of its Jacobite past. It also became a key institution for socialising middle-class English immigrants into Scottish civil society.

Even more than the men, women were influencing Scotland by the devices of civil society. Later in the century, some middle-class women also gained the vote in local elections, for example for municipal councils in 1882 and for school boards in 1873. In some places, women therefore constituted a sizeable proportion of the local electorate, for instance seventeen per cent in Glasgow as a whole in 1901, and higher in middle-class areas. From 1873, women were also allowed to stand for election to school boards, and some of them achieved significant educational advances for women and for the working class: an example is Flora Stevenson in Edinburgh.

What united the diversity of middle-class social groups who were promoting social welfare was committed Christianity, and in this the common principles mattered more than the institutional fissures. R. D. Anderson has described the resulting civil society as being far closer to the 'German idea of the ethical state' than to the hostility to state action that dictated social policy in England, or at least in those parts of England not dominated by Methodism (R. D. Anderson, 1992a, p. 69). He cites the view of the prominent evangelical leader and social reformer Thomas Chalmers, speaking in 1826, that 'the principles [of laissez faire] applicable to trade could not be extended to education' (p. 70). Such a judgment could be replicated across the spectrum of social policy. For example, in public health, a belief grew in the nineteenth century that the responsible middle class ought to tackle the social causes of disease. In education, the wealthy would provide schools and bursaries to enable at least the academically able poor to make progress. It was the duty of the strong to protect the weak, and the role of state was to provide the institutions by which that philanthropic vocation could be pursued.

In these senses, the state and ideology which the middle class established in Scotland was more interventionist than in England. But it did share one important characteristic with England: it was above all local. This was as true of philanthropy as of the structures of government, and indeed the civic activities of a city such as Glasgow were a partnership between wholly voluntary activities and the local state. Localism and voluntarism were the ways in which an enthusiasm for public intervention could coexist happily with a liberal scepticism about the role of central government. It was also the way that Scottish self-government could remain acceptable to England: Scotland was not claiming a state of a formal type, but was able to pursue statist ends by civil-society means.

CULTURE AND NATIONALISM

It was not only the economy that flourished in this framework; a variety of Scottish cultures did too. Some of this was the direct product of an explicit nationalism which was in practice very similar to the nationalisms of small countries all over Europe. Indeed, with Walter Scott, it was actually prototypical for these. His novels had the effect of creating the community of Scotland by imagining it. In certain respects, he gave birth to a new definition of that community: now that Jacobitism was no longer a serious political threat to the state, he and his followers could build a newly unified national culture around the symbols of the Highlands and Gaelic. The audience was receptive partly because of the general romantic appeal of the Highlands and the lost cause of Jacobitism. But there was, too, an attenuated loyalty to the Highland social system: the new clan societies were not only immensely popular among Lowland Scots with Highland names, but also played a national role in famine relief in the middle of the century. That they had the resources to do this ironically reflected the business and social success of people who had left the Highlands behind.

If the tone of the culture derived from Walter Scott was elegiac, that too was common among liberal nationalists elsewhere: the point of invoking the past was, in their belief, to address the present: *reculer pour mieux sauter,* in the phrase used by Tom Nairn to characterise this Janus-faced character of modernising nationalism. The Scots looked to a partly imaginary past, not because they doubted who they were or had some sense of inferiority in their relationship with England, but because they knew that they would discover in the new received version of their own history great national deeds which would demonstrate the strength that they were sure they had for the future.

From this emerged that strangest of phenomena, unionist nationalism, something that is not wholly dead even in the late twentieth century (Morton, 1994). Unionism and nationalism were mutually dependent. To be a true unionist, it was necessary to be a nationalist, because otherwise Scotland would not be a partner in a Union but become dependent on England. Thus the exploits of national heroes such as Robert the Bruce and William Wallace – whose leadership had liberated Scotland from English dominance at the beginning of the fourteenth century – were celebrated as a unionist achievement. Without them, it was argued, Scotland would not have had the historical strength to negotiate a Union with such a powerful country as England.

On the other hand, to be a true nationalist it was also necessary to be a unionist. This version of the argument was a pragmatic recognition of the limitations on the sovereignty that is available to small nations. The best way of defending Scotland's national interests was to maintain the alliance with England in foreign affairs; only in that way would Scotland be able to develop its own society and culture free from outside interference. What is more, this developing Scottish culture would then be exportable. Scots made a substantial contribution to British culture in the nineteenth century – not only in Scotland, but also in England and throughout the Empire. The Scots became renowned for their hard-headed realism – collecting statistics, running Mechanics' Institutes for the education of skilled workers, and contributing to the great engineering works that were transforming the British landscape. The epitome and instructor of the practical Victorian bourgeoisie, Samuel Smiles, came from a dour Protestant background near Edinburgh. From his teaching, it was believed, and not just by Scots, came Britain's greatness.

The nationalism also had the recognisably European effect of reviving or inventing popular culture. The late nineteenth century was the all-time high point in writing in Scots, which had been the language of the Scottish court before the Union of the Crowns in 1603, but had since become a patois. The removal of special taxes on newspapers and magazines in 1855 opened the way for a rapid growth in the number of titles. Donaldson (1986) shows that they carried many and substantial articles in Scots, often on themes relating to the social conditions of the working class, or to radical politics, or to the kind of foreign affairs that would interest a liberal readership. Some of the magazines serialised novels of social realism, and carried poetry and songs. The belief that Scottish popular culture in the nineteenth century was parochial and reactionary cannot be sustained:

the literature of which that is true – the kailyard – was produced largely for a market of expatriates.

The radicalism of some of this writing was associated with recurrent bouts of radical politics, and as in the eighteenth century this was directed against an indigenous elite. Examples include the agitation for extending the franchise, first to wider groups of men, and then later in the century to women. The protests in the Highlands against evictions of people by landlords in favour of sheep and grouse-moors evolved into one of the most successful radical movements in Britain, achieving at least as much in the way of land reform as the Irish Land League on which it was modelled. Some of these radical movements did advocate a Scottish parliament, especially towards the end of the century. But others – notably the Chartists – did not, and in general the nationalist dimension of the campaigning was subordinate to the main aim of social reform or revolution. The enemy was the Scottish ruling class, who seemed to be in such undisputed control of Scotland that there was no easy equating of radical protest with separatism. For workers or peasants who found the Scottish conditions unbearable, there was the desperate option of emigration, a crucial social safety-valve throughout the century.

Scottish culture was not only populist or even radical, however. The Enlightenment continued to have its effects, again despite some modern claims that it had died around 1820. There was, it is true, a change of direction towards science and technology, the most visible legacy of which is in the emphatically Scottish public architecture which still dominates most Scottish towns and cities. But that was merely to follow the logical conclusions of the dominant common-sense school of philosophy, which taught that knowledge should be in the service of human beings. Science and practical theology suited the national spirit – especially of the solidly practical bourgeoisie – and yielded in politics that highly effective evangelical liberalism that we have discussed.

So, if we ask where Scottish nationalism was in the nineteenth century, we can give two answers. One comes from the institutional and religious developments that we have surveyed earlier in the chapter: Scottish nationalism was a successful, practical and official nationalism, engaged in building a state to rival in its modernity the most advanced in Europe. It believed itself to be at the forefront of social development, and the economic success which Scotland enjoyed seemed to confirm this self-confidence. It was a nationalism which did not demand a parliament for the simple reason that it believed that it could get what it wanted without a parliament – economic growth, free trade, liberty, cultural autonomy.

And that last is the other place where we find Scottish nationalism, although the political relevance of this cultural activity was contested. Certainly there remained the view that culture should be free from politics: as Henry Cockburn put it in 1853, 'the features and expressions of a people cannot be perpetuated by legislative engraving' (Smout, 1992, p. 261). In this respect, the Scots shared a common belief of European romanticism that the essence of the nation lay in its people and culture, and that state forms were superficial. As we have seen, this view also had firm Scottish origins in the eighteenth century.

But the cultural revivals and reinventions could not but contribute to national politics, just as they did elsewhere. Hanham (1969) dates the founding of modern Scottish nationalism to the 1850s, in the sense that this was the time when Scots started to articulate their nationalist demands in something like a modern form. There were campaigns to restore what were believed to be historical Scottish rights, fuelled by what was still a vibrant school of Scottish historical writing. There was also pressure for more Scottish representatives in parliament. All this rhetoric has parallels elsewhere – for example, in the recurrent demands for Czech rights against Viennese centralism.

The key difference in Scotland, however, is that these demands largely worked. The National Association for the Vindication of Scottish Rights (1853) wanted institutional reform to enable the pursuit of social reform. Thus, because the grievances were managerial, they could be satisfied by the expanding boards that we discussed earlier. Later in the century, the same kind of nationalist discontent produced another managerial solution, the founding of the modern Scottish Office. The issue then was the alleged neglect of Scottish business by the existing administrative arrangements. By the 1880s, this frustration was widespread enough to produce a political consensus for a separate Scottish Secretary: in January 1884, the Convention of Royal Burghs organised a large and representative meeting in Edinburgh, which convinced the government that change was indeed wanted in Scotland. The outcome in 1885 was the inauguration of the Scottish Office, which in the next decade took over the central government role in all the main areas of Scottish administration – local government, education, social policy, law.

The campaign for the Scottish Office was both instrumental and nationalist. It sought a new government department in order to get certain things done; but the framework in which the campaigners imagined their proposed solutions was nationalist, in the sense that they sought to advance the interests of the nation of Scotland. Their opponents shared this framework: the reason why Lyon Playfair opposed transferring education to the Scottish Office was a fear that Scotland would thereby become provincial – an example of the belief that Scotland could be a full nation only in union. The dispute was not about whether there was a Scottish national interest; it was about how best to serve it. After the Office was established, its nationalist role grew. It quickly became the focus of all Scottish campaigning, even in policy areas where it had no formal remit.

Repeatedly, therefore, nationalism was about the inadequate treatment of Scottish business by the state, not about imposed policies, far less about oppression. A nationalism of this sort is satisfied if it gets the instruments which it thinks it needs. In rhetorical flights of protest, the Union might be questioned, but it was never really threatened even by those who had temporarily lost an argument, for example the factions in the church disputes. The unity of parliament remained largely unchallenged until the last decade of the century because it still had in its favour the powerful arguments about international security, free trade and a common British culture.

Not that the Scots were as straightforwardly enthusiastic for assimilation to England as in the eighteenth century. A more sceptical attitude to English culture emerged in the 1820s. The Scots still insisted on making the Union as complete as possible, but now more emphasis was placed on mutual respect between the partners. The particular incident that provoked these feelings then was a proposal to remove the rights of banks to issue their own notes – a response to a liquidity crisis that was confined to England. The Scottish middle class did not like the proposal, and, as Phillipson points out, the discussions that took place were conducted in a newly Scottish context – 'almost as though Scotland were an independent country'. He judges this to be 'a sure sign of latent nationalism', and it was a nationalism appearing at the highest levels of society (Phillipson, 1969, pp. 181–2). Walter Scott wrote some influential public letters on the matter, which included the jeremiad about the threat to Scotland's soul which I quoted in chapter 1.

So this was a defensive action, and Phillipson implicitly contrasts it to a more self-confident nationalism because it was limited in its aims: Scott's letters, he says, were 'not a call to action, but a substitute for it' (p. 184). But we can doubt the judgment without dissenting from Phillipson's characterisation of the limited nature of the protest. The point is that the action which was taken did work in the terms which it set itself: Scottish banks retained their rights to issue banknotes. This kind of thing happened again and again in Scotland in the nineteenth century: specific demands were met to the satisfaction of those making them.

Usually this success was achieved readily because the English had no particular interest in imposing on Scotland, as we have seen earlier in this chapter. Because the main political schisms were between parties, not between Scotland and England, the Scots always had prominent allies in the English Liberal Party or among English religious dissenters. The worst that could be said was usually that the English acted in ignorance of Scotland, and were willing to rescind a policy only when the Scots complained loudly enough and with enough of a consensus. Elsewhere in Europe – the 'normal' nationalisms to which the Scots' is sometimes invidiously compared – national demands often started off in exactly the same low-key way. They escalated only when the particular grievances were not met, and even then, as we will see in chapter 5, liberal nationalism usually tried to avoid the most extreme path of separatism.

Nevertheless, although less adulatory of English culture than before, the Scots continued to project their destiny – both cultural and political – in close association with England. The main pressure for assimilation now came from commercial interests: the merchants of Glasgow, for example, were less interested in the ancient rights and culture of Scotland than in free trade under common legal conditions. But to argue that this assimilation of commercial law was imposed on such self-confident people as the Glasgow bourgeoisie is implausible. The pressure was indigenous: as Rodger puts it, 'Scots law changed in character in the nineteenth century precisely because of changes in Scottish society' (Rodger, 1992, p. 571). English commercial lawyers were in fact indifferent to what went on in Scotland: it was only Scottish pressure which forced the extension of the main commercial legislation to Scotland, culminating in the Sale of Goods Act of 1893. The campaign for harmonising commercial law was led by the Glasgow merchants but also included, for example, the Aberdeen Chamber of Commerce, the Faculty of Advocates and the distinguished legal academic and Liberal politician John Dove Wilson.

Although the development of commercial law was seen at the time as an adoption of English measures, it was also believed to be merely the first step in an eventual international code, an aspiration shared by liberals everywhere (including nationalist liberals). The discussion in Scotland often drew parallels with Germany which, in 1862, adopted a common commercial code for the whole federation. Scots business people, pointing out that Germany had thus achieved more uniformity than the UK, urged on politicians and lawyers the continued pursuit of that familiar utopia, full completion of the Union.

Assimilation in general was also supported by the emerging principles of professionalism: for example, the Public Health Act of 1867 was the result of pressure on the Lord Advocate by the Board of Supervision to extend the public-health laws of England and Wales to Scotland, where sanitary legislation was especially weak. This is a fairly early example of the ready surrender of Scottish distinctiveness in favour of the putatively universal claims of science; plenty more such instances have occurred in the twentieth century, as we will see in chapter 6, and these continue today. There also survived the types of assimilationist pressure that dominated the eighteenth century: thus Scots law was seen as authoritarian and out-of-date, and, to the liberals, English law was a modernist paradigm.

But if assimilation continued, it also continued to be advocated on nationalist grounds. As in the times of Dundas, the assimilation can be seen as having been chosen by the Scots, or at least by the elites that governed Scotland. A Scots tradition could be given up because the interests of the people of Scotland were believed to be more fundamental than mere custom. Thus we find the Glasgow Law Amendment Society arguing in 1853 that 'the fitness of the Scotch laws to the Scotch people has scarcely been less than at present' (Hutchison, 1986, p. 93). This is a nationalist argument, and occurred at a time when the first nationalist movement was emerging, even though it is also part of an appeal to adopt English laws: it posits an entity called the Scottish people, whose integrity is never in doubt. The dominant Whigs were usually nationalist in this sense, and were self-confident enough to choose assimilation to England when that seemed appropriate.

In choosing England, of course, they were also choosing a successful empire, which was generating its own external influences on Scotland. Writers such as Robert Louis Stevenson and Violet Jacob epitomise the link between imperial culture and colonial experiences, a Scottish instance of a very general phenomenon which has recently been analysed by Edward Said. Popular culture imbibed imperialism not only from writers such as these, but also from a whole variety of sources – exemplary tales of missionaries such as David Livingstone, celebrations of British military patriotism as subsuming Scottish nationalism, and racialist myths about the civilising effects of Scottish Protestant culture on benighted natives.

Thus, to cast the key conflict in nineteenth-century Scottish politics as being the nationalist resistance to assimilationist pressure from England is to miss the whole point. If there was a political contest involving nationalism, it was between two types of nationalism. On the one hand there was the Tory inclination to preserve ancient Scottish institutions; through Scott, this engaged with similar tendencies elsewhere in Europe. In the realm of culture, it was quite successful, but culture was believed to belong to the private realm by the liberal majority. In public politics, the dominant nationalism was liberal and therefore universalising, and liberals interpreted that as adopting English models because these had cultural prestige. Pressure for assimilation can even be said to have become a distinctive characteristic of Scottish culture. The Scots felt that they had invented rationalism in the Enlightenment; reason told them that ancient distinctions, however privately attractive, should give way in the face of progress. Thus the Scots had incorporated rationalism and universalism into their culture, and so that culture now contained the seeds of its own denial; and it still does so.

Out of this dual nationalism arose the dual identity that twentieth-century Scotland has inherited. Scots were British and Scottish: British for formal and public matters, Scottish for the family and home and community. In much of the imagery and symbolism, this duality became gendered. Britain was male, Scotland female. As throughout the UK, foreign affairs and the Empire were for men, domestic matters for women. What distinguished Scotland from England, however, was the coincidence of the gender dichotomy with the national one, and in this respect Scotland resembled other similarly placed nations in central Europe, where the essence of the nation was believed to lie in the family.

Dual identity was not the only outcome of such a process; so also, it has been suggested, is the aggressively masculine image of twentieth-century Scottish nationalism. Cairns Craig has argued that the nineteenth-century association of Scotland with femininity produced a reaction among the intellectual founders of later political nationalism, such as Hugh McDiarmid. They believed that, to have a true nationalism, Scotland had to become more manly; this, they thought, demanded all or nothing: they had forgotten about the partial, negotiated, but nevertheless real autonomy of domestic sovereignty.

EDUCATION

The story of education policy is worth examining in some detail for three reasons. The most important is that it is a very clear example of the delicate Scottish balance between autonomy and constraint, or nationalism and chosen assimilation. The second is that education has always been a Scottish icon: its autonomy having been preserved by the Union treaty in 1707, it has been seen as a main bastion of Scottish independence. The third reason stems from this: ever since the publication of George Davie's eloquent book *The Democratic Intellect* in 1961, nationalist polemic has accepted that Scottish education underwent an unprecedented and fatal anglicisation in the late nineteenth century.

Three particular issues can clarify the processes: the campaign for a national system of elementary schools, the reform of the university curriculum, and the introduction of domestic science into the school curriculum for girls. The general conclusion that emerges has been summed up simply by Sydney and Olive Checkland: 'the debate on education was recognised by many [in the nineteenth century] to be not a question lying between England and Scotland, but between two views of how Scotland should respond in educational terms to a rapidly changing world' (S. and O. Checkland, 1984, p. 8).

Scotland did not get a national system of elementary schools until 1872, two years after a corresponding English Act, despite there having been Scottish agitation since the 1830s. Many historians – for example Smout, not usually thought of as a nationalist – have taken this to show that Scottish wishes could be frustrated until the English wanted the same. But a different story can be told.

Certainly there was widespread Scottish campaigning, starting at the time of the debate which led to the Disruption of 1843. The confusion which the split in the church caused to the long-established system of parish schools led many campaigners to believe that the state should take over. This argument was combined with some of the same case that the secessionists in the Free Church had made – that it was no longer adequate to have just one school in each parish when industrialism had led to some parishes mushrooming. An especially influential intervention came from George Lewes, whose pamphlet *Scotland – a Half-Educated Nation* argued that most of the children in the new industrial areas were not receiving any education at all. The campaign was coordinated by the National Education Association of Scotland from 1850, still over twenty years before the eventual success.

Why was there the delay from the 1830s to 1872? There were three reasons, and all of them are by origin internal to Scotland, although they spilled over into debates in parliament. The first and most simple was that the established church opposed it. It feared that the loss of its schools would be the end of its formal established position, having already lost control of the poor law in 1845. The proponents of a national system were predominantly supporters of the Free or United Presbyterian Churches. The established church used its influence with MPs to delay and defeat legislation; some of these MPs sat for English constituencies, and the argument which the church used with them was that a state system in Scotland would presage the ending of the Church of England's role in education too. The initiative in this lobbying came from the Scottish church, however.

The second and third reasons for the delay were disagreements between these other two Presbyterian churches, and between both of them and the secularists in the campaign. Most simply, the Free Church wanted a more extensive religious curriculum than its allies. It secured the defeat of bills in 1850 and 1851 on these curricular grounds, and it did so by enlisting English evangelical MPs. Again, though, the initiative came from a Scottish faction.

The third reason was the most fundamental of all, and was over the principle of establishment (rather than the particular fears of the Church of Scotland). The Free Church continued to favour establishment; its difference from the Church of Scotland was essentially the sectarian one of which body should be that establishment. The United Presbyterians were voluntarists, and so favoured only non-statutory religious intervention in any school system. The secularists, of course, were opposed to any religious involvement at all. These disagreements posed a dilemma for the Lord Advocate, James Moncrieff, who drafted bills for a national system between 1850 and 1855. He was a member of the Free Church, and his proposals were seen as being partisan, 'a scheme for taxing the entire people of Scotland to the benefit of the Free Church', as the liberal and non-conformist Edinburgh *Evening News* put it (Hutchison, 1986, p. 78). The combined forces of the voluntarists therefore recruited English non-evangelical but also non-conformist MPs, and again defeated the bills.

The ultimate reasons for the delay in legislation can be seen, therefore, to have been Scottish disagreements rather than deliberate obstruction instigated in England. Certainly the various Scottish factions needed English allies, but that can be understood as an instance of a general phenomenon within small nations, however formally independent they may be. Factions in such places always have the option of calling to their aid the superior force or wealth or prestige of their allies in neighbouring big nations. If we blame the delay on English obstruction, then we would have to find a Scottish consensus so broad and stable as to be called national, and we would also have to find its being thwarted by English voting power again and again. That picture would be a caricature, implying a quite implausible degree of subservience to England by one or other of the Scottish factions (and a quite unlikely unanimity in England). Scottish majorities were temporary because the factions kept allying themselves in different groups. But none of them were English agents.

Furthermore, the eventual national system in England can be reasonably attributed to Scottish campaigning anyway. This is another strategy which campaigners in small nations can adopt: seek to persuade a sufficiently influential faction in the larger nation to support them. We will see this happening at several points in Scottish twentieth-century history in chapter 6. The internal divisions among Scottish Presbyterians had become less acrimonious by the 1870s, and so the same tactics were not used as in the middle of the century. But even the outcome in 1872 reflected new religious tensions: the Catholic Church, beginning to grow following large-scale Irish immigration, preferred that the board which governed Scottish education should share a president and secretary with the corresponding English board, because they feared Protestant bias. For the first thirteen years after 1872, this Catholic preference was satisfied. But the Catholics could not prevent the legislation coming about, because their allies in England were not powerful enough.

The second example is reform of the university curriculum, probably the most famous instance of alleged anglicisation. George Davie argues that the 1876 Commission on the Scottish universities sought to impose English ideas by inaugurating an entrance examination (thus restricting entry), by sacrificing curricular breadth to specialism, and by displacing philosophy from the central place which it had always enjoyed.

Davie's analysis of the Scottish tradition in philosophy and the curriculum is persuasive and undisputed, but he is not convincing on anglicisation. The members of the Commission would have been astonished to have been told that they were culturally dependent on the English. Most of them were solid Scottish academics and professionals looking for a way of modernising the curriculum in response to changes in the economy and society, according to their own definition of modern. The anglicisers in Davie's account – T. H. Huxley and Lyon Playfair – in fact took little part in the proceedings.

An important external change which had to be dealt with was indeed British: the competitive examinations for gaining entry to the newly professional imperial civil service required a higher degree of specialist knowledge than was being provided to Scottish students. But it is significant that this pressure was British, not English, concerning the career route into the Empire which the Scottish middle class cherished as their destiny. The main external models were not, in any case, English, but rather German and French. Both these states, moreover, were seen to be more successful economically than the UK, and (as repeatedly since) education was believed to be the key to this lead.

We may judge the Scots on the Commission to have been wrong in their definition of modernisation or in their assessment of the educational needs of the economy; but we should recognise that they were genuinely choosing their strategy on the basis of sincere beliefs, not succumbing to external pressure any more than would the education system of any small country that is faced with the need to accommodate pressures from the economy and the educational models of its neighbours. Assimilation to English models was acceptable when that seemed in the best interests of the Scottish people. Playfair, as we have seen, was a Scottish nationalist in the sense that he had in mind a conception of the Scottish national interest. In other contexts, he was ready to denounce what he felt to be inappropriate anglicisation, for example in the debate over the 1872 Education Act. Scottish advocates of curricular reform even argued in parliament that the situation demonstrated the need for a Scottish parliament: only such a body, they believed, could give the matter the attention it was due.

The outcome of these debates did not actually have the effects which Davie and others have said it did. In practice, because more students followed the full course to graduation, more of them pursued broad studies, and more took philosophy. Merely comparing the official regulations before and after the reform cannot tell us this, because they do not tell us how many students were governed by them. Students attending university came from a broader range of social classes than before, partly because of improvements in the secondary-school system; and women were admitted to graduation around the same time. (Davie and his followers always define breadth of access to mean social-class breadth, rarely mentioning gender.)

All of this explains why universities never generated the same intensity of nationalist campaigning in Scotland that they did elsewhere – for example, in central Europe, or Ireland, or Wales. The Scottish middle class already had what the middle class were agitating for in these other places: the Scots had an indisputably national system which they, in effect, controlled through the local governing bodies of the universities and through Commissions such as that of 1876.

The final educational example is the introduction of domestic science for schoolgirls. This too has been described as anglicising recently: Moore has said that it was imposed on a reluctant Scottish working class by an anglified upper class of mainly female philanthropists. It is undoubtedly true that the Scottish advocates were influenced by the popularity of domestic science in England. It is also true that prominent Scottish campaigners for girls' education objected, notably Flora Stevenson.

Again, though, we cannot see this as a matter of English imposition, unless we are to dismiss these self-confident Scottish campaigners as puppets. They were not: they were choosing a model of education for girls that seemed to them to be modernising, and indeed incipiently feminist in that it would attach educational value to women's traditional activities. The modernising, at least, was recognised by influential Scottish politicians such as Henry Brougham, who had also advocated a national system of elementary schools. It is not plausible to describe him straightforwardly as an underminer of Scottish values on the domestic-science issue when he had been on the nationalist side earlier on.

In all these three instances of educational reform, the disputes were not simply between Scotland and England. They are best characterised as showing one Scottish faction using the power of the state to impose on other Scottish factions. The successful factions were, in their own terms, modernising; and from the analysis presented earlier in this chapter we should not be surprised to find that modernisation always went along with choosing some elements of the English system. But that does not make these educational victors the mere tools of a putative English rule over Scotland. They were factions in the Scottish elite; they had their own ideology, some of which advocated the emulation of English practices; and they, like all influential elites, could impose their will on weaker segments of society – for example, working-class girls. But the imposition was indigenous: the oppressors, if there were any, were Scots, not the English.

CONCLUSIONS

Thus Scotland was indeed normal. That claim has been controversial for many decades now: at least since the nationalist cultural revival of the 1920s, the belief has gained currency that Scotland in the nineteenth century was subservient to England. This belief assumes that the only sure sign of not being subservient would have been a developed demand for an independent parliament. My argument has been to the contrary, and in that respect it is close to the image that middle-class Scots of the nineteenth century had of themselves. They had real autonomy. The mass of the people did not, but then neither did their counterparts anywhere else in Europe. As Scottish radicals knew well, the ruling social groups in Scotland would still have ruled even if a Scottish parliament had been set up.

These groups built up the institutions of civil society to coordinate the services which they believed firmly that the state had a duty to provide. As far as they could, they did this in a non-partisan way; even more surprising, they mostly did so in a way that was not religiously sectarian, as between different brands of Protestantism. In other words, drawing on the Enlightenment invention of reason, they began that process of rational government which was to have its culmination in the welfare state of the twentieth century. Scotland, then, was a paradigm of Poggi's legal state, a place where access to the government that mattered domestically depended on technical legal expertise rather than on winning elections. The governing institutions were part of civil society and were often informal; as was common throughout the highly decentralised British state, they were the creation of localities rather than impositions from the centre. At the time, this would have been seen as a significant achievement: the goal of laissez-faire liberalism was to reach the utopian condition where society regulated itself.

Was this system of government a Scottish state? There is not a simple answer, because states are not the clear-cut entities which some political theorists have assumed. If we define a state to be something which has a monopoly of violence, in Weber's famous dictum, then Scotland did not have one, although it did have full control over a share of one (insofar as it controlled internal policing). But states are more fissured than Weber allowed, except in the extreme case of external war. Scotland did have a domestic state, and its governing structures did command symbolic authority. Scotland also formed a realm of shared meanings, in the sense that discussion about social policy took for granted a Scottish realm.

We could say that this had to be 'allowed' to happen by the English, and therefore depended on their goodwill. The Scottish system of government evolved to reassure English politicians that Scotland could be kept quiet as far as foreign and imperial matters were concerned. But to say this without qualification is to misrepresent the self-confidence of the Scots. They chose quietness, because they genuinely believed in the common destinies of all the British peoples. Liberals that they emphatically were, they wanted free trade, free speech and Protestant hegemony; and they saw the British framework as the best way of attaining these ideals. Political conflict within Scotland was about how these should be interpreted, rather than about how they should be secured. The example of the campaign for a national system of schools shows this well. If one faction was able to use the power of the UK state to defeat a larger faction, the losers never reacted by seriously questioning the whole British connection. They believed that, at the next attempt, and with different English allies, it would be their turn to be the victors. All factions found this expectation to be true sufficiently often for their continuing loyalty to the system to be worthwhile.

The general conclusion, then, is that national assertion could take a variety of forms, including the form of chosen union. Building the new state was not the only Scottish activity that was felt to depend on staying in the Union. So also was the development of Scottish culture. This was partly because of the same argument about protection: for example, Scotland's distinct brand of Protestantism might be endangered within other arrangements. Partly also, however, it was because the culture itself grew to contain elements of chosen Britishness – for example, the continuing emulation of English traditions, or the new enthusiastic imperialism.

In these pragmatic cultural responses, moreover, Scotland was not the only place that developed a tradition of accommodation in pursuit of liberalism: as we will see in chapter 5, Poland in the nineteenth century recurrently opted for cooperation with Russia, Germany or Austria-Hungary, and it did so for the thoroughly nationalist reason that Polish society and culture might be allowed to flourish under safe protection. If Scotland was unique, it was only in the relative dominance of pragmatism: there was almost nothing similar to that other version of Polish nationalism, the romantic rejection of cooperation. Scotland eschewed this, not because of dependency, but because of success: romantic nationalism seemed futile because, quite simply, pragmatism worked.

5

The Autonomy of Small Nations in Nineteenth-Century Europe

So far, my argument that Scotland was relatively autonomous has been based mainly on showing the extent to which indigenous ruling groups could take decisions largely free from external interference. The purpose of this chapter is to set the Scottish case in a wider European framework. Autonomy is a relative concept, especially for small nations. Part of the problem with much nationalist rhetoric is that it compares Scotland's situation with a utopia of unfettered independence. More interesting is to ask whether Scotland's autonomy in the nineteenth century was greater or less than the country might have reasonably expected in the Europe of the times.

The conclusion of the chapter is not simple. I am certainly not suggesting that Scotland was as independent as large states. But I will argue that in some important respects it was as independent as places which enjoyed a degree of formal autonomy that Scotland did not have – notably the retention of a parliament. Thus Scotland was not as independent in all areas of policy as Finland, Norway or Hungary, but in many ways its semi-independence did resemble theirs. Scandinavia is discussed at the end of the chapter. More complex is the comparison with the realms of Austria-Hungary: apart from Austria and Hungary themselves, even the most autonomous of the national groupings there, such as the Czechs, did not enjoy the independence of Scotland. Something the same can be said about Catalonia in the Spanish state. Poland's situation was even more ambiguous, split among Austria-Hungary, Germany and Russia. For some of the time, some of its territory was more independent than Scotland in many policy areas; but for most of the time, all three parts were uniformly less independent. These examples are discussed in the central sections of the chapter. The first example is closer to Scotland: Ireland undoubtedly had less independence than its close neighbour.

A country can therefore be autonomous in some areas of policy while being dependent in others. What is more, most European nationalist movements recognised this for most of the nineteenth century. They usually did not campaign for independence, preferring autonomy in domestic matters, frequently administered by the local middle class, notably the lawyers. The goal of autonomy was usually economic development and cultural freedom, things which, as we have seen, Scotland had little difficulty in obtaining. Where autonomy was already quite strong, there was as little pressure as in Scotland for outright independence. Only when a nationalist movement met repeated oppression by the empire that ruled its territory did it start demanding more, but even then statehood did not usually became a common goal until after about 1900.

The countries which are discussed in this chapter have been selected to represent the types of autonomy that were available to small nations in nineteenth-century Europe. These types cannot be represented on a simple continuum, but the range can be crudely thought of as running from fairly full autonomy (in Scandinavia) to a high degree of constraint (for example, Poland for most of the time). The countries have also been chosen to be fairly comparable to Scotland in varied social and political respects: Catalonia and Bohemia were heavily industrialised, Hungary and Catalonia were partners in empires, Norway developed the forms of liberal democracy early on, and Ireland shared with Scotland the same central state. In other respects, of course, these places did not resemble Scotland. But the point is to show that Scotland was not as special as is sometimes claimed: other places experienced similar degrees of partial autonomy. The map in Figure 5.1 shows the location of the countries discussed, and so provides a context for the analysis of their external political situation.

The theme of the chapter is therefore negotiated autonomy. An associated idea is that a qualitative change took place in small-nation nationalism around the beginning of the twentieth century, when its goals shifted from being primarily limited autonomy to being primarily independence. This was, in turn, a reaction to the stronger national assertion of the ruling big powers. When people say in the late twentieth century that we are living in an era of 'nineteenth-century nation states', what they really mean is that we are still subject to that eventual and intransigent form that national demands took. For most of the nineteenth century, nationalists were as willing to accommodate their aspirations to reality as the nationalist proponents of European union are today.

IRELAND

The Irish parliament remained in existence until 1798, but up to 1782 its independence was severely circumscribed. Governmental power lay in the hands of the British viceroy, who manipulated the Irish parliament and exercised extensive patronage. The viceroy in turn was frequently overridden by the British Prime Minister or Home Secretary: from 1720 the British parliament could legislate directly for Ireland, and all acts of the Irish parliament had to be approved by the British one.

FIGURE 5.1: Europe in the late-nineteenth century. *Drawing by Taryn Keogh.*

So for most of the eighteenth century, despite the existence of an Irish parliament, control of Ireland was exercised by London politicians through patronage. In this, the system resembled Scotland's. But in important respects, Scotland was more autonomous. Ireland had no counterpart to the self-governing Presbyterian Church, its majority population of whatever social class being Catholic and therefore barred from government office. This religious divide between Ireland and Britain was the main reason why the British were wary of granting autonomy to anyone in Ireland. The invariably British viceroy intervened in local affairs more readily than the Scottish managers did in Scotland, and British Home Secretaries took a closer interest in Ireland than they ever did in Scotland.

Irish demands for lost rights to be restored were triggered by the American declaration of independence. But an equally important cause was the withdrawal by the British government of a promise to give the Irish access to trading opportunities in the British colonies; the withdrawal happened because of pressure from industrialists in England. In Scotland, as we have seen, access to the empire was guaranteed by the Union.

The outcome of this 'gentry nationalism', as Foster calls it (1988, p. 241), was the granting of greater independence to the Irish parliament in 1782. Nevertheless, Irish politics continued to follow the conflicts that dominated English politics, and English politicians continued to see Ireland as an appropriate place for interference. The parliament that sat between 1782 and 1798 continued to be monopolised by the Protestant ascendancy, and the viceroy continued to manage it. It has even been argued that Ireland lost economic independence by this change, because the British parliament now debated trade matters without reference to Ireland.

The most that can be said, therefore, for the century during which Ireland had a parliament and Scotland did not is that Ireland's autonomy was no greater than Scotland's. Demands for change intensified in the 1790s, coming from the liberal United Irishmen. They were modernisers – analogous to the Scottish Whigs; but unlike these Scots, they eventually conducted an armed rising against the government. The reaction by London was to abolish the parliament altogether in 1798. Thereafter, Ireland sent MPs directly to Westminster.

This Union became the reference point for Irish nationalists throughout the nineteenth century. But it can be doubted that the abolition of the parliament made much difference to Irish society. The administration of Ireland remained separate, through the office of the viceroy, which continued to run the country's local affairs. Unlike anywhere in Britain, there did not evolve a set of intermediate institutions to develop education or public health: such matters were dealt with by the viceroy. Irish local government was regarded as ramshackle, and the Protestant gentry as inadequate; the parishes were too poor to finance their own social development. In the face of this, centralised government by relatively impartial administrators was believed by the British rulers to be preferable. Attempts by the viceroy to sponsor civil-society bodies failed in the face of religious division, at least until 1898: for example, his proposed National Board of Education in the 1830s collapsed when the Protestant churches refused to take part and the Catholic Church withdrew. The absence of a local ruling elite of the Scottish (or English) type meant that reform of local government to make it more efficient was bound to involve centralisation, for example in the poor law.

Economic development required some intervention by the state, because outside the Protestant areas around Belfast there was a dearth of indigenous sources of capital. The economy was dominated by landed classes, which extracted profit for spending elsewhere. The small middle class was rural or professional, not entrepreneurial. Thus the economy was 'permanently subservient' (Lyons, 1973, p. 69). The partial exception of Belfast produced a Protestant business class, and a Protestant working class, sharing much of the aggressive unionism (but also some of the radicalism) of their Presbyterian cousins in Scotland.

Most of Ireland, in other words, had many of the characteristics of a colony, and protests against the underdevelopment took an increasingly nationalist form as the century progressed. After the secular and rationalist United Irishmen, nationalism became firmly Catholic (although not without significant supporters among the Protestant intelligentsia). The shaping political event of the nineteenth century can be seen as Catholic emancipation in 1826, which allowed the emergence of a Catholic middle class. This produced a political leadership for nationalism, in the form of MPs organised loosely as the Irish Party. But equally fundamental was the potato famine in the middle of the century, a devastating blight which caused widespread emigration and death. The effort at famine relief was carried out by the British state, and so its failures triggered anti-state protests. As in any colony, the credibility of the administration depended on its continuing to work. In Scotland, by contrast, blame for administrative failures lay clearly with autonomous Scottish bodies.

The Irish Party was nationalist, but despite the colonial situation, and despite the extremities of the famine, it remained utterly constitutional. Much of its activity was not even directly aimed at securing autonomy, but rather at exerting leverage on Westminster: for example, one of its leaders, Fintan Lalor, argued in 1847 that the repeal of the Union was less important than the protection of the economic interests of Irish tenant farmers. It was, in a sense, a somewhat incoherent coordinator of pressure groups, taking advantage of schisms in English politics and society to extract concessions for Ireland (a move reminiscent of the Liberal party's activities on behalf of Scotland). Throughout its dominance of electoral politics between the famine and 1914, the Irish Party never advocated full independence: it wanted Home Rule, a compromise recognising what was felt to be the inevitability of dependence on England.

Partly in response to this pressure, the British government developed a programme of 'constructive unionism' from 1898. (They were also seizing the tactical opportunity offered by the debacle over Gladstone's attempt to introduce Home Rule, and by the political collapse of the Irish leader Parnell over a divorce scandal.) This was, at last, an attempt to do in Ireland what had always worked well in Scotland: that is, encourage civil society by setting up truly autonomous local government. It was emulating developments which were taking place in various parts of east-central Europe (as we will see later). The response by the nationalists was pragmatic: for example, Horace Plunkett applied his nationalism to setting up cooperative rural industry. The strategy nearly worked: the material conditions of the population slowly improved (although still far behind those of Britain). But it came up against an inherited bitterness: in the rural areas, it provoked a fundamentalist nationalism, and the north-east unionists refused to cooperate because of paranoia about even the minor degree of devolution proposed by the British government in 1904. It also failed to address the social problems in the towns. The strategy was thus too late to satisfy nationalist demands by material means: separatist nationalism then wiped out the pragmatists after the 1914–18 war.

Ireland was thus a failure of UK liberal democracy, in the sense that the country was fully represented in the UK parliament, and yet found that position permanently frustrating. Why did the UK state not allow Ireland the political freedom that Scotland could enjoy? There is, of course, no simple answer. But the main theme of an answer is that Ireland could not, in fact, be straightforwardly described as belonging to the UK political realm at all. To claim otherwise is to place too much weight on parliamentary representation, and to ignore the importance of the informal workings of civil society. In fact, Irish Home Rulers would have been quite ready to forego that representation in return for control of their own domestic policy, even if the country had remained within the British Empire. But that control was not available. Civil society, unlike in Scotland, developed sporadically and slowly. This was partly because Ireland did not have a recent history of independent statehood, and therefore lacked the institutions which that might have bequeathed. But the problems were exacerbated by British policy, for example by the delay in Catholic emancipation. As a result, outside the north-east, there never emerged a middle class that would rule the country and have a material and ideological stake in the Union. The British authorities tended to deal with social problems only in emergencies, and then inefficiently; failures such as that over famine relief alienated the mass of the population. Underlying all this, and feeding it, were the colonial attitudes on both sides – the racist sense in Britain that Ireland was inferior, and the Fenian demonology in Ireland representing England as irredeemably evil. Divisions between Protestants and Catholics in Ireland also discouraged compromise, especially because the Protestants, being powerful, could impress their suspicions on the British government. In Scotland, by contrast, where it was the Catholics who were suspicious of indigenous government, they were too weak to have much influence: we saw this in their failure to prevent the setting up of a Scottish Education board in 1885.

Thus Ireland illustrates two important points. First, it shows how privileged was Scotland's position within the same central state. Scotland retained at least as much autonomy as Ireland in the eighteenth century, and much more in the nineteenth. The other conclusion is about the nature of nationalism in the two countries. Scotland had its own institutions, and so its nationalism was official and successful. Ireland's was oppositionist, and yet its most notable feature was still its pragmatism. Nationalists even in semi-colonial situations were not necessarily much more inclined to push for parliamentary independence or even autonomy than were the Scots.

AUSTRIA-HUNGARY: GENERAL THEMES

The most acute nationalist conflicts in Europe arose in the Habsburg Empire, although some of them – such as in Poland – impinged on other states as well. Four phases can be distinguished in the century-and-a-half up to 1914. The first is increasing centralisation from the late eighteenth century onwards, partly in reaction to the French Revolution; the key imperial figures in this were Maria Theresa, who ruled from 1740 to 1780, Joseph II (1780–90), and Metternich, who held various senior posts in the government between 1809 and 1848. This culminated in the liberal revolution of 1848, which inaugurated the second phase: there was a mixture of further repression and military disaster up to the defeat by Prussia in 1864. The third phase started with the granting of autonomy to the Hungarian Magyars in 1867; this precedent was cited by national movements among other peoples for the next fifty years. The fourth phase emerged towards the end of the century, as the Empire slipped again into chaos and oppression.

Autonomy and nationalism waxed and waned in inverse relation to each other as these phases developed. We will find, therefore, that there are several general themes in our discussion of individual nationalities. The first is that there was always central control of local government, by means of centrally appointed local bureaucrats. The result was that 'the appointment of every teacher, porter, doctor, or tax-collector was a signal for national struggle' (Taylor, 1964, p. 114). The second point arises from this: for most nationalists, local autonomy mattered more than national parliaments (or diets). For most of the period, nationalists campaigned for a federation of the Empire.

The third point is that the centre interfered with culture – notably religion – whenever cultural activists asserted differences from German or Magyar practices. The idea that a union could foster diversity was not popular in ruling groups: the most that could be hoped for by smaller nations was that, by keeping quiet, their differences would be ignored. Thus defence of local government and the churches were both powerful motives. But so also, more positively, was liberalism, which is the final theme. A principal cause of the revolutions of 1848 was the nascent middle class's wanting liberal freedoms in order to pursue industrialisation.

These themes can be illustrated by considering the Magyars and the Czechs, and so the next two sections are devoted to them. On the one hand, the Magyars were the most privileged nationality after the Germans of Austria, and although their nationalism was directed primarily at securing autonomy from Vienna, they acted also as oppressors to the smaller nationalities which they in turn ruled. This instance of imperialist small-nation nationalism has much in common, therefore, with Scotland's. The Czechs, on the other hand, found their autonomy being continually undermined by the imperial government in Vienna. Their nationalism is therefore prototypical of movements which had to defend essentially local rights before they could even contemplate statehood. The other nationalities in the Empire also suffered impositions from the centre (whether Vienna or Budapest), and so studying the Czechs gives us insight into the general experience of central Europe. However, Poland is dealt with separately later because only a relatively small part of its territory was ruled by the Habsburgs.

THE MAGYARS

The Magyars were the ruling class of Hungary, although there were also large numbers of Magyar peasants. They had more or less voluntarily bound themselves to the Viennese Habsburgs in 1723, for military protection, but they retained substantial autonomy in local affairs. They had their own national diet, which could propose legislation to the Emperor. The Magyars secured this relatively privileged position partly because their historical institutions were stronger than those elsewhere (such as in Bohemia), and partly because there were fewer Germans in Hungary than in other parts of the Empire. Furthermore, the Magyar ruling elite, having their base in large rural estates, favoured an economic caution that was not threatening to Vienna.

This is not to say that the Magyars were left free of challenge by the Empire in the eighteenth century. Both Maria Theresa and Joseph II tried to centralise further, by a mixture of attempting to undermine the powers of local government and of attracting the Magyar aristocracy to base themselves in Vienna. But the resilience of Hungarian civil society resisted this and provided the basis for the liberal nationalism of Kossuth under Metternich. Thus Magyar nationalism was partly a defence of autonomy, not only a claim for it.

The revolution of 1848 produced a brief liberal constitution. Its main features were the leitmotivs of nineteenth-century liberal nationalism: a ministry responsible to the diet rather than to Vienna, autonomous local government, a property-based franchise, the enshrining of civil liberties and the emancipation of the peasants. The repression which followed 1848 crushed this, brutally, and imposed administration from Vienna. But the 1848 scheme was revived after 1867, when Austria was forced to concede permanent autonomy following its defeat by Prussia. Thereafter, there were two parliaments in the Empire – in Vienna and Budapest – and neither was subordinate to the other. Hungary had complete domestic autonomy; foreign affairs, the military and joint financial matters were dealt with in common. The only opportunity for Austrian interference in Hungarian affairs was the ten-yearly renegotiation of the financial settlement; this did become increasingly difficult, but most disputes were resolved by Austrian concessions to Hungary.

Thus in several respects Hungary resembled Scotland. It had much the same degree of domestic autonomy until the early nineteenth century, through autonomous local institutions and through relatively privileged access to the ruling circles of Vienna. So, given this relatively successful defence of autonomy, the question arises as to why political nationalism was a force at all. There were two reasons for this, neither present in the Scottish case. The first was precisely the imperial repression that grew in intensity up to, and then after, the revolution of 1848. Because the centre of military and administrative power was in Austria, the conflict could be represented as being on national lines – Germans versus Magyars. Conflicts of this national type simply never occurred in Britain: if there was repression, it was class-based, and even then it was relatively mild compared to the severity of the Austrian action after 1848.

The second reason for the intensity of Hungarian nationalism was the sense that the Magyars had to defend their culture from below as well as from the Germans. They believed that only Hungarian autonomy would allow the defeat of what were perceived to be threats from the Slavs or the Romanians. The Magyars used their new institutions to impose Magyar culture throughout that part of the Empire for which their parliament became responsible after 1867. In one sense, Scotland had nothing like this: it did not rule any other nationalities directly (rather than through the British Empire). But in another it did. The immigration of large numbers of Catholic Irish labourers in the late nineteenth and early twentieth centuries produced much anguish about a threat to Scottish integrity. But Scotland did not need to demand new institutions to counteract this immigration because it already had the religious autonomy that it needed; moreover, as we saw, Britain was underpinned by Protestantism, and so the Union could be believed to be the best defence against Catholicism. There was never that degree of cultural unity between Magyars and Germans.

Thus the Magyars were defending a privileged position against not only oppression but also rebellion. They were also resisting any radical transformation of their economy by industrialism: again unlike the Scots, their economy was too agricultural for the Magyars to feel that they belonged to an international movement of capitalist modernisation. It may seem to us to be somewhat ironic that Hungary should have achieved more independence of a formal sort after 1867 than Scotland, when it undoubtedly also suffered more severe oppression before then; and this irony can easily lead to the belief that Scotland would eventually have fared better if it indeed had been truly oppressed. But the opposite conclusion is more plausible because it pays more respect to the motives of the people involved. The Scottish middle class were quite happy with their situation because it was able to deliver to them the things they wanted: local autonomy and economic growth. As Kossuth and many other central European nationalists recognised, Britain already enjoyed those freedoms for which they were fighting. The idea that Scotland should declare independence from a Britain with these achievements would have seemed ridiculous.

THE CZECHS

If the Hungarians were fortunate, the Czechs were not. But the recurrent theme throughout the story of the Czech lands is of compromise: despite severe restrictions on their autonomy, the Czech middle class for most of the nineteenth century were happy to settle for limited autonomy.

Between the middle of the eighteenth century and the middle of the nineteenth, the Czech lands – Bohemia, Moravia and Silesia – suffered from the increasing centralisation of the Empire. The old balance between the monarch and the estates broke down, and there was 'ever-tightening control over the lower echelons of public administration – the manors and the towns' (Kann and David, 1984, p. 185). Maria Theresa abolished the Bohemian Court Chancellory in 1749, the body that had been the supreme source of administrative and judicial authority. She and Joseph II steadily emasculated the estates, until the diets which rested on them became purely advisory bodies (and even their advice could be given only when invited by the monarch). Local officials were subjected increasingly to regulation by the central state. They were required to have formal legal training, which came to be more closely controlled by Vienna after the abolition of the Chancellory. Town councils could be elected only from a list supplied by the centrally-appointed bureaucracy.

Matters deteriorated further for the Czechs under Metternich, who ruled directly through the *gubernia* of Prague and Brno, and their imperial bureaucracy. Indeed, after 1815, the civil administrators were secondary to the police directorates. For all but the most trivial of municipal matters, local elected councillors were replaced by people appointed by the *gubernia*. The diets remained, but were consulted only on minor local laws and taxes.

All this produced a cultural and nationalist resistance, which was independent of local government and the diets because they were seen as being creatures of the central state. Indeed, it was independent too of the privileged classes, and sought the essence of the Czech nation in the people and in their Slavonic language and ethnicity. This concern was also directed against the large population of resident Germans: the ratio of Czechs to Germans was sixty to forty in Bohemia, seventy to thirty in Moravia and thirty-five to sixty-five in Silesia, where, moreover, there were almost as many Poles as Germans (Kann and David, 1984). The supporters of nationalism were an odd mixture of people threatened by modernisation and those in favour of it. Catholic priests, manorial officials and small craftspeople and shopkeepers resented Germanisation, the last commercial groups especially because the Germans dominated the emerging large industrial enterprises. Students and teachers, on the other hand, were liberals of a different sort, being less concerned with the trading threat from expanding industry, and more with civil liberties; they saw the imperial state as impeding such progress.

Yet the programme of these nationalists was for limited autonomy within a reformed empire organised federally on ethnic principles. This remained the case even when both repression and nationalism intensified up to 1848. The leader of the Czechs, Palacký, did not challenge Habsburg rule. Neither did he favour popular sovereignty: the federation that he and his associates envisaged would have derived its authority from above. One reason for their wanting to retain the link with Austria was again their liberalism: the vast imperial market was needed by Czech industry.

When this modestly radical programme collapsed with the repression of 1848–59, even more of the remaining limited Czech autonomy was eroded. The administrative and judicial functions of the manors and towns were now wholly taken over by officials who were directly answerable to Vienna, and a policy of imposing German culture was pursued. As in Hungary, this was the low point of Czech autonomy.

The Czechs did not manage to secure as favourable a settlement after 1867 as the Magyars. Local self-government was re-established, supervised by the executive arm of the elected diets. In this respect, the Czechs enjoyed a key component of liberal freedom. But parallel to that was the administrative structure imposed by the central state, in the form of the provincial governors and the district captains; they repeatedly came into conflict with the elected bodies. In the absence of an independent judiciary to resolve these disputes, the imperial officials usually won. They had the power to dismiss local officials, whether elected or not; and they could back this up by their control of the police force. As a result, the local councils restrained themselves to avoid conflict.

The diets and local councils therefore had a merely administrative role, rather than much of a political one. Nevertheless, this did allow them to achieve some of the programme of the Czech national revival, for example establishing a national system of elementary schools within a general framework set by Vienna. Czech nationalists, like the Scots and everyone else, believed that the essence of a people lay in its culture, which could therefore be developed without recourse to politics and constitutions. This environment encouraged writers, artists, composers, folklorists and historians to construct new national identities (even while usually claiming to be rediscovering ancient roots).

The other aspect of Czech life that flourished was the economy. Bohemia was the most economically developed part of the Empire: in 1880, for example, it had only twenty-five per cent of the territory of the lands ruled by Vienna, but thirty-seven per cent of the population, and as much as sixty-four per cent of the industrial production (Kann and David, 1984). This was heavily dependent on external capital, however, mostly from Austria and the newly unified German states. Unlike Scotland, therefore, Bohemia was tied to an imperial core that was less economically developed than itself.

The economic situation created a dilemma for the Czech middle class. The National Liberal party which they supported, and which dominated Czech politics in the last part of the nineteenth century, was torn between pragmatism and patriotism. As Garver puts it in his history of the party: 'Czech businessmen were proud of their Czech heritage and identity, but wished to do nothing that might so inflame national passions that the tranquility necessary for profitable business would be impaired' (Garver, 1978, p. 101). Indeed, they – like the Scots and the dominant faction in the Irish Home Rule party – believed that indigenous development mattered more than constitutional forms or even cultural activism: the National Liberal party chairman, Emanuel Engel, said in 1903 that 'twenty more Czech millionaire industrialists would better serve the national cause than the best legislation on language rights' (Garver, 1978, p. 142). Their programme resembled that of the Liberal parties of the West, and indeed they held up Western Europe and the USA as models of how to organise a society in the interests of business. They would have preferred a federal solution, mainly because independence threatened free trade as much as did a reactionary empire, but also because they genuinely had a dual cultural loyalty. They valued German as an international language (which is why such distinguished authors as Franz Kafka chose to write in it): all they wanted for Czech was recognition.

Fortunately for their political peace of mind, however, they did not have to choose between their liberalism and their nationalism: the free trade and civil liberties that their economic programme required were not readily available from Vienna. The liberals controlled local government, but the imperial restrictions meant that that was not enough for them to create the social context best suited to their interests. There was growing conflict with Vienna over civil liberties – freedom of speech and of the press, for example. Pragmatism, as favoured by the National Liberals, depended on continued imperial goodwill, and this broke down at the end of the century as the Austrian state became increasingly centralised and authoritarian. Only then did it seem to be finally clear that federation was not a feasible option.

Thus the key difference between the Czechs and the Scots was that the Scots held securely what the Czech liberal nationalists were demanding. There are five areas of political conflict where this is evident. The first is that there was no parallel in Scotland to the national conflict between Czechs and Germans: there was no attempt by England to impose its officials or its legal system on the Scots, and Scottish local government was thoroughly independent. Second, there was no threat to the Scots' exercising their own cultural choices, for example in education. As we have seen, the Scots had to sort out among themselves the extent to which religion would have a place in any new system of elementary schools; Vienna, by contrast, tried to force clerical influence on the Czech schools. There was, third, no British or English persecution of Scottish cultural organisations or activities, so that these became depoliticised: after the death of Jacobitism, Scottish national symbols ceased to be threatening to the very existence of the state. Thus, for example, we can contrast the Austrian government's obstructing the building of a monument to the fifteenth-century religious reformer Jan Hus in Prague, in the 1890s, with the freedom that the Scots had to build explicitly nationalist monuments to the likes of William Wallace or John Knox. But above all – the fifth point – there was no incompatibility between remaining in the British Union and free trade; indeed quite the opposite.

One of the few things which the Czechs did have and which Scotland did not were nationally representative bodies, the diets. But their functions were circumscribed, and their role was mainly consultative. In that case, we have to compare their activities with those of the Scottish Faculty of Advocates, Convention of Royal Burghs, general assemblies of the Presbyterian churches, and county meetings. Scottish autonomy may not have been vested in a single national body, but in practice – and that is what mattered to the realistic middle class – it was more real than anything that places such as Bohemia enjoyed.

POLAND: GENERAL THEMES

Poland was forced to develop to the full the opportunities for negotiated autonomy within external constraints, because it was partitioned at the beginning of the nineteenth century among Russia, Prussia and Austria. The medieval kingdom of Lithuania-Poland had itself been a great power, but by the end of the eighteenth century, Polish society was ruled locally by the gentry, the *slachta*. The partition took place at the Congress of

Vienna, which ended the wars against Napoleon. This gave only limited autonomy to any one part of Poland, a situation which shaped modern Polish nationalism in three respects that are common to the different parts of the country. The first is that exiles were important in forming the very idea of modern Poland. Thus the popular historical novelist Kraszewski, similar to Walter Scott in some ways, differs from him in being forced to live abroad. The exiles could not avoid their fate; but, living elsewhere, they tended to the romantic rather than the realistic.

The second characteristic is religion. The Catholic Church had always been important to Poland, but became increasingly so in the nineteenth century because it provided a unifying institution. Its political role was all the more significant because the two most powerful of the partitioning states – Prussia and Russia – were not Catholic.

The final point is related to the first and second: Polish nationalism (and not just in the nineteenth century) oscillated between the realistic and the impossibilist – the 'positivist' and the 'romantic'. The romantic vision was radically liberal, and was based outside Poland except in revolutionary moments: 'the intellectual émigrés looked upon themselves as the leaders of a nation deprived of its freedom of expression and fettered in its cultural development' (Wandycz, 1974, p. 180). The positivist tradition, in contrast, was developed by pragmatists who, mostly, lived in Poland itself. It involved working with one or more of the partitioning powers, often against the others. On the whole, this was the approach adopted on the ground by the Church. The purposes of such cooperation was social reform: 'foregoing the heroics of soldiers, the positivists extolled the heroism of physicians struggling against sickness or of teachers fighting obscurantism' (Wandycz, 1974, p. 263). By the end of the nineteenth century, this pragmatic tradition had virtually abandoned nationalist ideals.

Thus there are common themes in nineteenth-century Polish history. But the partition was not for nothing: the stories of the three parts have to be told separately too. This, indeed, was partly a consequence of the positivist tradition. The middle class in each part of Poland was increasingly integrated into the society and economy of its local great power: many inhabitants 'resented the political and cultural repression, but at the same time enjoyed the economic benefits derived from membership in a vast empire' (Dziewanowski, 1977, p. 59). This was true also of leading socialist activists (Rosa Luxembourg, for example), and of the nascent feminist movement, although the political opportunities which they saw were, of course, rather different from those which attracted the middle class.

The themes are seen most clearly in the large part of Poland that was ruled by Russia. But some general points – especially about positivism – can be drawn from the history of the other two parts, which are dealt with briefly first.

The part of Poland which was ruled by Austria – Galicia – became increasingly autonomous as the century progressed, until eventually it had more independence than any part of the Habsburg Empire apart from Hungary and Austria. But that was not how it started. Even before the partition at the Congress of Vienna, Galicia had experienced the same centralising tendency as we have seen operating throughout the Habsburg lands. The diet was abolished, and the elected town councils were placed under administrative control. Between the Congress and 1848, the Habsburgs exploited Galicia fiscally, and the Galician assembly had no more than token powers.

The opportunity for nationalist gains expanded as the Empire became weaker, in the same way as in Bohemia and elsewhere. The structures of limited self-government that emerged were similar to those in Bohemia. There was a diet with restricted powers, and elected local councils again, but all of these were under the supervision of the imperial governor. The diet had to rely on the imperial administration to implement any legislation. In practice, however, tensions were fewer than in Bohemia because Vienna chose to interfere less. Galicia was felt to be small, relatively atypical of the rest of the Empire, and also in the safely conservative hands of the gentry. Allowing autonomy to the much more economically developed and socially radical Bohemia, by contrast, would have risked setting a precedent.

One result of this relative freedom in Galicia was that nationalism never became separatist, and was not even in favour of strong autonomy. From 1867 on, Polish nationalists in Galicia worked for limited autonomy within a federalised Austrian state, and Polish union was no more than a distant aspiration. Indeed, the main national demands were for universal suffrage and social justice in the Austrian state as a whole. In this respect, Polish nationalism in Galicia resembles the nationalism of liberals in nineteenth-century Scotland, although the parallels cannot be taken further than that because of the vastly different economic situations.

AUSTRIAN POLAND

PRUSSIAN POLAND

The eighteenth-century experience of Prussian Poland was similar to that of Galicia. The provincial diets and administrations were abolished in the period of enlightened despotism after about 1770. The Prussian legal system was enforced, and German immigration was encouraged by the state in order to foster economic development. The resulting large German minority then were suspicious of Polish nationalism.

A limited form of autonomy was introduced after the Congress of Vienna into the Grand Duchy of Posen, but the elected diet could only petition and give advice, not legislate. Moreover, in western Prussia, which was historically regarded by Poles as part of Poland, there was no autonomy, rather systematic Germanisation. After 1830, the state became more oppressive. The gentry were deprived of the right to elect the provincial captains, who instead were appointed by the Berlin government. The judicial system became wholly subordinate to Berlin. And German was made the official language in education.

Nevertheless, the unified Germany was federal, and so its provinces enjoyed considerable autonomy. Posen was one of these. It, like the rest, retained autonomy in the administration of domestic policy. Johnson judges that the substantial decentralisation was feasible because Germany had adopted many Western European ideas of separating the state from society: 'legal developments in Germany had already resulted in a sophisticated body of public law which embodied such a strong sense of the rationality and necessity of common, general conditions that decentralised administration presented few serious risks of fragmentation' (N. Johnson, 1991, p. 11).

As a result, positivism was more successful in German Poland than in the Russian or Austrian parts. Economic development was encouraged, and – with Bismarck – social welfare too. It was the success of these policies that made Germanisation acceptable: the economic and social goals which were the pragmatic purposes of positivist Polish nationalism were, it was believed, being achieved by means other than independence or reunification.

RUSSIAN POLAND

In contrast to the other two parts, Russian Poland became less autonomous as Russia slipped into autocracy. To start with, in the late eighteenth century, there was little attempt by Russia to impose its policies, and it did not interfere with Polish institutions or the Polish legal system. This experience produced an early example of positivist policies: after the Napoleonic invasion, there was a strand of thinking led by the influential Prince Jerzy Czartoryski that Poland should join Russia in a union analogous to that between Hungary and Austria.

The Congress of Vienna produced a government consisting of five ministers appointed by the Tsar, and presiding over a system of commissions and boards. The Polish parliament – the *sejm* – could only make representations. But partial autonomy did not satisfy the romantic nationalists, who in 1830 rose in emulation of events in Paris and Belgium. This was the first effective instance of revolutionary nationalism in nineteenth-century Poland. The *sejm* declared independence and dethroned the Tsar.

But there were tensions, as recurrently in the history of the romantic strand in Polish nationalism. The conservative majority wanted compromise, believing that Poland could not gain independence from Russia without the support of another neighbouring great power. The likelihood of support from Prussia or Austria was small, considering their reluctance to set an example to their own Polish populations. The political left, on the other hand, wanted the national revolution to go further and become a social one.

Russia then invaded. It was nervous about the threat to its western border, and realised that the political disagreements among the Poles could be exploited. And, as a result, the semi-independence that had been put in place by the Congress of Vienna came to an end. Almost all the administration was put in non-Polish hands, and assimilated to the ministries of the Russian Empire. Education, for example, was run by a Russian ministry in such a remote way that most of the school inspectors could not speak Polish. The Russian criminal code was imposed on the courts, and tariff barriers excluded Polish goods from the Russian market.

The centralised nature of the new regime helped to shape the new phase of Polish nationalism: demands for educational reform and for economic liberalism dominated, and for a while positivism made some progress in re-establishing Polish law and Polish culture in the schools. But the second significant Polish rising of the nineteenth century took place in 1863, and this was replaced by even more severe repression than in 1830. The viceroy was replaced by a governor-general. All the remaining administrative institutions were abolished. The Polish banks were taken over. And – again – the legal system and the schools were russified.

Yet, despite this, the dominant theme of Polish nationalism from then until the 1890s was positivism again. In particular, it was believed that pragmatic measures could help to develop Polish industry. Only when the Russian Empire again and finally became much more repressive at the end of the century did the romantic tendencies once more become strong.

Two contrasts are worth drawing here. The first is with Finland, which will be examined in more detail later in this chapter. By negotiating a union with the Tsar, Finland never suffered this degree of Russian imposition, and continued to benefit from access to the huge Russian market. The other is with Scotland. The autonomy enjoyed by Poland under the Congress settlement bore some resemblance to the Scottish situation – autonomous local boards and legal system, with limited interference from the imperial centre. Scotland, like Finland, did not challenge this, and that is one of the reasons why they both kept their autonomy.

The pragmatic Poles appreciated such matters, which helps explain why, despite recurrent Russian repression, positivism was always strong. The dichotomy between romanticism and positivism may have been peculiarly acute in Polish nationalism, but it was present everywhere. The appropriate response to repression can be brave resistance, or sensible accommodation; and each of these positions can be cogently denounced by the other – as histrionics, or as surrender. We saw the same ambivalence in Scotland in the eighteenth and nineteenth centuries. For most of the time, accommodation dominated Scottish politics, partly because it was believed to have worked. But we could also see the occasional assertion that true Scots should fight if they were to preserve the national spirit. The big difference is that the Scots only speculated about fighting, usually in song, whereas the Poles combined their singing with ultimately tragic action.

If Scotland shares something with Hungary and, for some of the century, with Russian Poland, its situation also bears comparison with Catalonia, at the other end of the continent. In the nineteenth century, Catalonia was the most economically developed part of Spain, and on the whole believed its interests to be well served by the connection to the rest of the state. Catalonia enjoyed a considerable amount of informal autonomy, and so the dynamism of its middle class ensured that its social development was fairly indigenous. As a result, Catalan nationalism did not develop a strongly separatist strand until the Spanish state began to collapse completely at the end of the century. But that disaster – epitomised by the loss of the colony in Cuba – indicates that there is an important difference from Scotland: economically developed Catalonia was tied to a state that was decrepit, mainly rural, and still suffering politically from the collapse of its empire.

In the late Middle Ages, Catalonia had been the centre of the Aragonese kingdom, and so was instrumental in the dynastic union of Aragon and Castile in 1479 that founded the Spanish state. The Spanish Empire was the most powerful state at the time, and so there was little temptation for Catalonia to leave it: the Union was not challenged until the seventeenth century. A Catalan republic was declared in 1640, but – unlike Portugal at the same time – Catalonia was not able to secure independence. After several periods of warfare, a new Union was imposed in 1714 following Catalonia's decisive military defeat in the War of the Spanish Succession. The repression that followed was severe. Catalan laws, institutions and rights were abolished, the Catalan parliament and government were suppressed, and the Catalan language was replaced by Castilian. Catalan merchants were prevented from trading with the Spanish colonies.

Some of these measures were relaxed over time: for example, access to the colonies was granted after 1778. But under the Bourbon and then liberal centralisation of the early nineteenth century, assimilation went even further. What is interesting from the point of view of our themes, however, is that in the first part of the nineteenth century there was much less protest here than there might have been in east-central Europe. The most convincing explanation of this refers to the strength of civil society, as noted by Giner: he argues that small countries – Catalonia or Bohemia, for example – that are more 'advanced' socially and economically than the states that rule them 'must find their collective identity by falling back on the institutions of their civil societies, as public and state institutions are alien and often hostile to them' (Giner, 1980, p. 10). Catalonia in the nineteenth century, he says, had a much more vigorous life of voluntary associations than other places in southern Europe, creating a relatively open and pluralistic society.

This development was also, paradoxically, reinforced by the very severity of the Union. Because the Castilian measures destroyed the power of the aristocracy – the traditional ruling class – the middle class were free to flourish, and to absorb cultural influences from abroad. As a result, Catalan capitalism was indigenous. The Catalan economy was based on textiles, brandy, paper and soap, all goods which required large markets. Access to the Spanish and colonial market therefore ensured the loyalty of the entrepreneurs to the regime, despite the vast subsidy which Catalonia gave to the rest of Spain. The Catalan industrialists demanded – and got – protection to keep out mainly British competitors. They also needed Spanish military support, either against invasion (as during the Napoleonic wars) or against their own proletariat.

The local government that developed in the nineteenth century resembled Scotland in the eighteenth century. It grew out of the centralised system set up by Napoleon, and was run by the *caciques,* local political bosses who dispensed government patronage in their districts, in return for turning out the local votes for government candidates. But – in contrast to Scotland – this system was supplemented by the same type of central constraints as in Austria-Hungary. Elected officals were subject to the supervision of the administrative representatives of central government – the *jefe politico,* whose power increased towards the end of the nineteenth century. The *jefe* was transformed into a civil governor, usually now a party hack, and the mayors were government servants. Utterly trivial matters had to be referred to Madrid: 'every country postman, village schoolmaster, and customs official [owed] his appointment to the minister in Madrid' (Brenan, 1943, p. 19).

The situation resembles Austria-Hungary, and is in sharp contrast to Britain. Brenan judges that the system of *caciquismo,* which lasted until 1917, was analogous to the governing structures that were abolished in Britain in 1832. Genuinely autonomous local government became the goal of Spanish reformers, explicitly seeking to emulate Britain.

This was even more true of Catalan radicals than of those elsewhere in Spain, precisely because they were aware that their industrialisation had created many similarities between their situation and Britain's. Catalan nationalism was forged during the dynastic Carlist wars of 1820–3, when for the first time a sense of a distinct Catalan interest developed against Madrid control of local government and trading conditions. But for most of the nineteenth century, nationalism was confined to the intellectuals, whose political programme in any case asked for no more than the reform of local government, and whose main concerns were cultural (a discovery of ancient Catalan culture, inspired by Walter Scott and the German romantics). This movement was largely ignored by all the politically significant social groups – the bourgeoisie, the aristocracy and the emerging working class.

The main wave of nationalism came in 1898, and it was caused not by cultural politics but by a change in Catalonia's material interests. Spain was defeated by the USA and allies, and as a result it lost the remnants of the Empire and with it Catalonia's main markets and suppliers of raw materials. Catalan nationalism then became a mass movement for the first time. Between 1898 and 1919, the most significant political force in Catalonia was the Lliga Regionalista, a nationalist party with strong support in the middle class. But its programme was limited, even in this situation. It sought to negotiate autonomy from Madrid, not to declare independence, and it settled for Madrid's administrative decentralisation in 1911: thereafter, local government was supervised by the Catalan Mancomunidad, not by the central state, in a structure that was somewhat similar to Scotland under the Scottish Office. More important to the Lliga than these constitutional reforms, however, were the new trading tariffs introduced between 1907 and 1913: this gave Catalan industrialists a complete monopoly of the Spanish market.

Thus Catalan nationalism in the nineteenth century resembled Scotland's quite closely. It was essentially cultural for most of the time; even when its demands became more political, it was willing to settle for administrative autonomy. As in Scotland, the social classes that might have been expected to support political nationalism were more interested in securing the conditions that would allow the industrialised Catalan economy to flourish. And all this resemblance to Scotland was despite a governing system that gave to Catalonia much less autonomy than Scotland enjoyed. Constitutional change, in the eyes of the Catalan middle class, would be desirable only if their more fundamental liberal and economic goals could not be achieved by other means.

SCANDINAVIA: GENERAL THEMES

Of the small nations we have examined so far, only Hungary after 1867 could be said to have enjoyed a degree of autonomy that was greater than Scotland's. We now come to a group of nations which did have at least as much autonomy as Scotland: the countries of Scandinavia, in particular Finland and Norway.

Sweden had been a major European power until the seventeenth century, and was still important in the nineteenth. But its power was declining, and as a result of military defeat it lost control of Finland to Russia at the beginning of the nineteenth century. At almost the same time, Norway took advantage of Denmark's weakness to declare independence, immediately however transferring allegiance (under duress) to Sweden. There is no doubt that Sweden and Denmark were independent states, although both – and Denmark especially – could not afford to annoy both Prussia and Britain at the same time. So there is also no doubt that they were more autonomous than Scotland. The interesting questions for us, then, concern Finland and Norway. In all respects they were much more independent than places such as Bohemia, Poland or Catalonia, not least because they retained their parliaments throughout the century. But were they more independent than Scotland?

The other important theme here, as well as the nationalism of Finland and Norway, is Scandinavianism, a form of unifying nationalism. Most of our discussion of this belongs to chapter 7, because it grew in strength mainly in the twentieth century. But even before the separation of Norway from Sweden in 1905, Scandinavian union was coming to be seen as an alternative framework of external security for these small northern nations, a voluntary agreement among culturally very similar people to avoid the more or less involuntary dependence on Russia, Prussia or Britain.

FINLAND

Finnish history is a story of balancing between the demands of Poland, Lithuania, Denmark, Sweden, Russia and the German states. It is therefore a paradigm of the external constraints which international relations place on a small country's development. But it is also an example of the ways in which astute national elites can exploit the rivalries of great powers to carve out for themselves a limited but significant area of independence.

Sweden ruled Finland from the late Middle Ages onwards, but it did not interfere with Finnish practices and institutions. Throughout Europe, nationality conflicts before the nineteenth century tended in any case to be territorial, not ethnic: thus it was the Swedish aristocrats of Finland who first asserted Finnish rights in the seventeenth century. These claims were made because the Swedish monarch was gaining more control of Finnish trade and was imposing the Swedish language on Finnish institutions.

This centralising pressure intensified in the middle of the eighteenth century, but more significant in the development of Finnish attitudes were the wars between Sweden and Russia in 1741–3 and 1788–90. In each of these, Sweden came off badly, and Finland was invaded or occupied by Russia; a weak Sweden was no longer able to protect Finland from its immediate neighbour. There grew a feeling in Finland that Russian domination of Finland was probably inevitable, and that Finland would secure better terms if it actively sought union than if it was forced into one. (The argument is familiar from our discussion of the Scottish-English Union of 1707.)

After the next war, in 1808–9, Finland was permanently annexed by Russia. In some respects, Finland was now worse off. It had no say in the administration of Russia, where it had historically had some influence on Sweden through the Swedish nobles who were resident in Finland. But in domestic matters Finland was autonomous.

Executive power rested with the Tsar, but he needed the approval of the Finnish diet before he could change any Finnish laws. But until the very end of the nineteenth century (a period of centralisation to which we will come later), no Tsar had any inclination to interfere: the purpose of the Union was to create a buffer state that would protect the new Russian capital in St Petersburg, which was dangerously close to Russia's Finnish border. Finnish executive power lay, then, with the senate, which was appointed by and chaired by the governor-general (who in turn was appointed by the Tsar). The main powers of the governor lay in his control of the police and armed forces. Otherwise, the senate rarely met as a whole, being concerned mostly with the efficient administration of internal government.

In these respects, Russia could in principle exercise more control over Finland than England would ever have done over Scotland: as we have seen, there was no equivalent of the Irish governor-general in Scotland. But control of the military or even the police is a power of last resort; and in the day-to-day running of Finland the Tsar did not interfere at all. Finland, like Scotland, kept its legal system, its religion and its social structure – all things which Finns believed would have vanished had they not entered a Union voluntarily. There was little nostalgia for what went before: 'Finland's myths do not include a golden age' (Engmann and Kirby, 1987, p. 12).

Finland came to regard itself, therefore, as a state allied with Russia, not as a province. Within this external security, it could develop its own modern government, which consisted of a system of administrative boards coordinated – as in Scotland – by lawyers. So the purpose of Finnish nationalism for nearly all of the nineteenth century was to defend and reinforce these structures, not to demand anything more. So much did the Finns feel that they had created this administrative system for themselves that they did not change it when Finland eventually became a fully separate state in 1917.

Like the Scots, too, Finland had substantial cultural autonomy. In contrast to other parts of central Europe, Finnish assertions of national identity did not attract the ire of a great power, essentially because Russia did not doubt Finland's political loyalty. As a result, the Finnish national poets – such as Runeberg – transformed the Swedish-Russian war of 1808–9 into a war of national liberation for Finland. Russia even approved of the middle class's learning Finnish, because this was seen as a cultural underpinning of the military buffer against Sweden. The Finnish cultural nationalists went along with this: they generally believed that a Scandinavian Union would have provided a weaker external framework for Finland than the Union they had.

In one important respect, however, Finland might appear to have been more independent than Scotland: it kept its diet. Nevertheless, this body was not a significant forum for most of the century. It did not meet at all between the Union of 1808 and 1863. From then until 1906, it was elected on a very limited franchise, and had few powers. Between 1863 and 1886, it had no right to initiate legislation: its only function was to petition the Tsar, except when it had to approve proposed changes by him to traditional Finnish institutions and laws. But since he still had little wish to do so, that power to withhold assent was not used. Change to this system did not become an issue until the beginning of the twentieth century, and then the main pressure was not directly nationalist, but rather for democratisation, as we will see.

The new diet after 1863 did have a significant cultural impact: it became a forum for expressing liberal ideas. The dominant parties there were in favour of free trade, free speech and all the other freedoms that formed the standard programme of European liberals. These were largely granted – certainly to a far greater extent than in Russia itself, or than in its other satellites such as Poland. Finnish industry had free access to the enormous Russian market, and was allowed, moreover, to exclude Russian goods from Finland. The Finns achieved this because of their foreign-policy loyalty and their caution.

So there is no straightforward answer to the question of whether, for most of the nineteenth century, Finland was more independent than Scotland. Scotland, too, had national bodies with a right to petition – the Faculty of Advocates, the Convention of Royal Burghs, the county meetings, the churches. Scotland had autonomous administrative agencies, which could petition as well. All these Scottish bodies also proposed legislation with a reasonable chance of its being accepted, and in effect had control of it. Scotland did not have a parliament as a forum for expressing its liberalism, but it had plenty of substitutes. Scotland had these freedoms because it, like Finland, was utterly conservative in foreign affairs, never seriously challenging the Union with England, and showing itself to be an enthusiastic partner in the Empire. We might be able to say that Finland had more sovereignty simply because the diet existed as a national symbol: we are back to Geertz's charismatic centres. But in Finland as in Scotland, theoretical powers mattered far less to the realistic bourgeoisie than actual ones: the informal constitution was what counted.

It was the erosion of these actual powers that provoked Finnish political nationalism at the very end of the century. Russian nationalism became more aggressive from the 1890s onwards, and the Russian state became more centralised. In Finland, the effects were felt as russification. Finnish autonomy was gradually eroded, and liberal freedoms were curtailed. The response was nationalist partly because of the cultural renaissance that had been taking place since the middle of the century, and partly because the national argument became tied up with the democratic one. It seemed clear to the social democrats that their participation in Finnish government would be impossible unless the franchise were reformed, and the likelihood of that happening was diminishing as the Tsar assumed increasingly dictatorial powers.

The outcome of the centralisation and the nationalist reaction was Finnish participation in the Russian Revolution of 1905: a significant precipitating event of that was the assassination in 1904 of the autocratic Finnish governor-general Bobrikov. After the defeat of Russia in the war with Japan in 1906, the Tsar conceded reform, and the Finnish diet instituted a highly democratic franchise (including, for the first time anywhere in Europe, votes for women on the same terms as men). Thereafter, the Finnish diet experienced the same conflicts with renewed Tsarist autocracy as the Russian reformers did, and the Russian Revolution of 1917 was welcomed as providing an opportunity for Finnish independence.

Nevertheless, even this centralising and democratising phase cannot be interpreted in straightforwardly nationalist terms. The impetus for protest did not come directly from the cultural renaissance, but from Russian policies. These policies, moreover, were centralising as much as deliberately russifying, and that was why much of the protest was about gaining democracy rather than national freedom. Finland in fact never ceased to have its own distinctive state, even at the height of Bobrikov's rule. As we have seen, the Russians never wanted to destroy Finnish culture, because it was a bulwark against Sweden.

Indeed, we cannot understand why the democratic arguments did eventually take on a national form unless we recognise the continuing relative autonomy of Finnish society and culture. The cultural nationalists despaired in the 1880s because, they believed, the Finnish people were too happy with their autonomy: the nationalist intellectual Snellman, for instance, lamented that the Finnish people were unwilling to assert themselves 'as a single-minded nation' (Jutikkala and Pirinen, 1979, p. 194). Even under Bobrikov, the traditional political nationalists argued only for further compromises with Russia: they were less concerned with the fate of the diet than with ensuring that the senate and administrative machinery remained in Finnish hands. They continued to defend the institutions that had served Finland's national interests well for a century. The political demands that won in 1906 rose to prominence because Finnish society had been changing, and the new forces of social democracy had arisen to challenge not only Russian centralisation but also the old Finnish nationalism as well. These new democratic demands were therefore never simply nationalist: for example, even as late as the eve of the 1914–18 war, separation from Russia remained the goal of only that small minority who favoured Scandinavian union in place of continuing with a limited, though reformed, link to Russia.

A similar story can be told about Norway: as in Scotland and Finland, nationalism in Norway was based on the successful defence of relatively autonomous national institutions.

From the late Middle Ages until 1814, Norway was ruled by the Danish monarch. On both sides, this was a convenience for foreign-policy reasons – such as to maintain unity against the power of the north German Hanseatic League. There was no interference by the monarch in Norway's laws and social customs.

The Norwegian national assembly declared independence from Denmark in 1814, and drew up the constitution that has remained in force ever since. But, for continuing reasons of external security, the assembly was immediately forced to enter negotiations for union with Sweden. This was not the preferred outcome in Norway, but was accepted because of pressure from Britain, Russia and Prussia, and because the Swedish monarch agreed not to try to change the new Norwegian constitution.

The constitution was liberal: the monarch was head of state, but there was an independent legislature (the *storting*) and judiciary. The monarch had responsibility for administration, foreign affairs and church matters. He also had the right to propose legislation in the *storting,* and to suspend laws which he did not like. As in Finland after 1863, then, the formal constitution suggests that Norway had substantial independence, even though that was ultimately constrained by the foreign monarch.

But in practice the nature of Norwegian autonomy had a great deal in common with Scotland's (and so, again, with the practice in Finland too). Although nominally responsible to the *storting,* the Norwegian cabinet was a self-renewing corporation: until 1884, no minister resigned or was dismissed from office. The members of the *storting* itself were predominantly either farmers or professional members of the bureaucracy, such as lawyers, teachers and the clergy. In practice, the apex of the bureaucracy was the supreme court, which made appointments and resolved disputes. The members of the cabinet did not interfere very much in the administration, and their main role was to act as advisers to the monarch in Sweden.

This administration by an indigenous elite resembles Scottish government in obvious ways, for example the role of the courts in making appointments and in regulating the conduct of the bureaucracy, or the importance of autonomous professionals. The same can be said of the local institutions which shaped Norwegian society, and indeed some of these were deliberately modelled on British practice. Local government controlled poor relief and public health, and the new education system of 1848 was based on Scotland's. The local courts were embedded firmly in local society when juries were inaugurated in 1889.

The ruling ethos of this system was professional paternalism, informed by a Lutheran morality that resembled Scottish Calvinism. The goal of the middle class was to protect Norway's position in the Union, and to develop the economy. Separation (or democracy) would have interfered with that. Indeed, the Union with Sweden was believed to have the advantage of opening up a large market to Norway. In foreign policy for most of the century, Norwegian and Swedish interests were believed to be so much in harmony anyway that there was no point in pursuing separate goals.

Cementing the Union was the belief in a Scandinavian realm, although for Norwegian nationalists this wider framework would have had the advantage of allowing them to play off Denmark against Sweden. Scandinavianism was similar to the movements for German and Italian unity, politically as well as culturally. Thus Norway and Sweden were closest in foreign policy when the external world seemed most threatening, as for instance during the Crimean war between 1853 and 1856, or when Germany invaded Schleswig in 1848. A currency union was formed in 1875, and Swedish capital became important in Norwegian economic development. The cultural component of Scandinavianism impinged on the political: regular academic conferences of lawyers set harmonisation of legislation as the goal from the mid-century onwards. They achieved most progress in commercial law and the law governing the family, influenced by the common culture of capitalism and of Lutheranism. Solem judges that the only reason that the movement did not lead to Scandinavian Union was that no state was strong enough to impose its will on the others. This was true, but equally important was that Scandinavia was not so much an alternative to the separate nations as a shared context for their own identities. Voluntary cooperation was therefore believed to be the natural expression of Scandinavianism, in contrast to an artificial project of common statehood imposed from above.

It was Sweden's relative weakness in international affairs that led to the end of the Union with Norway in 1905. Norway feared that Swedish opinion was moving towards protectionism, while Norway's economy continued to depend on trade. The *storting* therefore believed that Norway needed separate trade delegations because its economic interests could not be protected by Sweden. When Sweden refused to grant these, and thus in effect refused to grant Norway control of its own trade, the *storting* opted for independence.

The Union ended, not because Sweden was interfering in Norwegian society, but because the instrumental reasons that had brought the two countries together in the first place had changed. The fear of Russia remained strong (reflecting current Finnish experience), but not strong enough to outweigh the frustrations over trade. The Swedish market may have been large, but its attractions to Norway were not as great as the attractions of Russia were to Finland, or of England to Scotland.

Thus Norwegian independence is unlike all the other cases we have been looking at. Norway sought independence essentially because its interests were no longer being met in the Union. One way of putting that is in nationalist terms: to be treated as an equal of Sweden, Norway had to be independent. But the nationalist rhetoric of equal treatment is always balanced by the instrumental benefits which union is believed to bring. The simple fact was that Sweden was no longer as powerful internationally as it had been, and the Swedish market was no longer attractive enough on its own to satisfy Norwegian trading needs. At the same time, Norwegian politicians could neither persuade nor cajole Sweden into the economic programme that was favoured by Norwegian traders. Persuasion failed because Norway and Sweden did not share the political outlook of laissez-faire liberalism, unlike Scotland and England; and, unlike Catalonia in Spain, Norwegian capitalists were not powerful enough to impose their will on the Union as a whole. When all these arguments came together – when the lack of Swedish international influence on behalf of Norway threatened to frustrate Norway's attempts to develop new markets outside Scandinavia, and when Sweden did not come round to Norway's point of view – the instrumental reasons for independence became stronger than those for union. But even then, independence could seem attractive only because it would not face Norway with an international catastrophe. Swedish policy, although conservative, had nothing of the repressiveness that contemporary Russia or Austria or even Germany showed, and none of these powers – or Britain – was willing to come to Sweden's aid.

CIVIL LIBERTIES

So, when Scots looked around Europe, they would have seen a variety of forms of autonomy, some greater than Scotland enjoyed, and many much weaker. The fate of places such as Poland was a standing reminder of the dangers that would confront a small nation if it sought more independence than was compatible with the security of its neighbouring great powers.

But the really important lesson that would have been drawn from our survey by a nineteenth-century liberal would have been a reinforcement of the belief that state forms mattered less than the scope which the state gave to the autonomous operation of civil society. The nationalist movements that we have discussed pursued national autonomy because it was a vehicle for liberalism. A Scottish liberal would have been more inclined to celebrate the common liberal framework of Britain as a whole than to detail the institutional autonomy which Scotland enjoyed. Scotland had freedom mainly because the UK state let civil society function autonomously. Thus Scottish autonomy was a by-product of something that was regarded as much deeper. Scotland was not the only place, moreover, where the middle class eschewed separatism because they felt that their liberal interests were being satisfactorily met within a wider Union. In many places, only later in the century did nationalism become the means to liberalism. In some places, as in Scotland, separatism was never needed: in the Rhineland, which was incorporated into Prussia at the Congress of Vienna in 1814, the business elites never pressed for autonomy, because they had the political and economic conditions that they wanted. As in Scotland, too, the Rhineland managed to secure a compromise over the independence of its church.

We have become used in recent years to regarding claims of the UK's uniquely liberal constitution with great scepticism. But if there has been a late-twentieth-century stagnation of the governing institutions of the UK, this should not blind us to the genuinely distinctive freedoms that Scots and other Britons celebrated in their system. On the whole, political oppression was less severe in Britain than in most of the rest of Europe. Even in Ireland, British policy was relatively benign compared to Russia in Poland, or Hungary in Croatia.

Goldstein (1983) provides a comprehensive analysis of the civil liberties that were available in Europe in the nineteenth century. He concludes that only in Switzerland and Scandinavia was political repression insignificant. At the other extreme, where repression was severe except during revolutionary interludes, were Russia, Spain, France, Italy, Germany, Austria-Hungary, Portugal, Serbia and Romania. In the middle were Belgium, the Netherlands, Greece, Bulgaria and the United Kingdom. But if we examine the UK case more carefully, we find that it was, on the whole, at the free end of the spectrum for those civil liberties that were likely to concern the middle class: it had freedom of expression and of assembly, academics were never imprisoned or even dismissed by the state for their teachings, and by the middle of the century political liberals were never imprisoned or exiled. Where Britain was indeed somewhat repressive was in areas that all but the most radical liberals would have regarded as acceptable for maintaining public order and the integrity of the state – for example, by restricting the activities of trade unions or revolutionary politicians, although even in these respects Britain was fairly liberal by the end of the century.

Thus it was no wonder that mainly middle-class nationalists throughout Europe held Britain up as a paradigm of liberty, nor that Britain could pride itself on being a haven for political refugees, many of them nationalists – people such as Louis Kossuth from Hungary, Giuseppe Mazzini from Italy, or the most famous of all, Karl Marx. Protection of foreign radicals was believed to be part of Britain's destiny as a uniquely free state. And so it is no wonder, too, that Scottish liberals felt that their British connection was a prize to be cherished.

CONCLUSIONS

For small nations throughout Europe, then, autonomy had to be continually negotiated and compromised. They could not affect the governing framework, where international relations were determined by five large and multinational states along with some moderately powerful others. The big diplomatic issues were always settled by the UK, France, Germany (or Prussia), Russia and Austria-Hungary, with some contribution from Spain, Sweden, Italy or Turkey when their regional interests were involved. In this power bargaining, places such as Bohemia were little more than pawns, and Scotland or Catalonia could feel that being able to make some contribution to imperial affairs was worth the sacrifice of the more ceremonial of local institutions.

Symbolic national bodies like a parliament were, in any case, less important than the relative autonomy that could be negotiated using whatever local forums that were available. Nationalists were realists: the capacity to compromise which the Poles called positivism was evident everywhere, although in some places, such as Poland itself, it was occasionally overwhelmed by romanticism. But the great powers were realists too, appreciating that granting some autonomy was likely to avoid trouble: the constructive unionism of Britain in Ireland responded to, and inspired, the positivism of the nationalists. The scope for nationalists' making a success of this strategy depended on whether autonomy for the small nation disrupted the interests of the large one. This was easier to achieve in Scotland or Finland than in such a strategically crucial part of Europe as Poland.

When we ask whether the nationalists were successful, we therefore have to pay as much attention to civil society as to formal independence. Certainly it helped if the nation had indigenous institutions: they had a legitimacy and experience that helped coordinate national efforts. That was why local government was so important, because much of it had a far longer pedigree than national parliaments. Local institutions, moreover, helped in that central goal of nineteenth-century liberalism – the separation of the state from civil society. Important in this respect also was the professionalisation of local government and of the civil service: it was this which prevented Scottish or Norwegian or Finnish local government becoming the site for acute political conflict of the type which dominated Bohemia or Poland or Catalonia.

The separation of civil society from the state mattered to liberals essentially because they wanted to free the life of the nation from politics. Culture, the economy, and all the other relations that constituted everyday life were believed to flourish only when the state did not interfere. The liberal ideal was then that the state should create conditions under which its role was barely felt. If this could be managed without national independence, then that was probably preferable, because separation did sometimes have the effect of disrupting markets.

Thus nineteenth-century nationalists – a group which has come in for much rhetorical abuse in the late twentieth century for being obsessed with the nation state – actually turn out to be far more subtle than many of their successors. From one point of view, it can certainly be legitimately objected that the groups who achieved formal power under the systems of autonomy that I have described were mostly middle-class, professional and male, and that the power they exercised was often bombastically comic when it was not tragic. But to stop with that analysis would be to ignore the important concomitants about the autonomy of civil society. Nowhere in Europe did the working class exercise political power, and women had at best only very exigent access to it. But if the essence of the nation lay in its life beyond politics, then the liberal nationalists were not as hypocritical or self-contradictory as has been claimed. They might have been thoroughly paternalistic in their belief that these middle-class men could free everyone else from the imposition of politics; but they were not insincere. And, when we look at the mess that politics (and its extension into warfare) did make of ordinary people's lives at moments of crisis in places like Poland, we must acknowledge that creating the conditions for the relatively free conduct of private affairs was an achievement of which the Finns or the Norwegians – or the Scots – might reasonably be proud.

6

Scottish Autonomy in the UK Welfare State

The autonomy which small nations within large empires could enjoy in the nineteenth century was bound to come to an end in the twentieth, as the state took over the administration of larger and larger areas of social policy. These changes are discussed in this chapter and the next. This chapter deals with Scotland, chapter 7 with other places. Thus the main questions to be asked are: did Scotland retain autonomy in the era of the welfare state? And how did its position compare with that of other small nations?

The recurrent theme of the present chapter is that the UK welfare state which emerged between 1910 and 1950 took a distinctive form in Scotland, to such an extent that Scotland can be described as having had a welfare state of its own. The argument is not that Scotland had control of its own legislation (although it could influence that). The key point is the one we took from Poggi in chapter 2: the politics that mattered were those of the bureaucracy, in the sense that the autonomy and distinctiveness of any country in the mid-twentieth century rested more on the way that its bureaucracy interpreted legislation than on the legislation itself. This is what Poggi describes as technocracy – rule by experts. Thus the argument of this and the next chapter is that Scotland had as much scope for national distinctiveness as many other small nations – especially those embedded within federations – because Scotland had its own welfare-state bureaucracy. Moreover, even in policy areas where Scotland did not have its own branch of the welfare state, the decision not to seek that distinctiveness was chosen by Scottish politicians responding to the Scottish electorate, not straightforwardly imposed from outside.

The first sections of the chapter provide a chronology of the first half of the century, describing the emergence of the overall constitutional structures, at the British and then at the Scottish level. The most important aspect of the Scottish discussion involves describing the growth of the Scottish Office. The significant moments in these changes were the reforming Liberal government of 1906–14 and the Labour government of

1945–51, and so the origins of the new state are firmly embedded in social democracy. But, increasingly from the 1930s onwards, both the British and the Scottish changes were linked also to a new form of official national-ism, built by the ideology of 'middle opinion' in the 1930s. This new official Scottish nationalism continued to maintain that Scotland was a nation in a voluntary Union with England, that Scotland's problems of industrial decline were so acute as to require special treatment, and that the new welfare state should reflect Scotland's national status and national emergency.

Developments in the first half of the twentieth century therefore provided the context for the new Scottish politics that emerged after 1950. The later sections of the chapter fill in the constitutional context with details of particular areas of policy. The degree of autonomy varied, and in some topics barely existed at all. Scotland had considerable independence in education and housing; in health and social work, its freedom was more constrained but still substantial. In economic policy, the Scottish Office was highly constrained, but made a distinctive contribution to UK policies on regional development. In social-security policy, there was almost no Scottish distinctiveness at all.

Britain also retained prestige. The Empire was declining, but had not yet collapsed, and it was still possible to believe that Britain had a special mission in the world – of mediating among the USA, Europe and the Soviet Union. The monarchy became even more popular than before, sym-bolising the unity that was achieved during the 1939–45 war and after. It is hardly surprising, therefore, that assimilation remained an attractive option to many Scots; as in the previous two centuries, this could be justified on the nationalist grounds that the Scottish people would be best served by being able to compete equally with the English. Traditions should be maintained only if they did not interfere with that.

This chapter takes the story up to approximately the middle of the 1970s. The decay of the social-democratic world from then on is the subject of chapter 8.

THE TWENTIETH-CENTURY UK STATE

The reform of the UK state in the first few decades of the twentieth century was partly a response to pressure from political parties and other campaigning groups, although the system which emerged was not at all participatory. Both the political and the industrial wings of the Labour Party became much stronger than ever before, eventually replacing the Liberal Party as the main vehicle for reformist opposition to the Conservat-ives. Even though Labour achieved power only briefly until 1945, the threat of political disaffection by the newly enfranchised segments of the electorate – women and the working class – shaped the attitudes of Liberal and Conservative politicians as well. Many of them were receptive for other reasons: nineteenth-century philanthropy had evolved into a paternal-istic belief in the moral duty of the state to correct the excesses of capitalism.

At the very least, a healthy and well-educated population was believed to be desirable in the interests of national efficiency. The Empire would have to be organised if it was to survive, and a wealthy Empire would in turn finance the social reforms that were needed at home. This view had supporters from all parts of the political spectrum, from Joseph Chamber-lain (who left the Liberals over Irish Home Rule in 1886 to lead the new Liberal Unionist Party, and who eventually ended up in the Conservative Party), through Lord Rosebery (who continued to be a Liberal until well into the twentieth century), to Sydney and Beatrice Webb, founders of the Fabian gradualism that became the ideology of the Labour Party. Even though they might not have agreed about the interpretation of democracy, the paternalism which these people had in common was much greater than the gulf which separated them from the revolutionary socialists or the declining band of laissez-faire individualists. The purpose of demo-cracy, in fact, was to produce material welfare, not necessarily to encourage participation: the Liberal leader Lloyd George argued that 'we must demon-strate in practice [free institutions'] greater efficiency in dealing with the conditions of life among the people' (Marwick, 1964, p. 292).

These ideas crystallised into what has been called 'middle opinion' in the 1930s, which laid the ideological basis for the post-1945 welfare state. The central features of the ideology were beliefs in the mixed economy, the welfare state, and state planning. The economy would be run as a partnership between private and nationalised industries; the purpose of the state would be to use public expenditure to overcome the effects of poverty, unemployment and ill-health; and the different agencies of the state and of private initiative would be coordinated by means of coherent national and regional plans. As with the ideology of national efficiency, these views embraced everyone from reformist Tories such as the later prime minister Harold Macmillan to the leaders of the Labour Party such as Herbert Morrison; they were willing to place enormous faith in the proposals that came from 'non-party reformers and leaders of the profes-sions' (Addison, 1975, p. 40). Planning, in particular, seemed to offer scope for the application of the new sciences of society. The British Association for the Advancement of Science even proposed a new house of parliament recruited from among scientists who would be, they rather naively hoped, 'devoid of politics' (Marwick, 1964, p. 292).

The apotheosis in practice of this dirigiste ideology came between the 1930s and the 1950s, receiving added impetus from the successful planning of the economy and society during the 1939–45 war. The trade unions and the Labour Party were finally accepted as partners of the state, welfarism thus being the means by which the state retained legitimacy in an era of mass electorates. Between 1945 and 1951, the Labour government nationalised significant industries, established a fully public health service, instituted a system of state insurance against sickness and unemployment, and extended secondary education to all children. The outcome was impressive, no matter that the problems of this system have become glaring more recently. Nearly all the goals which middle opinion set itself had been achieved by the late 1940s. Addison (1975) notes that even by the end of the 1930s, the successes of British social reformers were envied by social democrats in Sweden, New Zealand and the USA. What is more – and more long-lasting – these achievements were mostly taken for granted by Conservatives.

All of this had profound implications for Scotland, as we will see in the sections which follow. The general drift of the policies was accepted in Scotland. Eradicating unemployment or using the state to develop a healthy population were Scottish goals as well as British ones, and if the UK state could be used to these ends, then that mattered more than hanging on to what was coming to be seen in influential circles as the outdated policy of Scottish home rule. Moreover, there was significant Scottish input to the formation of middle opinion, which will be discussed later.

The central state also intervened directly in people's private lives for the first time. For example, family allowances gave a source of income to mothers to support children, but were accompanied by a patriarchal ideology in which women were expected to do all the caring and home-making. Insofar as the essence of Scottish social distinctiveness in the nineteenth century lay in people's private lives, this change therefore laid the basis for the state to shape Scottish society to an unprecedented degree. The effect was also to politicise family and private matters as never before, providing new terrain on which Scottish nationalism could build (for example, housing and health). In this sense, the traditional Scottishness of the private realm prevailed over the new Britishness of the welfare state, causing these social policies to be debated in a Scottish context.

Nevertheless, although Scottish political nationalism was strong at times, it did not pose a threat to the new UK state that was emerging. The centre continued to tolerate diversity. Bulpitt argues that the main purpose of the state was still to disentangle itself from local involvement so as to be able to concentrate on foreign policy; as a result, the periphery (in which he includes local government throughout the UK) was also autonomous from the centre. Bernard Crick, writing about the centralising strand in the much later Conservatism of Margaret Thatcher, reminds us that 'many of the old English Tories had a clear and politic sense of the diversity of the UK' (Crick, 1991, p. 91). Marquand calls this the 'whig imperialist' vision of Britain: 'civil society is a majestic river, flowing in a uniform direction. The role of the state is to administer the occasional glib rectification of the banks' (Marquand, 1993, p. 213). According to this view, the state agencies which did come to intervene in people's lives – the doctors, social workers and unemployment benefit offices – are best thought of as part of the local state, not the centre. That left them scope, in Scotland, to be distinctively Scottish.

THE FOUNDATION OF THE TWENTIETH-CENTURY SCOTTISH STATE

The general pressure for reform at the beginning of the twentieth century which affected the UK state as a whole had a particular version in Scotland, responding to the distinctive legacy from the nineteenth century. The institutional outcome was consequently distinctive too. Scotland in the 1920s was the only part of the UK which continued to be ruled by a system of specialist boards that were separate from a professional civil service: despite the existence of the Scottish Secretary, and despite the upgrading of that post to a Secretary of State in 1926, the boards continued to devise and execute policy as if they were wholly autonomous. This was not popular with the Labour Party, who saw them – especially most of the local poor-law boards – as agencies to allow the conservative middle class to deny welfare to the poor.

Reform was instigated by Sir John Gilmour, who was Secretary of State for Scotland in the Conservative government of 1926–9. By the late 1930s, most of the boards had come under the aegis of the Scottish Office, which was believed to be the appropriately modern replacement. In achieving this aim, Gilmour was at pains to construct a consensus. The committee which devised the new system included representatives of the Labour and Liberal Parties as well as Conservatives and others: one notable member was Tom Johnston, a leader of the Scottish Labour Party, and eventually to become Secretary of State for Scotland in Churchill's coalition government of 1940–5.

But this mere chronology of modernisation does not fully explain why the mechanism for reforming the boards was so distinctively Scottish: why a Scottish Office, rather than, say, field offices of the London departments?

The first explanation is nationalism. As we saw in chapter 5, the Scottish Office had been founded in 1885 in response to nationalist campaigning. The opposition to Gilmour's proposals often took a nationalist form too: for example, as we saw in chapter 1, the former Labour Scottish Secretary, William Adamson, claimed that the changes were centralising power on London. On the political right, too, there were doubts: Walter Elliot criticised the 1929 abolition of parish councils as removing a 'foundation stone of Scottish society' (Levitt, 1988b, p. 160). Gilmour insisted that there would be no transfer of authority out of Scotland altogether, and that policy would remain as distinctively Scottish as before. Parish council powers would go to the new councils of the burghs and counties. And he accepted a proposal from the Convention of Royal Burghs that the relevant legislation would stipulate that the Scottish Office would be sited in Edinburgh. This provided something of an answer to the nationalist concern about the risk of the Scottish Office's being anglicised if it remained based in London. It therefore also removed an argument from the case for a Scottish parliament: hitherto, it had not been thought possible to have a branch of central government operating so far from Westminster.

The other reasons for a Scottish Office appear to be more straightforwardly instrumental, but nevertheless interacted with nationalist arguments. The main consideration was an early sign of the emergence of technocratic criteria: the old system was judged to be inefficient. The first serious proposals to reorganise the nineteenth-century Scottish boards came from a Commission chaired by Lord MacDonnell, which reported in 1914. It saw Scotland's institutions as being inadequate to cope with increasingly complex and technical legislation. The political nature of the boards was actually felt to be a disadvantage: it prevented professional knowledge from being brought to bear on social problems. Slightly later, in the reform of 1929, the local authorities were similarly felt to be too small and ineffective to deal with the social effects of industrial decline, far less with regenerating the economy. This belief was quite widely held in the Labour movement as well as in official circles: although some parish councils were captured by radical socialists, and were able to use this local base to improve the level of public support for unemployed people, there was a more general feeling on the political left that only large local authorities would be efficient enough to instigate extensive improvements in the social infrastructure. Thus, in the same parliamentary debate where William Adamson objected to the centralising effects of the Gilmour reforms, other Labour MPs complained that the Scottish Office did not have powers to require local authorities to build hospitals.

It was even believed that the lack of scope for Scottish professionals led to creeping anglicisation, because Scottish politicians – many of whom were regarded as carpetbaggers from England – could not appreciate all the myriad technical ways in which there ought to be differences between Scotland and England in the implementation of legislation. This was accompanied by a degree of special pleading by civil servants: their status (and pay) would improve if they were attached to a government department rather than a board, and would rise even further if the head of that department became a Secretary of State.

Alongside these doubts about the old institutions, however, was the nationalist assumption that the new framework would be Scottish: yet again, we are reminded that Scottish nationalism was partly official, providing a taken-for-granted context in which Scottish politicians operated. It was this which allowed Gilmour to propose that the Scottish Office be moved to Edinburgh. Thus the debate about reforming the boards was primarily about efficiency and technical effectiveness, but also took place in a context of assumed Scottish nationhood.

The other instrumentalist reason for setting up a Scottish Office was a response by the authorities to what was believed to be the threat of bolshevism. During and after the 1914–18 war, the revolutionary left attracted quite substantial support in Glasgow – 'Red Clydeside' – and to a lesser extent other parts of central Scotland. It was believed that an interventionist Scottish Office would help to defuse the political discontent, for example by eradicating slum housing. It was also believed that replacing the parish councils by larger local authorities would prevent the radical left from coming to power locally. This response to socialist strength was typical of much of Europe: thus it is another example of a key policy's being shaped by a distinctive Scottish national ethic. This Scottish penchant for state corporatism as a means to social reform was soon to become the dominant ideology of the Labour Party.

Thus, as Harvie puts it, the increase in state power meant, in Scotland, the growth of Scottish Office power. If there was a challenge to traditional Scottish institutions, it came from within Scotland. It might not have taken this form had there not been nationalist pressure for a Scottish parliament, or socialist pressure framed in a Scottish context; but whatever the motives of the reformers – and they all believed themselves to be staunch patriots – the effect was to start the building of a new Scottish state for the new century.

THE GROWTH OF THE SCOTTISH OFFICE UNDER ELLIOT AND JOHNSTON

Much the same story can be told about the growth of this new institution between its transfer to Edinburgh in 1939 and its consolidation there by the mid-1940s. There were two key politicians in this: Walter Elliot, who was Conservative Secretary of State between 1936 and 1938; and Labour's Tom Johnston.

Elliot took full advantage of the Gilmour reforms to make the Scottish Office into Scotland's government. When he could construct a Scottish consensus on social policy, he could get his way, provided that the direction he was pursuing did not deviate too far from government policy in London. As a result, the real power in Scottish politics came to lie with the Scottish Office bureaucrats, because it was by means of their committees and networks that Elliot could sound out and mould Scottish opinion. This 'fostered a kind of one-party-state ethos bridging businessmen, professionals, and even collectivists' (Harvie, 1992, p. 247).

Elliot contributed significantly to British middle opinion. He was an intellectual as well as a politician, and so his influence was wider than his administrative role on its own could allow. He argued for the fusion of the traditional elites with the emerging social strata of scientists and social scientists. The new civil servants whom he had in mind were already receptive to this view: being products of the Scottish universities of the decades spanning the beginning of the century, they had absorbed the reformism that was then popular. Elliot's was not the only Scottish contribution to middle opinion: Robert Boothby, Harold Macmillan, James Lithgow and Tom Johnston were active too, and they and several others shaped the economic policies which developed during the 1930s. As a result, these policies and beliefs had nationalist implications in Scotland: for example, there were distinctly nationalist – but non-partisan – motives in the setting up of the Scottish Youth Hostels Association, the aim being to promote national efficiency by developing the fitness of the nation's young people. Other examples were the Association for the Protection of Rural Scotland, the Saltire Society, the National Trust for Scotland, and the Scottish Council of Social Service. In between them and the state were such semi-official bodies as the Scottish National Development Council, the establishment of which was encouraged by the Scottish Office to promote industrial renewal. Likewise, the town-planning movement fused a nationalist revival of Scottish architectural styles with a reformist attack on slum tenements. The effects of these people and organisations on the economy are discussed later: the point to note here is that the new Scottish state was emerging in an atmosphere of consensual Scottish nationalism.

Johnston continued Elliot's policies. Churchill wanted him in the wartime Cabinet to keep Scotland quieter than it had been in the 1914–18 war. Johnston agreed to serve provided that he was given freedom to pursue what he wanted on the basis of whatever Scottish consensus he could manage to produce. His vehicle for this was initially his Council of State, consisting of all living former Secretaries of State, but he soon bypassed that in favour of more technical committees staffed by industrialists and experts. Johnston had been a supporter of Scottish home rule, and had been on the left of the party, but he had little time for sentiment. He believed that the Scottish Office could allow reforms to be distinctively Scottish without being a threat to the Union. Johnston now preferred to keep the Union because, he believed, Scotland was too weak economically to support itself. He also saw state intervention from the Scottish Office as offering the chance to be collectivist without being socialist: building better houses in the present was preferable to fighting for a distant utopia. Given the emphasis placed by middle opinion on technocratic solutions to social problems, it is hardly surprising that Johnston – along with a majority in the Scottish Labour Party – believed that it was getting everything it wanted by maintaining the British connection. In any case, developing an interventionist Scottish state within the Union could be seen as the first steps on a road to eventual home rule or socialism.

For these compromises, however, Johnston earned the ire of nationalists and socialists. One member of parliament from the leftist Independent Labour Party described the Council of State as being packed with 'die-hard Tories' (Campbell, 1979, p. 1), and the activists of the Scottish

National Party (the SNP, formed in 1934) denounced him for selling out the cause of home rule. But Johnston was going with the grain of Scottish opinion, and the radical critics had no practicable programme to offer as an alternative. Moreover, as in the nineteenth century, there was always the safety-valve of emigration, which lessened the pressures on Scottish government to solve social problems at home.

Johnston was achieving things because mild collectivism had always been acceptable to Scottish Conservatives with their recent origins in the Liberal-Unionist breakaway of 1886. Acceptable also, as we have seen, was a similarly mild nationalism – the ideology of what Harvie calls 'the patriotic party of the "Anglo-Scottish" Empire' (Harvie, 1992, p. 247). Thus Elliot – leader of the Scottish Unionists – played an enthusiastic part in several of Johnston's committees, just as Johnston had done in Gilmour's. Placing the implementation of collectivism in the hands of reliable Scottish civil servants and other experts was reassuring to most Scottish politicians, fearful at once of socialism and of London encroachment. And all the electoral evidence was that the vast majority of the Scottish people had come to agree with this too: Unionists and the increasingly cautious Scottish Labour Party won far larger numbers of votes than the far left or the SNP.

With such a basis in consensus, the Scottish Office became the mouthpiece of Scottish civil society. This was most obvious in public: Scottish organisations of diverse sorts started to put pressure on the Secretary of State to represent them in government or more widely, even in policy areas where the Scottish Office had no remit. The reason why such pressure continued is that it worked: in the private discussions inside the government, Secretaries of State took up these grievances, and used them to try to convince their colleagues that concessions should be given to Scotland. These processes had already been noted by the Gilmour committee in 1936: 'there is an increasing tendency among Scottish people to appeal to the Secretary of State on all questions affecting the social and economic life of Scotland' (Levitt, 1994). In the early 1930s, for example, the Secretary of State persuaded the government to appoint an independent Scottish commissioner for the depressed areas (alongside one for England and Wales). He mixed technical arguments with political ones: Scotland had a separate legal and administrative system, and political sentiment in Scotland was turning increasingly nationalist in the sense that politicians of all types were casting Scotland's problems in national terms. When in office, Elliot and Johnston, too, exploited this to the full, and the convention continued for long afterwards. Indeed, so high did the status of the Scottish Office rise that all government offices in Scotland were to some extent answerable to the Secretary of State, even those which were branch offices of London departments.

THE SCOTTISH OFFICE AND NATIONALISM AFTER 1945

The evolution of the Scottish Office between 1945 and the mid-1970s continued to be conditioned by nationalism. There was the official national-ism of the Office itself, celebrating its achievements on behalf of Scotland and helping to maintain and develop a Scottish social identity through the distinctive agencies of social policy that it set up. But this nationalism was always set against a background of more radical agitation, pressing for a Scottish parliament or for full Scottish statehood. Neither side in this political dependency liked to admit the importance of the other. But each significant extension of the powers of the Scottish Office was in response to current nationalist campaigning – usually spreading across the political spectrum – whatever the official rhetoric about administrative rationalisa-tion may claim. And, although the campaigns did not achieve their overt goal of a parliament, these changes to the Scottish Office were actual victories. The purpose of this section is to outline these processes.

After the end of the Labour government in 1951, the Scottish Office continued to operate by constructing consensus, a task made necessary by Scotland's diversity. A united front remained the most effective way of putting pressure on London, and was especially effective if it combined a large amount of nationalist rhetoric (the Scottish Office's defending Scot-land's interests) with a large degree of secrecy in negotiations with London. This style of national bargaining encouraged the Scottish Office to sponsor the formation of interest groups, so that it could readily find out what the range of opinion was: Kellas (1983) cites examples such as the Transport Users Consultative Committee, and the Advisory Council on Education and its successors. Fry (1987) notes that the continual expansion of consult-ative bodies is ironic considering that the Scottish Office was set up to abolish boards; but that may be the inevitable reality of bargaining within a small country that has no national and public political forum. As McPher-son and Raab (1988) point out in their analysis of this process in Scottish education, interest groups acquire a special legitimacy in the absence of a parliament. The Scottish Office also continued to coordinate the activities of the Scottish branch offices of all government departments, something which became easier as these were upgraded to be headed by people who could take decisions without referring back to London. Kellas sums up the system over which the Secretary of State presided as 'the vast apparatus of advisory councils and committees dominated by professionals and busi-nessmen' (Kellas, 1983, p. 192).

He could have added representatives of trades unions. The mechanism by which labour was incorporated was the Scottish Trades Union Congress, which was fully independent of the London-based Trades Union Congress. The STUC astutely expanded its influence by the apparently paradoxical route of encouraging amalgamations between Scottish unions and English ones: by this means, affiliation to the STUC became normal for British unions, and so Scottish government had no option but to treat the STUC as the representative of labour. The other way that labour people were involved was through the Labour party's role in local government: many of the consultative committees had statutory representatives from the Convention of Royal Burghs and other similar bodies, and so were bound to contain Labour members even when the Conservatives were in government.

Official sponsorship also stimulated the formation of autonomous Scottish sections of professional bodies, because the consultative dialogue tended to take place among professionals. Thus middle-class organisations tended to become more Scottish, even while trades unions were amalgamating into British ones. The middle class could feel that they owned the Scottish state because they managed it. Indeed, whole new segments of that class were produced in the new state institutions such as health, education, social work and the nationalised industries. Middle-class people staffed the boards and committees in the policy network, reaching these positions through technical competence rather than the capacity to win elections. When he was Secretary of State in the Labour government of the 1960s, Willie Ross defended his appointment of Tories to official boards on the grounds that there were no socialists who were competent enough (Marr, 1992, p. 107). The Scottish professions felt that they controlled the rules by which these committees worked. Scottish civil servants tended to be overwhelmingly Scottish, as had been hoped by the MacDonnell commission in 1914.

Scottish education was especially important in shaping this new system of governing Scotland. Both Poggi and Daniel Bell have argued that the character of the welfare state depended above all on the education that produced its ruling staff. If that is true, then the Scottish state was thoroughly Scottish. As we will see later, education remained one of the most autonomous areas of Scottish policy-making, and it continued to inculcate a distinctive social ethic based on the residue of Protestantism. It was the duty of the well-off to provide for the less fortunate, and the new welfare state created a new opportunity for this ethic to be put into practice.

The Scottish Office thus became the focus of Scottish national and nationalist debate. It could speak for the policy networks which it sponsored, a form of home rule which was favoured in the 1950s by the influential Secretary of State James Stuart, and his deputy Alec Douglas-Home (later the prime minister). Almost the whole political class had thus accepted the conclusion, reached by Tom Johnston, that Scottish interests could be advanced without national self-determination. This view even extended, at times, to leaders of more militant nationalism: for example, in 1944, R. E. Muirhead declared at a meeting of the SNP national council that Johnston had been 'more useful to Scotland than almost any other man' (Harvie, 1981b, p. 16).

The oppositionist nationalism might use the ancient symbols of nation-hood, and the state might borrow them on ceremonial occasions. But the nationalism that had any lasting political effect was modern, based on the new Scotland that was being shaped by social democracy and the unprecedented economic prosperity of the 1950s. The Scottish Office depended on this nationalism, but still rarely admitted it in terms which campaigning nationalists would accept. Transfers of powers to the Scottish Office were always justified in technocratic terms: it was claimed that matters could be organised more efficiently or rationally if they were dealt with from Edinburgh. The same arguments were used for changes in the ways that Scottish business was dealt with in parliament. For example, devising ways of considering Scottish legislation separately in Westminster was justified on the grounds of relieving the congestion of parliament as a whole. But all of these changes were responses to an actual or feared challenge from nationalism, something of which Scottish Office ministers were ready to take advantage in private. For example, in the debate over where to place a new steelworks in 1958, the Secretary of State conceded in Cabinet that 'purely economic' considerations would indicate a site in Wales, but nevertheless threatened his colleagues with the spectre of nationalist disaffection: failure to choose Scotland 'would subject the relations between England and Scotland to a new and severe strain' (Levitt, 1994). Similarly, the new procedures for Scottish legislation were a reaction to nationalist campaigning for home rule, especially by the cross-party Scottish Convention in the late 1940s. The Grand Committee of Scottish MPs which resulted was frequently described as a 'Scottish parliament within Westminster', a substantial exaggeration of its rather cursory powers (J. Burns, 1960). It was for essentially nationalist reasons, too, that there was no transfer of administrative powers away from the Scottish Office after 1945. If the allocation of responsibilities had indeed been purely 'rational', then we would expect such reversals whenever the nature of the economy and society changed.

The reason why these responses to nationalism did manage to appease it is that nationalism remained diffuse. All the political parties used it. Under the Labour government of 1945–51, the Conservatives opposed centralisation on nationalist grounds. They continued to present themselves as the most truly Scottish party right through the 1950s, achieving, probably as a result, the most striking electoral success that they had ever had (far better than they have had since): they reached a peak of just over half the vote in 1955. They linked this Scottish nationalism with loyalty to the Empire, and with a defence of the distinctively Scottish tradition of Protestantism: they thereby captured large segments of the Protestant working class, who were attracted by this continuing tradition of collectivist Unionism.

Much the same can be said of Labour, although with the important difference that it relied on Catholic votes as well as Protestant. As we saw, the social and economic reforms of the post-war government were interpreted as fulfilling Scottish national aspirations: if Scotland was fortunate enough to be in a prosperous Union where the main partner had come round to its point of view, then breaking the link seemed futile to socialists (especially, moreover, when the Union could reasonably claim to have played a significant role in the defeat of fascism). Labour believed in internationalism, but that was not an evasion of its Scottishness: it inherited that assimilationist Scottish nationalism which we have seen among modernisers and liberals throughout the eighteenth and nineteenth centuries. Labour people campaigning under the Conservative governments of the 1950s continued to argue in terms of the Scottish national interest: that was one reason why the Secretary of State could press the nationalist case for a new Scottish steel plant. Similar points are true of the Liberals, although they had been temporarily eclipsed after the war.

Thus there emerged a sense of a common Scottish interest, embracing most political points of view as well as the policy networks and interest groups whose thinking had evolved from the middle opinion of the 1930s. All the Secretaries of State were centrist in their beliefs, maintaining the collectivist Unionism which Elliot had embodied earlier.

This consensus was evident even in parliament, that hothouse of manufactured conflict. In the 1950s, three quarters of Scottish bills were passed without opposition, and for the remainder the government frequently accepted amendments proposed by the opposition. A sign of this was that decreasing numbers of Scottish bills were debated by the whole House of Commons: to be referred to the Scottish Grand Committee (or the new Scottish Standing Committee), they had to be judged to be non-partisan. English MPs were expected to keep out of Scottish business, leaving the Scots to get on with developing their consensus.

HOW INDEPENDENT WAS SCOTLAND?

Of course, none of this could have worked if there had been fundamental political divisions between Scotland and England. But, for all but three years between 1945 and 1970, the Scottish and English majorities were of the same political complexion: Labour from 1945 to 1950, Conservative from 1951 to 1964, and Labour again from 1966 to 1970. The parties agreed on most matters anyway, and so the supporters of the minority did not feel alienated from power. Thus political debate was about ways of implementing policy, rather than about fundamentals. This, then, is a clear instance of Poggi's general point about the role of the technocracy: national autonomy lay in the scope for implementing legislation, because the legislation was widely agreed. This would have remained true even if Scotland had had its own parliament: that international consensus around the welfare state would probably have produced much the same legislation as came from Westminster, and so the Scottishness of policies would still have rested on the implementation, not on the broad principles.

This is not to say that Scotland was independent; its autonomy was circumscribed, sometimes severely so, because its freedom related always to the means of implementation, not to ends. Midwinter et al. (1991) argue that the system cannot even be described as devolution, because, they claim, the Scottish Office has never been able to take authoritative decisions. Moore and Booth, similarly, criticise Kellas's use of the word 'system' to describe Scottish politics: a system, they say, would have to have a distinctive sovereignty. According to this argument, the strongest statement that could be made about Scotland is that it had a 'differentiated pattern of political communication, and a subsidiary administration mechanism' (Moore and Booth, 1989, p. 15). Scottish Labour, in particular, settled for administrative autonomy partly because British leaders such as Herbert Morrison were unwilling to grant them more; to have achieved a Scottish parliament in the face of this opposition would have risked a split in the Labour Party which might have endangered the gains which the Scots saw coming from the first-ever majority Labour government.

So I am not claiming that Scotland had the freedom to pursue separate political goals. My point is, simply, that it chose goals which were common throughout Britain, and even further afield, and retained control of implementation. To say that Scotland did not have a political system is to take a limited view of what politics is, to restrict it, essentially, to formal sovereignty expressed in the public realm of parliament. That is a very British view, shaped by the characteristically British obsession with parliament's sovereignty. It would not be shared by politicians in federations, as we will see in chapter 7. Scotland settled for control of a different kind of politics (while never failing to remind its partners that it could, ultimately, fall back on an assertion of sovereignty if it failed to achieve the autonomy that it wanted).

Some elements of sovereignty did remain, most notably in the legal system, which was more independent than the systems of the component parts of any federal states. Lawyers no longer exercised the virtual monopoly of government that they had enjoyed in the nineteenth century, but they continued to set the framework within which all legislation had to be placed. There continued to be a separate stream of Scottish legislation, required to fit common policies into Scots law. And the lawyers were prominent in the policy networks, either as individuals or through the Scottish Law Commission, set up in 1965 to make its own proposal for reforming the laws.

But if formal sovereignty was not the main expression of Scottish autonomy, then to find that autonomy we have to examine particular policy areas, precisely because it was in the details of implementation that the scope for independent Scottish action lay. This is done in the next few sections, for the economy, housing and education, with some further comments later on social work and health.

ECONOMIC AUTONOMY

Whatever the nationalist sentiments, and however important the whole range of social policies, the new constitutional framework that emerged in Scotland in the 1930s was bound to be judged ultimately on what it did for the economy. The manufacturing industries which had dominated Scottish employment since the 1860s were declining, losing markets to Germany, France and the USA. Control of what remained was shifting to London or overseas, and so indigenous sources of new capital were increasingly unavailable.

That was the main reason why Scottish middle opinion in the 1930s and after turned to the state. The state in question was that amalgam of British resources and Scottish agencies which we have been looking at; both of them were informed by a theory of regional development that was the geographical counterpart to the welfare-state aim of redistribution between social classes. This programme, moreover, can be reasonably claimed to have originated in the thinking of the Scottish elites, and therefore to have been the policy that Scotland's governing system had evolved autonomously.

On the face of it, it is true, the Scottish Office did not have much control of economic policy after 1945. The new Keynesian convention was for state intervention at the macroeconomic level, through its control of prices, labour supply and the external balance of payments. Nationalisation was believed to be an essential tool, and this seemed to entail centralisation. The point was to control the 'commanding heights' of the economy, which could not be done from the Scottish foothills. These new assumptions about economics arose from the collectivism of middle opinion of the 1930s, and (until the 1970s) were accepted as thoroughly by the Conservatives as they were by Labour. In this respect, the British consensus resembled that in most of Western Europe and North America.

However, given that the framework was so widely accepted internationally, we have to ask what scope a small country – even a formally independent one – could have for influencing the development of its economy. Was the Scottish situation really so dependent in this context? A clue to an answer is in the economic aspects of the system of boards and committees that was described earlier. At both a British and a Scottish level, the system provided a mechanism by which interest groups could be coordinated in the pursuit of Keynesian aims. These groups would involve leaders and bureaucracies, not popular participation: at the British level, therefore, the key groups were the leaders of the Confederation of British Industry, the Trades Union Congress, and government. The ideology of the resulting consensus at that level was, moreover, British nationalist. The unit of management was the national economy, which coincided also with the territory covered by the nationalised welfare state. According to this welfare-state nationalism, the state now had a duty to further the national interest through managing the economy, and thereby developing the society.

Scotland was part of this, but also constructed its own separate national economic interest. In fact, if British socialism was indeed intent on decreeing uniformity (as its Scottish nationalist critics alleged in the 1940s), then it signally failed to do so. The very existence of Scottish policy networks helped to ensure that economic debate would take place in an increasingly Scottish framework as the 1950s and 1960s progressed. If any national unity was strengthened in this period, it was Scottish attitudes to the development of the Scottish economy, fed not only by the policy networks of the elites, but also by the new mass audiences for the new Scottish national broadcasting media.

The Scottish Office led the way in promoting this notion of a Scottish national economic interest, no matter that it was part of the UK government and therefore nominally subordinate to the British national interest. The purpose of British welfare-state nationalism in Scotland was to serve the Scottish national interest too – a plausible argument given the still growing tendency for Scottish businesses to be taken over by British concerns. It was this general equating of Scottish and British interests that allowed Scottish ministers to speak on the whole range of economic matters affecting Scotland, even those topics for which they had no formal responsibility. Frequently, they were merely articulating the messages which they were receiving from the Scottish corporate networks that they had constructed. Furthermore, this Scottish nationalism was furthered by being embedded in Britishness: if Scottish politicians could be seen to be enthusiastically backing British economic interests, then they might be listened to in London when they went on to argue for redistribution in favour of Scotland within Britain.

The core of their arguments was based on the ideas of regional development. Kellas (1983) notes that the intellectual impetus came from the Scottish universities in the 1950s, notably Glasgow. This fed into bodies like the Scottish National Development Council (SNDC), one of the consensual committees set up by middle opinion in the 1930s. It was established by the Convention of Royal Burghs, with the backing of the Scottish Office and involving not only the highly influential industrialist Sir James Lithgow but also trade unions, churches, political parties and numerous professional groups. At the same time, the Secretary of State was persuading the Cabinet to appoint the Scottish commissioner for the depressed areas, and so his activities fitted well with these autonomous Scottish initiatives. The SNDC in turn formed a Scottish Economic Committee which became the focus for Scottish thinking on the economy and for the activities of planners such as Frank Mears and Patrick Abercrombie. It investigated Highland problems, advocated a Scottish development agency, organised the Empire Exhibition in Glasgow in 1938 and founded Films of Scotland (1938); and the commissioner for the Scottish special areas developed sewerage schemes and an industrial estate at Hillington near Glasgow. These activities were the immediate practical outcome of the middle-opinion thinking of the 1930s. The lessons were fed into the Barlow Commission on the Distribution of the Industrial Population, which in turn shaped the basis of UK regional policy after the war. The lobbying activity made the case for Scotland's being treated as an entity, and thus bolstered the economic nationalism implicit in the development of the Scottish Office.

So respected had the SNDC become by 1940 that Johnston involved it in the planning aspects of his Council of State. The Industry Committee which he set up – and which was more active than the Council – fused with the SNDC to form the Scottish Council Development and Industry in 1946; this marriage blurred even further the distinction between Scottish civil society and the new Scottish Office state. Among the achievements of Johnston's committees was the Hydro-Electric Board, which extended electricity to most of the Highlands and Islands by using the region's vast supplies of water power. But the main effect of Johnston's rule was felt after the war: the committees which he had established had created the climate for state development of the economy that remained dominant until at least the 1960s.

It was in the nature of such a policy in Scotland that it had to be furthered by first of all persuading the centre to concede resources and to compel firms to relocate; that was not a mark of dependency, but rather an instance of the bargaining in which a small economy would be bound to engage. The Scottish Office itself sponsored some of this work, for example the Clyde Valley Regional Plan of 1949 and the report of an investigation into the Scottish economy chaired by Sir John Toothill in 1961. That the centre did grant resources was partly a consequence of the political leverage which the Scottish Office could exercise, and that leverage in turn was feasible partly because of recurrent nationalist sentiment across the parties. Thus the mood that created the Toothill report also caused electoral losses to the Conservative Party in the 1959 general election, as Labour began to have success in its argument that the Government was not serving Scotland's interests well. But the success of the Scottish Office in its negotiations with London was partly also due to the alliances which it could form between Scottish interests and those of the economically declining parts of England and Wales; and to achieve that, nationalism had to be tempered with realism.

In Scotland, the effects of regional policy were felt increasingly through policies devised and implemented by the Scottish Office. The Scottish

Office worked with the Scottish Council Development and Industry to promote planning and economic growth through sponsoring such initiatives as new bridges over the Forth, Tay and Clyde estuaries, electrification of railways in Glasgow, the building of a new Glasgow airport, and the encouragement of 'growth points' for new industry. It also made lasting institutional changes: most notable were the two nationalised electricity boards (1940s), the Highlands and Islands Development Board (1965) and the Scottish Development Agency (1975). The five New Towns became a particular focus of Scottish Office sponsorship of new industry: by 1975 they contained about ten per cent of all Scottish manufacturing employment. They were most important in attracting small projects, which some writers have judged to have had a more lasting impact on Scotland's economic performance than developments such as the Ravenscraig steelworks, the car manufacture in Bathgate, or the aluminium smelter in Invergordon.

The high point of this type of economic activity came with the technocratic socialism of the 1964–70 Labour government, when the Scottish Office prepared a national plan on the basis of the Toothill report. From 1975, the Scottish Office had control of regional development grants, taking over from the Scottish branch office of the London-based Department of Trade and Industry. The Scottish Office also played an important role in coordinating the infrastructural needs of the development of North Sea oil from the early 1970s.

How much effect these regional policies had is a matter of controversy. But Gavin McCrone, who was chief economic adviser at the Scottish Office from 1972 to 1991, has pointed out that in this period the performance of the Scottish economy relative to that of England improved (G. McCrone, 1985). Whereas the Scottish growth rate was slower than the UK's in the 1950s, it kept up with the UK in the 1960s and 1970s, and surpassed it in the early 1970s. The Scottish gross domestic product per head and average earnings moved closer to the UK average, as did its unemployment rate.

McCrone concedes the difficulty of estimating the extent to which this relative improvement is due to the regional policies pursued by the state; much of the growth, for example, was attributable to services or to North Sea oil, the development of neither of which was a major concern of regional policy. The industries which were established in the New Towns were usually branch plants of American companies, and so – especially from the 1970s onwards – had few research and development functions and did not trade extensively with the local economy.

But McCrone also points out that even these successes were helped by the infrastructure which regional policy provided. If the policy failed to arrest the decline of the traditional manufacturing industry, that is hardly surprising: nothing short of outright protection could have prevented that, and Scotland's open economy would probably have suffered a far more serious decline if tariffs had been imposed. Thus the net increase of 90,000 jobs attributable to regional policy up to 1979 may seem small in a workforce of 2,100,000, but is much more significant when compared with the loss of 152,000 manufacturing jobs between 1954 and 1979 (Buxton, 1985, table 6). Randall, despite his doubts about the effectiveness of the New Towns, argues that 'it is not clear that it was realistic to expect a much more favourable outcome given the strength of the constraints' – constraints which would have been faced regardless of the constitutional position of Scotland (Randall, 1985, p. 268). Even an independent Scotland would have been peripheral to the main markets, and would have had to cope with a legacy of declining industry. It might have been formally separate from England, but the slow growth there would have continued to affect Scottish exporters (as they did Ireland's: see chapter 7). Saville points out that the encroachment of foreign ownership on Scottish industry was not as severe as in some other small European countries, including some of those which were independent.

For Britain as a whole, Maclennan and Parr writing in 1979 conclude that regional policy had been a relative success:

> [it] has diverted a considerable number of jobs to the assisted areas and . . . employment prospects in such areas, though still relatively poor, have been considerably enhanced by the policy. (Maclennan and Parr, 1979, p. 324)

They remind us also of the balancing of Scottish and U K interests which regional policy required: unless the U K economy was thriving, then regional policy could not work:

> Undoubtedly, a greater expenditure commitment to regional policy in the past could have further offset continued economic decline in the problem regions, though the possible adverse impact on the non-assisted regions and on [U K] national economic performance is not clear. (p. 324)

Within this overall framework of regionalism, the Scottish Office regulated the Scottish economy in a system described as a negotiated order by Moore and Booth (1989). It was not independent: because it relied on regional policy, ultimately it depended on resources and legislation from the U K state. But it was more autonomous than an English region, notably because of the dense interconnections of all the policy networks.

Moore and Booth estimated that in the early 1980s there were about 4,000 positions of patronage in the economic sphere available to the Secretary of State – appointments to interventionist bodies such as the Scottish Development Agency, to the Scottish ends of British agencies such as the Manpower Services Commission, to advisory groups such as the Scottish Economic Committee, and to nationalised industries such as the electricity boards or various companies running buses or ferries. In some sectors, the Scottish Office devolved statutory powers to partnerships with private interests in which it did not have a controlling vote: an example is the policing of the dairy trade by the Milk Marketing Board, set up in 1933 to ensure a reliable supply of milk in the interests of raising standards of nutrition. Much later, the Scottish Office gave a statutory role to the Scottish Fishermen's Organisation in regulating the quotas on catches imposed by the European Community.

At the heart of the Scottish Office's intervention in the latter part of the period, from 1975 until the late 1980s, was the Scottish Development Agency. The characterisation which Moore and Booth give it is a neat summary of the limited autonomy which the Scottish Office enjoyed in economic policy:

> [although] the SDA clearly operates within the . . . market, it is poten-
> tially an instrument of planning within the market. It cannot overtly
> contradict central government policy, but it implements it in ways
> which are not ideally consistent with notions of a liberal market role
> for the state or a directive bureaucratic planning role. It brings together
> the public and private sectors at the Scottish level, but . . . relationships
> are typically bi-partite, voluntary, ad hoc, and based on a political
> exchange of resources. (Moore and Booth, 1989, pp. 142–3)

As a result of this sponsored network, interest groups had to pay attention to what the Scottish Office and the other parts of the network were thinking. For example, Moore and Booth calculate that the Confederation of British Industry in Scotland spent about one third of its lobbying time dealing with the Scottish Office. The CBI had closer links with the STUC than it had at British level with the TUC. And the Scottish Council Development and Industry resembled the economic councils of Spain and France, bringing together interest groups in a voluntary dialogue with government.

Thus Scottish economic policy between 1945 and the mid-1970s can be regarded as indigenous. Scottish thinkers – including the Scottish Office – contributed to developing ideas of regional policy. They then persuaded the UK state to their point of view, helped by allies in Wales and the depressed regions of England. The implementation of the policy – that is, how to spend the resources thus released – was in the hands of the Scottish Office and its policy network. The Scottish economy did continue to decline, relative to its main competitors, and in that sense these reformers could be said to have failed, although it probably did not decline as far as it would have done without their policies. But the important point for our discussion is that the reformers were, on the whole, free to pursue their own path. The ideas which informed Scottish economic policy may have been wrong, but they were not imposed; they were chosen by influential Scots, the same as would have run the country had home rule come about in the 1920s. Given the institutional and economic inheritance, and given the historically tight links with the English economy, it is difficult to imagine that a self-governing parliament would have pursued policies that were much different.

The housing which Scotland inherited from the nineteenth century was among the worst in Europe. So, state intervention to improve matters started early, with a Royal Commission which reported in 1917. This recommended that private enterprise had failed, and that the only way of solving the problems was by a partnership between the state and local authorities. The Scottish Office accepted this recommendation. There had already been state intervention to restrict rents during the war, following a campaign led by women in Glasgow against increases.

Subsequent Scottish housing policy was distinctive in two main ways: state subsidies, and state encouragement of house-building by public authorities. In both of these, the scope for independent action by the Scottish Office grew as the century progressed. The housing policy community – and in particular, later, the lobby for urban regeneration – became central parts of the policy networks.

At the outset of the discussion of subsidy, in 1921, the Scottish Office was not even being invited to Cabinet discussions of housing, and was not able to gain higher subsidies in Scotland than elsewhere despite evidence of poorer conditions. But this had started to change by 1925, when the Scottish Secretary did convince the Cabinet that a special subsidy could be justified. From then until the present day, the Scottish Office has successfully resisted the ending of the subsidy. Scotland was able to continue with it when it was being curtailed or ended in England in 1926, 1932, 1934, 1947 and 1952. This resistance thus took place equally under Conservative and Labour governments (as did the English pressures for reducing subsidy). In 1934, the Conservative Secretary of State argued that private enterprise simply was not functioning effectively. In 1947, the Labour Secretary, Joe Westwood, was able to use the twenty-year-old mainly Tory precedent to resist cuts that were being imposed by the Chancellor of the Exchequer, Hugh Dalton. Even today, in a completely different era politically, there remains a much-reduced government contribution to the Housing Revenue Account that has no counterpart in England.

The main purpose to which this extra subsidy was put was new building by public authorities, the second way in which Scottish policy was distinctive. Again, this was a programme that was advanced equally by Conservative and Labour Scottish administrations. Thus, from the 1920s until the 1960s, Scottish politicians of all types argued for the building of new houses rather than the renovation of existing ones. There was a widespread belief that renovation would merely subsidise inefficient or rapacious private landlords. In 1956 and 1957, for example, the Conservative Secretaries of State

James Stuart and John Maclay resisted cuts in building, arguing that private enterprise could not meet the targets. Labour favoured new public building because slum landlords were regarded with intense suspicion.

As a result, between 1950 and 1980, three quarters of new houses in Scotland were in the public sector; in the earlier period, between 1919 and 1937, the figure was over two thirds. In England and Wales, by contrast, the proportion was around one quarter. The agencies which were responsible for the building were firmly part of the Scottish Office's policy network – the local authorities, the Scottish Special Housing Association (set up by central government) and the New Town development corporations. Other technocratic rules made a distinctive mark too. Design of the new houses was left to architects and surveyors. This produced a recognisably Scottish style, at first for good in the solid, stone-built houses of the 1920s and 1930s, but later arguably for worse in the high-rise flats of the 1950s and 1960s.

The need to which these policies were responding was felt all over Europe, especially after 1945. In most places, the action taken was subsidy by government and encouragement of new building. Thus the scope for national distinctiveness was in the manner of this sponsorship, not in the principle. This was as true between independent states as between Scotland and England. Most of England preferred to encourage building by the private sector or by private housing associations, although there, too, public housing expanded to an unprecedented degree (especially in the north). This policy was closer to Denmark's than to Scotland's. That Scotland rejected some alternative routes is confirmation of the point: policy-makers chose not to join a partnership with the private sector because it was judged not to be effective enough. That decision may now seem to have been too narrow: renovation of existing stock could have been pursued more fruitfully in the 1920s and the 1940s. But the point is – again – not whether the decisions were correct so much as whether they were freely made; and the political consensus indicates that they were, indeed, not imposed from outside. Scotland's autonomy is shown by its ability to choose the means and not the ends, because the end of more housing was universally believed to be desirable.

The way in which the policy of state involvement in building came to an end in the 1980s was distinctive as well. When the Conservative government started to encourage home-ownership, two main types of transfer took place. One was common to England, the buying of former public-sector houses by their tenants. But the other was the buying of small flats in tenement blocks, thus creating a large sector of low-value owner-occupation that has no extensive counterpart in England. Again, we find a policy which is common – indeed, common throughout Europe, as Gibb and Maclennan (1985) point out – but which, for technical rather than political reasons, contributes to Scottish distinctiveness.

EDUCATION

The Scottish Office has had more independence in educational policy than in any other sphere, inheriting the autonomy that had been enshrined in the Union. The senior civil servant in the Scottish Education Department (SED) in the late 1960s, Norman Graham, claimed that 'I cannot think offhand of any important matter on which Scotland has been prevented . . . from taking a decision that ministers wanted to take' (Harvie, 1983, p. 229). This may seem to put quite tight limits on the scope for independent action: ministers, after all, were part of a government elected by an English majority. But, following our usual argument about the technocratic state, there was such political consensus anyway over education that the form which Scottish distinctiveness would take would be bound to be in the ways in which common ideals were implemented.

That consensus was especially strong in Scotland, essentially – once again – because the agenda was set by a tight group of civil servants, semi-official committees, and interest organisations. There were four key groups. The presiding influence was from the SED, in the form both of administrative civil servants and the professional inspectors of schools. The second group was local government, which was formally autonomous in its implementation of policy; in that context, the most powerful figures were the directors of education, who by statutory requirement had – like the inspectors – to be professionally trained as teachers. The third group was the teachers' trade unions, notably the dominant Educational Institute of Scotland (EIS). The fourth brought together representatives of all the rest: the advisory committees expanded rapidly in the 1960s, and had their origins in the Advisory Councils appointed between the 1920s and the late 1940s.

McPherson and Raab conclude from their study of this policy network that it was remarkably cohesive, partly because most of its influential members had gone through the same educational experiences. They tended to be male, from small-town rural backgrounds, and to have a teaching career that took them to schools that, through longevity, had acquired the status of national icons. They also all attended one of the four ancient Scottish universities.

The policy which they oversaw between 1945 and the mid-1960s (or even later) was substantially non-partisan. McPherson and Raab point out that there were no politicians among the main policy-makers in education; in this respect, an ideal of Tom Johnston's had been reached, because he wanted to remove education from local control. Ministers changed rapidly; bureaucrats were permanent. Thus they were more familiar with the networks than were the politicians, and they knew the detailed technical arguments in a way that only professionals could. Members of parliament other than ministers had almost no role at all, being concerned only with the local implementation of policies that had already been agreed.

Indeed, until the introduction of comprehensive education in 1965, ministers rarely even took initiatives: education was an uncontroversial subject that was nearly always referred without objection to the Grand Committee. The policy network used parliament as a sounding board: MPs would raise issues there relating to their localities, but what to do about them was decided by the Scottish professionals. Far from parliament dictating to the Scots, any imposition that took place was by professional men on everyone else. For example, the distinctive Scottish curricula and examinations – devised by the professional elite – helped to shape the cultural outlook of Scottish society: the dominant view of learning valued curricular breadth, intellectual rigour and meritocratic competitiveness for the academically able, but also dull confirmity and limited horizons for the majority. In this government by professionals, Scottish education did not differ formally from other European systems (including England's); but that meant that power, in practice, lay in Scotland.

Two examples can illustrate this, one from the 1960s, and the other to show that the relative autonomy lasted well into the 1980s. The first example is the reorganisation of secondary schools on comprehensive lines, the main effect of which was that children were no longer selected by intelligence test for different types of school. This had long been a goal of radical Scottish educationalists since the early twentieth century, and indeed in rural areas something like a comprehensive system already existed (insofar as all children attended just one public school). The Advisory Council which was appointed by Tom Johnston, and which reported in 1947, had advocated a system of comprehensives, but the Labour government had not responded.

But it was through the Labour Party that the policy was eventually implemented, and Scottish Labour MPs were prominent in persuading the party to adopt this goal. Among the British leaders of the campaign for comprehensives were the Scottish MPs Margaret Herbison, who was a junior minister in the 1945–51 government, and Willie Ross, who became Secretary of State for Scotland after 1964. Thus, when Labour won the UK general elections in 1964 and 1966, a policy was implemented that had been influenced by the thinking of radical critics of education in Scotland.

Despite this partisan origin, however, the striking feature of the Scottish developments thereafter was their basis in consensus, and their being led by professionals in the SED. The principle of comprehensivisation was widely agreed, so that the details of implementation were left to the SED in partnership with the mostly Labour-controlled local authorities. This entailed fitting the comprehensives into what was believed to be the Scottish educational tradition. For example, by more or less insisting on a standard pattern of six-year schools, the SED ensured that the long-established rural schools could adapt smoothly to the new system. (In England, secondary education was broken in many places into middle schools and high schools.) Another example was a continuing adherence to fairly traditional teaching methods, modified only in part by new thinking; again this contrasted to parts of England, where new methods provoked bitter political controversy. In Scotland, the Conservatives objected to no more than some details of reorganisation, not to the principles. Thus, when the Labour government lost the 1970 election, the new Tory administration did not attempt to reverse any local scheme of comprehensives, in stark contrast to England. By the mid-1970s, virtually all public-sector schools in Scotland were comprehensive, and – as we saw in chapter 1 – the system had already become a new and venerated Scottish tradition.

McPherson and Raab sum up the experience of comprehensive reform as showing 'the power of the Scottish centre, when supported by the local authority, to implement decisive and uniform organisational change' (McPherson and Raab, 1988, p. 397). This conclusion could be drawn also about the second example of technocratic autonomy: the reform of vocational education in the early 1980s, which provides a particularly graphic instance of how the Scottish policy community could close ranks against a perceived threat from outside.

The threat came from the new emphasis on vocational education in the Conservative government of Margaret Thatcher. The agency for this policy was the Manpower Services Commission, the activities of which seemed to endanger the SED's autonomy. Vocationalism was opposed also by the EIS, the local authorities, and the opposition parties, on the grounds that it would undermine the universality of comprehensive education. The SED used this national sentiment to have MSC incursions postponed or diluted. In the meantime, the inspectors developed their own alternative framework for vocational education, which was designed to preserve Scottish autonomy, and to defend comprehensives by maintaining a link between vocational and general education.

Thus, in this second example too, we see the importance of technocratic autonomy, even under the more divisive and radical Conservatism of Margaret Thatcher. Indeed, a perception by that government that the Scots were getting away with far too much in all areas of social policy provoked a much more centralising policy after 1986; this is the subject of chapter 8. The point to take from the discussion here is that, even in the early 1980s, Scottish education continued to be shaped largely by indigenous forces.

OTHER AREAS OF POLICY

Similar comments can be made about many other areas of policy. Social work, for example, was governed by the SED, producing distinctive practices such as the unique Scottish system of juvenile justice. A Scottish social ethic could continue to influence practice, as professionalism organised by the Scottish Office replaced Christianity as the organising principle.

In health, the Scottish Office acquired control of the new public service from the start in 1948, mainly because health services had previously been a function of local government, and therefore had always been the ultimate responsibility of the Scottish Office (and, before that, of the Board of Supervision and the Local Government Board). There were also technical reasons for a separate Scottish structure: for example, the teaching hospitals were much more important in providing care for patients than their counterparts in England, and the sparsely populated areas required special attention. Moreover, the doctors and the Scottish insurance companies resisted centralisation of all sorts, in a professional version of the Conservatives' Scottish nationalist opposition to Labour's nationalisation.

The health system that emerged therefore developed in ways that were different from the rest of Britain, even though the broad structure of a nationalised system was shared. For example, it was more unified in that general practitioners were not separated into a special administrative category. Partly for this reason, the system as a whole also had a firmer basis in the community, and there was less reliance on private medicine, even among the middle class. As in education, the policy decisions were evolved in distinctively Scottish networks: Kellas (1983) points out that, except over the negotiation of pay and conditions of service, Scottish doctors had almost no dealings with the Department of Health in London; all their communications were with the Scottish Office.

LIMITS ON AUTONOMY

Given the importance of controlling implementation, and the unlikelihood of any fundamental differences between Scotland and England in broad political goals, the limits on autonomy that made a difference to Scottish society were not in fact the absence of legislative powers, but the decision not to seek even administrative autonomy in some substantial areas of policy. These decisions, too, however, can be understood as voluntary: Scotland chose not to have bureaucratic supervision of some areas of policy because key groups in the country accepted the argument that control at the UK level would be more effective, and therefore would be in the best interests of Scotland.

Most notably, Scotland did not have control of social security – the benefits available to compensate for poverty or unemployment. But there was little Scottish pressure for anything different in the 1930s and 1940s. The political left had mostly opposed parish control of the poor law, as a form of middle-class policing founded on an objectionable morality and on an increasingly inadequate basis in the local economy. There emerged, therefore, a wide consensus that benefits should be uniform, and that only the greater resources of the UK state could ensure adequate support in Scotland. This argument is similar to some of those used in discussions of the economy.

Similar points about resources can be found in relation to other policy areas that did not come under the Scottish Office initially – for example, most of the nationalised industries, and most aspects of economic policy and of transport. The centralisation at a UK level was accepted by the Scottish Labour Party as necessary to achieve economies of scale; the Conservatives used a Scottish nationalist rhetoric to oppose this, but did not substantially reverse it when they came to power. The transfers which did eventually take place came about because of an awareness that the central state could be persuaded to release resources into the hands of an autonomous Scottish system of implementation. In that sense, Scottish independence has grown as the century has progressed.

Underlying the desire not to push for more than administrative autonomy – and even not to seek that in all areas of policy – was also a continuing desire for assimilation, the twentieth-century legacy of the anglicising enthusiasm we have seen prevailing in earlier times. A recurrent feature of Scottish political rhetoric in the welfare-state era was demanding parity with England. Scotland wanted to be taken seriously by British politicians: for example, when the modest self-government embodied in the Grand Committee was being proposed in the 1950s, Labour MPs objected that it might remove Scottish business from the main forum of the House of Commons – the only place, they believed, where it could have the status of a partner with England rather than a legislative afterthought.

As earlier too, the purpose of politics continued to be to free people to pursue the lives they wanted to lead. This was true even of this most interventionist of eras: after all, the point of the welfare state was to provide a safe material basis for the previously impoverished majority of the population, thus allowing them access to the freedoms which the middle and upper classes had long taken for granted. The Labour Party argued in the late 1960s, for example, that there was no need to link cultural distinctiveness to economic autonomy, and indeed that only the economic security of the Union could guarantee cultural choices. If the Scots used their new freedoms to embrace an Americanised culture, they did this to no greater extent than nominally independent peoples such as the Irish or the Danes. In any case, Scots retained some influential and distinctive features of popular culture – national newspapers, popular entertainment, sport. And the Scots also domesticated even the international elements: Smout points out that, as in other European countries, the Scots as often as not labelled the imports as Scottish – the Scottish National Orchestra or Scottish Ballet putting a Scottish packaging on largely non-Scottish music, or Scottish Television and BBC Scotland doing the same for broadcasting. These labels should not be lightly dismissed: they provided a symbolic framework for the social and political community, creating a cultural context for the society that the country's distinctive administrative agencies were constructing.

CONCLUSIONS

Scottish autonomy in the half-century from 1920 therefore consisted in exercising technocratic control of areas of policy which elite Scots can be said to have chosen to administer. The technocracy arose to accompany the welfare state: it was hoped to solve social and economic problems by removing them from politics and placing them in the hands of experts. The ultimate goals were shared between Scotland and England, and had indeed been shaped partly by Scottish middle opinion in the 1930s.

The scope for Scottish distinctiveness lay therefore in the ways in which these goals were implemented. This process was governed by the committees over which the Scottish Office presided. They coordinated the pressure coming from interest groups, and bargained with the UK state for resources and an appropriate legislative framework. In its relationship both with Scottish organisations and with the UK state, the Scottish Office articulated a concept of the Scottish national interest that was not in conflict with the Union, but which insisted that the Union was legitimate only because it served Scottish ends. In this sense, Scottish nationalism was official and successful, but it was also responding to populist campaigns for more autonomy. The Scottish Office that was inherited in the 1980s can then be understood as the residue of waves of nationalism, neither a straightforward victory for those people who wanted a Scottish parliament, nor a merely non-political response to technically-defined social needs.

Scotland can be said to have chosen its twentieth-century destiny in three ways. It chose to retain the Union, in order to gain access to economic opportunities and external security. It did this partly because the second of these choices – welfare-state ends – was shared by voters in England and Wales too. The fact that Scottish political preferences coincided with its partners' no more proves that Scotland was politically dependent than does the somewhat similar coincidence of these beliefs with the political choices of, say, Scandinavia or West Germany. Exercising autonomy does not require an assertion of difference.

But in the third set of choices Scotland was able to be distinctive: through the Scottish Office, it had control of the implementation of large and expanding parts of welfare-state legislation. In significant ways, Scottish society was therefore shaped by people and agencies who did differ in their beliefs from their counterparts elsewhere in Europe. If we ask why Scotland can still be recognised as distinct at the end of the twentieth century, the answer is much the same as would be given for any small European country: the character of a society is conditioned more by the daily interactions of human beings, drawing on a common history, than by the broad sweep of enabling legislation. If the state does have an influence in this respect, it is through the direct contact which people have with it – with its professional staff such as teachers or social workers or bureaucrats – rather than simply as a consequence of its laws; in Scotland, these professionals operated according to Scottish traditions and rules.

In any case, the great achievement of the welfare state had been to provide more people than ever before with the material security that would allow them some genuine freedom to shape the character of their own private lives. They may then have chosen to adopt the norms of England or America, but the point is that they now did have the opportunity to choose. The Scots' decisions may have been wrong, but they were their own.

7

Autonomy in Twentieth-Century Europe and North America

Scotland was not the only country where the nature of autonomy changed as the central state grew in importance in the twentieth century. This chapter traces the analogous processes in other places in Europe and North America.

As in chapter 5 for the nineteenth century, the countries that are dealt with here have been chosen to represent the kinds of autonomy which small nations could enjoy. Therefore only in some cases are the same places discussed here as in chapter 5: the criteria of selection are based on twentieth-century conditions. Nevertheless, the legacy of the nineteeenth century did continue to have an influence, and so some reference back to that earlier period is necessary in each case. The external political context is again summarised by maps: see Figure 7.1, which shows Europe after 1945; Figure 7.2, which shows North America; and Figure 7.3, which shows Europe in the 1920s and 1930s.

Four types of twentieth-century experience are dealt with: the component parts of federations; the satellite states of east-central Europe; Ireland; and Scandinavia. The discussion of federal systems is the most directly relevant to debate in Scotland, because a frequent claim recently has been that a federal system for the United Kingdom would give greater scope for diversity than the present centralised structures of government. This may be true for the late twentieth century, a point to which we will return in chapter 8. But as a claim about how matters could have been arranged for most of the century, the claim lacks subtlety. The first sections of this chapter argue that there were close similarities between the types of autonomy that were actually enjoyed by the provinces in federal states and the technocratic autonomy which we have seen being available to Scotland. Federations became, in Duchacek's words, 'fiscal and political centralisation interlaced by administrative decentralisation', a fair description of the UK at least until the 1970s (Duchacek, 1986, p. 154).

This development is traced for the Federal Republic of Germany, for the USA and for Canada. The story is not the same in all of these, and the scope for independent provincial action was greater in Canada than in the USA, and least in Germany. The point is not to prove that the provinces had no autonomy, but to show that the autonomy which they did have was related more to the implementation of legislation than to setting its principles. This is a better characterisation of the sharing of responsibilities than the rather trite one which figures in political debate in Scotland – that the provinces had control of domestic policy while the central government ran the economy and foreign affairs. Much of the legislative framework for social policy was set at the federal level, especially in Germany, but also in the USA and even Canada. As in the UK, this was a welfare-state response to the Depression of the 1930s. And the provinces, on the other hand, have engaged in foreign contacts of a technocratic sort: negotiating for inward investment, for example. The provinces went along with restrictions on their roles, not because they were coerced into accepting alien principles, but because the ultimate goals were so widely shared across the state that legislative variety was, by choice, limited.

The situation of nominally independent small countries was not necessarily that different. This is perhaps not surprising for the satellite states of the Soviet Union, the second type of experience discussed in this chapter. But by comparing Poland with Czechoslovakia we find that the degree of coercion did vary substantially. As in the nineteenth century, astute politicians could create space for their countries even when faced with overwhelming military power.

For the more thoroughly democratic nations of the West, independence in practice was often much less than its formal theory would suggest. The newly independent Ireland – our third type of autonomy – remained highly dependent on the United Kingdom until joining the European Economic Community in 1975. This switch of allegiance can be interpreted as the choice of exchanging one type of external constraint for another that was felt to be less severe. Choice of external constraints is found also in Scandinavia, the fourth area to be dealt with. Here there was no coercion at all, and yet the shared social and political values of the Nordic countries pushed them towards a closer Union than has ever been experienced among independent states anywhere in the world. This was a chosen Union, and the countries remained distinct: they were still able to choose the manner in which they put the common political ideas into effect, and they inherited somewhat separate cultural traditions.

As in chapter 5 on the nineteenth century, therefore, we can find a variety of forms of autonomy both within large states and between independent small states. This variety is useful for assessing the Scottish situation, just as was the analogous variety for small nations in the nineteenth century. Scotland was more autonomous than some other places – certainly Czechoslovakia and Poland, and, in important ways, also Ireland, the

German Länder and the US states. It was somewhat less independent than the Canadian provinces, but not all the time. And although the Scandinavian countries were undoubtedly more independent than Scotland, they chose to develop a common political path where the scope for national political variety was not substantially greater than within twentieth-century Britain. The main point about Scandinavia is, then, that shared policies do not necessarily indicate political dependence of one state on another: as in the component parts of federations, the sharing can have been freely chosen. In that sense, although the Scandinavian nations have pursued an extensive Union, the motives which induced them to do so are quite typical of influences on all small nations in Western Europe in the twentieth century.

THE FEDERAL REPUBLIC OF GERMANY

The FRG was established by victorious Western allies at the end of the 1939–45 war (Figure 7.1). A federal system was imposed in 1949 partly in order to prevent the re-emergence of another strongly centralised state of the type which had just been defeated. So decentralisation was a founding principle. The same system was adopted for the former East Germany when it amalgamated with the Federal Republic in 1990.

Nevertheless, the system which emerged over the forty years after 1945 was not as straightforwardly decentralised as could be assumed from the constitutional principles alone:

> One of the distinctive features of the German federal system is that the division of power between the centre and the member units coincides to a large extent with the division between law-making and law-application. (Forsyth, 1991, p. viii)

Virtually all federal legislation is administered by the Länder: the only exceptions are the foreign service, defence, the postal service and the railways; the social-security system is run by special bodies based in the Länder but under federal jurisdiction. Thus federalism is now 'administrative federalism', a term used by an author who concludes that the state is now, in effect, unitary (Klatt, 1991, p. 125).

In some respects, this destiny was determined from the start. Even in the original constitution, the Länder could make laws only for education, local government and the police. This circumscription created a precedent: no legislative power has ever been transferred away from the centre. On the other hand, frequent moves have taken place in the other direction, with the agreement of the Länder: for example, the Bund (the federal level) acquired legislative control of economic management, financial planning, higher education and protection of the environment.

The Bund would subsidise Länder activities not in order to impose tighter central control, but rather because the political consensus was so

FIGURE 7.1: Europe after 1945. *Drawing by Taryn Keogh.*

great that coordination could be taken for granted. The pressure for cooperation has come from a common political desire for

> ever greater uniformity in the provision of government services, co-ordinated planning for efficient use of resources, and centralised over-sight of public expenditure having regard to the need of economic management. (Blair, 1991, p. 77)

Thus the uniformity was chosen, not imposed: it was not like the dictatorial centralisation in the nominally federal Soviet Union, or in Spain after Franco ended the incipient federalism of the 1930s.

Even more fundamental than this shared belief in the welfare state in Germany was the somewhat artificial nature of most of the federation in the first place. Watts points out that the FRG is not a federal society, using the terms from Livingston that we discussed in chapter 2. With the partial exception of Bavaria in the south, there are almost no major cultural divisions, and, at least until the 1980s, few serious political ones. The belief in the central provision of social welfare dated from Bismarck's government in the earliest days of German industrialisation, in the second half of the nineteenth century.

Alongside this legislative centralisation, however, and for essentially the same reason of pursuing efficiency, the enormous administrative signi-ficance of the Länder was also established early on: indeed, they existed as adminstrative units of the occupying powers before they became political. Just as the centre has taken over legislative functions, the Länder have acquired administrative ones. The mechanisms of financial redistribution have had to involve the Länder, because they have been responsible for spending most of the money.

Thus, what Leonardy (1991) refers to as the 'working relationships' of German federalism happen in three ways: through the whole state (invol-ving the Bund and the Länder directly), through the federal state (involving the Länder in the Bundesrat, the second chamber of the federal parliament), and through horizontal coordination on technical matters between the Länder. These relationships take place in the several hundred committees which coordinate activities among the Länder, and between the Länder and the Bund.

The whole-state relationships come closest to resembling the negotiations that would take place between independent governments. Examples include the regular conferences between the federal Chancellor and the heads of government of the Länder, or among the presidents of the Länder parlia-ments. The federal foreign ministry coordinates meetings with the Länder whenever an international treaty impinges on the functions of the Länder.

But these whole-state relationships merely set a broad framework. The most frequent and detailed coordination happens through the other two types of relationship. The federal relationships are focused on the

Bundesrat, which consists of representatives of the governments of the Länder; the Bundesrat has acquired importance precisely because they have become the agencies through which policy has been implemented. Thus much ancillary legislation – for example, statutory instruments – requires only Bundesrat approval. The proceedings in the full Bundesrat are mostly limited to formal ratification of decisions already reached after technical discussion, which takes place in committees made up of the officials who staff the permanent offices of each Land in the Bundesrat administration. Politicians are involved in Bundesrat committees only to chair meetings, and this role rotates automatically among the Länder, regardless of party-political differences between the Länder governments. In these committees, and in the Committee of Mediation to resolve disputes between the Bundesrat and the Bundestag, the members of the Bundesrat are not subject to instruction from the Länder.

In the third type of relationship, committees of the Länder attempt to resolve difficulties in implementing legislation; these discussions take place in a similarly technical atmosphere to those in the Bundesrat. This system tends, therefore, to encourage a view that political issues can be settled by technical debate, a matter for cooperation between the executives rather than the legislatures.

The same style has also increasingly characterised German relationships with the European Union, and indeed the model of Bund-Länder negotiations has been seen as a model for the E U as a whole in its dealings with its component units. Through the Bundesrat, the Länder comment on all papers received by the E U's governing Council of Ministers. There are Länder observers at E U meetings, and Länder representatives on E U committees. The federal government has had to agree to this system again because of the role of the Länder in implementing legislation. But there has been an effect on the Länder too: they have found that their impact on E U processes can be stronger if they have reached a consensus, and so the E U has become another pressure towards legislative uniformity.

The new forms of E U government that were inaugurated by the Single European Act of 1987 have formalised the status of the Länder, but still their greatest role is through their civil servants. For example, they now have a right to be consulted on all E U matters, but this in itself has encouraged even more consensus, because a unified German front still helps the federal ministers in their bargaining in the E U Council.

The way in which the German constitution works is thus reminiscent of the relationship between the Scottish Office and London for most of the period after 1945. The nominal difference – the elected parliaments in the Länder – has been of less significance than some British federalists would claim. Watts comments that federation encourages bureaucracy precisely because, in order to work well, it requires a great deal of coordination, and hence a depoliticisation of decision-making. Klatt comments that the high level of bureaucratisation raises problems of democratic accountability in view of the inadequate public transparency of the decision-making process and the diffusion of responsibility (and therefore accountability) in a complex, multi-faceted institutional network. (Klatt, 1991, p. 127)

These points are familiar from the Scottish debate. The difference from Scotland is that in the Länder there has been almost no opposition to the growth of merely administrative federalism. As a result, policy among the Länder has been less varied than policy between Scotland and England. There is nothing as distinct as, for instance, the Scottish policies on public housing, or school curricula and examinations, or juvenile justice. The conclusion has to be that distinctiveness is not an inevitable consequence of having a separate legislature, and that – given a tradition of tolerance from the centre, as in the UK in the mid-twentieth century – autonomy can be exercised without one.

THE USA

Cooperative federalism has become the dominant characteristic of the USA too. The nineteenth-century constitution was described as dual federalism, in which the states and the federal level were equally and separately sovereign. But this worked only because government was limited, as in the UK and indeed in all places with a liberal constitution. It could not survive the growth of government activities in the twentieth century. There was a steady expansion of federal powers to meet the social needs arising from the 1930s Depression and from the welfare-state ideas of the New Deal that grew out of it. It was now accepted that government should regulate industry, agriculture and labour laws, and should have some responsiblity for social welfare. The political struggle in the 1930s was over how to interpret those clauses of the constitution which specify concurrent powers: President Roosevelt found resistance from the conservative judges in the Supreme Court, but his view prevailed, partly because the states simply did not have the resources to meet the growing popular preference for welfare-state spending. The resources available to the centre, by contrast, had grown rapidly after the inauguration of a federal income tax in 1913. The Supreme Court became less conservative as new justices were appointed by Roosevelt and his successors, and therefore it steadily relaxed its insistence on the rights of the states.

The greatest change in government from the 1930s onwards did not relate to legislation but to the growth in administration. Thus, as in Germany, the new federalism that emerged was founded on the states' administering federal spending. The extent of federal involvement varied according to the policy area, however, and in this respect the system never became as uniform as in Germany.

There was greatest standardisation in economic matters, where by the mid-twentieth century the federal government had largely replaced the states for policies on general economic management. The area of greatest cooperation has been in policies on social welfare. But this was not something which the states could force on the federation: cooperation came about because the federal government believed that it was the only way that its social policies would be administered efficiently, with appropriate adaptation to local needs. Thus the central government has set standards and provided resources through grants-in-aid, while the states and local government have taken charge of implementation. Whereas seventy-one per cent of all public spending in 1913 originated with the states and local government, by 1957 the proportion was only thirty-nine per cent, much the same as in Germany. The proportions have remained at these levels ever since. If defence and foreign relations are left out of the calculations, the decline in the relative role of state and local government was less steep, but still marked: from eight-two per cent in 1913 to sixty-three per cent in 1957 (Vile, 1961, pp. 11–12).

Whether we describe this as centralisation depends on what our standard of comparison is. Certainly the federal government had more powers than in the nineteenth century. But society and the economy had changed, as had political values. M. J. C. Vile comments that without the new rules of grant-in-aid, centralisation would have been much greater. He describes it, therefore, as 'the adaptation of federalism to modern conditions' (Vile, 1961, p. 174). The political relationships underlying the new system were intricate, shaped by the various elected bodies, the Supreme Court, and 'public opinion' as interpreted by all of these. Vile concludes that the USA does have the federal attitudes which Livingston described as being necessary for the operation of a true federation, and which were largely absent in Germany:

> the federal system is founded upon an attitude of mind which enables contradictory elements to be moulded into a single tradition, in which the elements of localism, sectionalism, and pluralism are inextricably interwoven. (Vile, 1961, p. 131)

This political situation 'requires institutional expression in complex ways', which are much more subtle than the merely formal division of powers between the centre and the states (p. 132). Political, not constitutional, reasons prevent the centre imposing on the states: for example, there was no equalisation of social welfare payments until 1958, because the states resisted it. The resistance did not, however, take the form of a legal defence of the rights of the states, but rather involved using the political processes of the centre, in the Congress. The federal level is not a unity, except during emergencies such as war. Thus if one branch of the federal government tries to encroach on state rights – for example, the president

– the other branches can be used to resist. The same point can be made as between the states and local government.

The political processes are mediated by the parties to some extent, but above all by the pressure groups in alliance with the bureaucracy. These groups are national in form, but local in their responsiveness. Interest groups have grown up in the same way as in other liberal democracies, and they – as Poggi argues – are the sources of ideas for legislation. They also determine how the laws will be implemented. Thus national organisations of tax administrators, highway officials, county officials or lawyers act as forces for uniformity. But, precisely because these officials work locally, the organisations are also forums in which tensions are articulated and resolved between diversity and uniformity. Thus the pressures from a federal society have been felt long before the legislation has been passed by Congress, and the same pressures continue to be effective while these same professionals are putting it into practice. Legislation is deliberately cast in very general terms, so that there can be administrative adaptation in the states and locally.

The USA is therefore more thoroughly federal than Germany, not directly because of its constitution, but because of the federal character of its society. The constitution has merely reflected this. But even here, the ways in which diversity has been maintained and promoted in the twentieth century have been as much through administrative politics as through the formal separation of powers between the centre and the states. The state legislatures have helped to focus state politics, although they have not been the only or even the most important means of doing that. And the consequences of these debates have been felt primarily in the administration of legislation and in the federal Congress. Once again, therefore, we have a system which resembles that in the UK: the scope for local distinctiveness is through the local bureaucracy, the politics that have most effect are bureaucratic politics, and the central legislature can be used as a sounding board for local concerns. This similarity has arisen because the UK, like the USA, has had to find institutional expressions for a society that is fundamentally federal in its attitudes.

CANADA

Federal attitudes do not only imply diversity; they also require an acceptance of unity. Canada shows some of the tensions that arise in a federation when the unity is in question. The biggest schism of all is between French and English speakers, which has had its political effects in the tension between Quebec and the other provinces (Figure 7.2). Nevertheless, even in Canada we can find the common pattern of federal centralisation.

The Canadian federation was founded with the British North America Act of 1867, when the provinces of Upper and Lower Canada, New Brunswick and Nova Scotia were united. Further provinces joined later,

FIGURE 7.2: North America. *Drawing by Taryn Keogh.*

the last being Newfoundland in 1949. The phases of the federalism that ensued bore some resemblance to developments in the USA, and, in significant respects, the Canadian story is, as there, one of centralisation in the interests of efficiency and uniform social welfare.

The crucial experience was the 1939–45 war, when there was an unprecedented degree of centralisation, accustoming people to paying federal taxes and to receiving federal grants. The argument for centralisation was expressed in the report of an official commission in 1940, recommending that powers over the economy and social welfare be transferred to the federal level. The report was never implemented, because of fears by conservative provinces that a unitary state would result. But, in practice, centralisation did proceed. The federal government assumed responsibility for using economic and fiscal policies to achieve satisfactorily low levels of unemployment and inflation: it was widely believed that only it could run the economy efficiently. A national welfare state was set up in cooperation with the provinces, rather than over their heads. And the federal government took the lead in developing transport and communication across the vast distances between the east and the west of Canada. The centre also acquired more powers over taxes. The provinces' reservations were met by a system of 'tax rental', whereby the federal government took over the running of the tax system. The proceeds were then returned to the provinces, having been reallocated by a complicated system of equalisation from richer areas to poorer. Many federal programmes did not depend on provincial cooperation at all, for example the promotion of better housing through national mortgages.

Other policy areas were centralised during the 1950s and 1960s. Hospital insurance became a federal responsibility in 1957, followed by general medical insurance in 1968. Old age pensions were transferred to the centre in 1951. The growth of education was financed and legislated for by the federal government, although the implementation of expansion remained with the provinces.

The continuing pressures for uniformity arose from the same sources as in the USA, Germany and the UK. There was the usual welfare-state belief that strong central government was needed to tackle unemployment, poverty and ill-health. Trade unions, for example, put pressure on the provinces to make demands of the centre. Thus, once more as in Poggi's account of the technocratic state, the main inputs to policies came not from the legislatures or even in the first instance from the bureaucracies, but from professional organisations which were organised across the whole of Canada. The system was based on 'widespread popular attitudes which are pragmatic and equivocal as to the appropriate level of government for carrying out particular public responsibilities' (Smiley, 1977, p. 372).

Hence there arose a version of the administrative federalism that we have seen operating in both the USA and Germany. Legislation became the result of joint decisions between the provinces and the federal government. There was continuous consultation between federal and provincial civil servants working on joint programmes, discussing the technical matters that were needed to make legislation work. Their committees grew rapidly after 1945. The federal parliament also delegated functions to provincial agencies, bypassing the provincial legislatures. And there were federal grants for provincial or municipal matters. The usually annual meetings of provincial premiers with federal ministers helped to achieve harmony in these activities, but – unlike the activities of the Bundesrat in Germany – these had no formal role.

The operation of all this required the evolution of working relationships between provinces and the centre. In response to this need, there grew up a pattern of constitutional conventions, which were ways in which the constitution was interpreted to enable its general framework to be applied to particular cases. These conventions were not merely customary patterns of behaviour, but political principles to govern the actual working of the system better than the theory of the formal constitution on its own could do.

But Canada's centralisation has never been as smooth or as thorough as in other places. The 1940 proposals for drastic centralisation were, after all, rejected, and this can be interpreted as a preference for public politics over technocratic rationality. Significant aspects of government are far more decentralised than in Germany, for example education. The share of public expenditure that is at the federal level is the lowest of any federation in the world, at forty-four per cent (Moreno, 1993). This is partly because some of the powers that were transferred to the centre in the 1950s have now been handed back to the provinces. Most significantly of all, however, there have always been strong pressures towards dissolving the Canadian federation completely, something which is not found in Germany or the USA. The most insistent secessionist tendencies are in Quebec, but the rich western provinces have reacted to that by asserting their own autonomy. Only the Atlantic seaboard remains reasonably happy with the federation: that is because, being poor, it benefits from transfers of resources within the Union. These views caused the rejection of the Meech Lake Accord in the referendums of 1990. The Accord was an attempt to give significant powers back to the provinces, but the various discontents with the Union seem to be too intense to allow a compromise to be workable. The regionally polarised result of the 1993 general election confirms this point.

As a result of these continuing pressures for provincial autonomy, relations among the provincial governments, or between them and the centre, have some of the characteristics of relations among independent states. Political conflict has remained overt and has not all disappeared into the secrecy of technical committees. Canada may therefore never be able to achieve as harmonious a federation as Germany or the USA, and some commentators now refer to Canada as a confederation, or a voluntary Union of sovereign states. In that respect, it is coming to resemble Scandinavia (as we will see) or the European Union.

There are two important conclusions for our discussion of Scotland. The first is similar to that from the USA and Germany. In the middle of the twentieth century, the shared assumptions of the welfare state produced pressures towards uniformity which kept the Union together. The scope for provincial distinctiveness lay mainly in the control of implementation. But the second is that the very existence of elected forums in the provinces has allowed the pressure for greater diversity to be expressed more readily than in the UK, and to be channelled into formal negotiations. This has allowed explicit readjustments of the Canadian Union, and might therefore have saved it from dissolution. On the other hand, by formalising the disunity, it might eventually lead to tensions that are so acute that the state will not survive. Scotland has not been able to negotiate formally in the way that the Canadian provinces have done, and so the accretion of powers by the Scottish Office has rarely been seen as the outcome of nationalist politics.

The difference from Canada is therefore significant, but at the level of symbolic sovereignty rather than everyday politics. Scotland has indeed lacked a crucial feature of autonomy, namely the formally guaranteed right to renegotiate its position: it has had to threaten secession if it is to achieve any greater autonomy at all. Despite the similar convergence in Canada and the UK towards merely administrative federalism, Scotland's lack of a forum in which renegotiation could take place must be judged to be a real relative restriction on the country's autonomy.

THE EUROPEAN SATELLITE STATES

The history of east-central Europe in the twentieth century can be divided into two main periods: there were the brief liberal democracies in the 1920s and 1930s (Figure 7.3), and then nearly half a century of control by the Soviet Union. Throughout this history, however, some of these countries were nominally independent. In the two sections which follow, therefore, the extent of that independence is assessed: did their formal statehood offer Czechoslovakia and Poland any greater autonomy in either period than Scotland had?

CZECHOSLOVAKIA

Czechoslovakia gained independence with the collapse of Austria-Hungary at the end of the 1914–18 war, even though the preference of most of its political parties was still for a federal empire. The new state faced enormous problems. Its frontiers were not yet recognised, and there was a threatened invasion from Hungary. The allegiance of the Slovaks and the Sudeten

FIGURE 7.3: Europe between 1921 and 1939. *Drawing by Taryn Keogh.*

Germans was problematic. The economy was in chaos, exacerbated by the general European recession. About two thirds of economic enterprises were owned from outside the country. There were widespread food shortages. The peasants were agitating for land reform. The returning soldiers wanted jobs.

And yet, by the 1930s, Czechoslovakia was the most successful, democratic and genuinely independent small state in the region. Despite its problems, it started from a strong industrial base: thanks to having been the industrial centre of the Empire, its economy was the tenth largest in the world. The new government adopted many left-wing and nationalist policies, socialising the ownership of industry, reforming the land-holding system, introducing extensive welfare provision, and insisting that Czechoslovakian citizens should form the majority on the controlling boards of large companies.

These measures stabilised the economy and the liberal-democratic constitution by 1923. Thus, when the new world recession came in 1929–33, the government was able to cope with discontent by reform of the type favoured in Western Europe, avoiding the dictatorships that emerged in neighbouring states. In this context, Czechoslovak cultures could develop free of political interference.

So, Czechoslovakia until the late 1930s seems to be a model of what could be achieved by an independent small nation, a vindication of the theories of nineteenth-century nationalist writers. But it depended for this on the tolerance of its large neighbours. It was sheltered by an optimal combination of circumstances that could not last: the temporary weakness of its main potential enemies, Germany and Russia; an alliance with France; and the support of the League of Nations. The astute president, Thomas Masaryk, was well aware of this dependence on external support when he said in the early 1930s that Czechoslovakia needs 'another thirty years of quiet, reasoned, and participatory development, and then our state is secure' (Korbel, 1977, p. 84). That was not available.

The main pressures came from Nazi Germany, seeking the 'return' of the Sudetenland. President Benes gave way at the Munich conference of 1938 because he was aware that Czechoslovakia had been deserted by France and the UK. He reasoned that to have fought Germany and lost, as would have been the inevitable outcome, would have been to have attracted severe punishment.

As it was, Czechoslovakia did indeed suffer less physical damage than many of the other countries that were occupied by Germany. It thus emerged in 1945 with its civil society relatively intact. There was a very high membership of political parties, and the press was free and flourishing. The largest party was communist, but it seemed to be pluralist and to advocate a distinctive Czechoslovak road to socialism. It pervaded public bodies in an open and democratic manner. The presence of Soviet occupying forces and the acceptance of Soviet food aid was merely a recognition by President Benes of the inevitability of Soviet influences, especially when American loans were not forthcoming. So, between the end of the war and the communist coup of 1948, Czechoslovakia could be said to be still in control of its destiny, even though choosing under enormous constraints.

Thereafter, however, the country became one of the least independent in east-central Europe, a reversal of its position before 1938. The communists remodelled the constitution along Soviet lines, taking instructions directly from Stalin; later, the government also had to employ Soviet advisers. The property of the Catholic Church was confiscated, and its priests put in concentration camps. All other bodies which were not affiliated to the communist party were dissolved or taken over. The party itself was severely purged between 1950 and 1952, removing those members who had contributed to its pluralism and its embedding in civil society. When its leader, Klement Gottwald, died at Stalin's funeral in 1953, his replacement was Antonin Norotny, a dull follower of Moscow.

There was fairly rapid economic progress until the early 1960s, but other aspects of economic reform were as disastrous as the similar policies pursued elsewhere in east-central Europe. The enforced collectivisation of agriculture caused production to stagnate, and the reorientation of trade towards the east led to a loss of Western technology. The result was increasing inefficiency, and hence an economic crisis in the mid-1960s. The resulting political discontent produced the popular rising of 1968, which was brutally suppressed by the armies of the Warsaw Pact. The political repression was not relaxed until the 1980s.

Thus post-war Czechoslovakia was far more dependent than the republic led by Masaryk in the 1920s. The thoroughness with which the Communist Party and Soviet advisers penetrated society means that we cannot even say that the country had control of the ways in which policies were implemented: the officials who were in charge were largely not adapting legislation to local needs, but shaping these needs to match a legislative pattern prescribed by Moscow. Bradley (1971) concludes that the history of small nations is inevitably about operating within constraints; they prosper when these are recognised, and when opportunities exist to take advantage of dissension among great powers. The country gained its independence in 1918 because of the defeat of Austria-Hungary. It lost it in 1938 because of the renewed strength of Germany, and it lost it again in 1948 and 1968 because of the military power of Russia operating through the USSR and the Warsaw Pact. The main difference between the 1920s and the later period was that Masaryk and his colleagues exploited the weakness of Czechoslovakia's enemies. This is what enabled the country to be more independent than Scotland in the 1920s. It shows the scope for imaginative independence if the international situation is favourable, and if (unlike Ireland at this time, as we will see) a country's leaders are determined enough. But the main point for our discussion is that Czechoslovakia after 1938 was an example of real subjection to foreign rule. Whatever limitations there were on Scotland's autonomy, they were far less than that.

The twentieth-century history of Polish autonomy followed almost an opposite trajectory to Czechoslovakia's. It was highly dependent between the wars, but became one of the most independent of the Soviet satellites after 1945. Even in the latter period, however, its autonomy was no more than Scotland's: it did no more than adapt standard Soviet policies to suit Poland's conditions.

Poland started the 1920s well. Its armies inflicted the only defeat that the Red Army ever suffered (until the withdrawal from Afghanistan in 1989). This secured Polish statehood for twenty years, and probably also prevented a more complete absorption into the USSR after the 1939–45 war. But the new state in 1920 was a 'precarious creation with amorphous frontiers' (Dziewanoswki, 1977, p. 74). Its problems were similar to those of Czechoslovakia. Both Germany and the Soviet Union were hostile. The economy was in a mess, partly because the positivism that had been pursued after 1863 had weakened the economic links among the three parts of Poland, in favour of ties to the centres of the three imperial powers. So dire was the external situation that the Polish leader Jozef Pilsudski even argued for a confederation of all new states of east-central Europe, to defend themselves against the USSR.

As the economy and society collapsed, Pilsudski led a coup in 1926. His political beliefs were an odd mixture. Before the war, he had been associated with the socialist party, but he had since moved to the nationalist right. Yet he retained cross-party support. Parliament and opposition functioned until 1935, although only on condition that they did not attempt to gain power. The system which he created has been described as 'directed democracy' rather than dictatorship (Dziewanowski, 1977, p. 90). Following the international fashion, technocratic efficiency was venerated; government was believed to be synonymous with good management. As in the west, this did achieve some economic progress and some gains in social welfare, education and culture.

But the country never prospered as Czechoslovakia did. Poverty was not overcome, especially in the rural areas, rates of emigration remained high, and the stifling of democracy eventually led to the emasculation of debate. Poland may have been independent as a state, but it did not have the independent civil society which was still taken for granted in the west, and for which its own liberals had agitated throughout the nineteenth century.

Worst of all, Polish resistance to German invasion in 1939 provoked far worse destruction during the war than was suffered by Czechoslovakia, or indeed almost anywhere else. Ascherson sums up the consequences graphically:

> One Pole in five had perished as a direct result of the war. Nearly 40 per cent of the national wealth had been destroyed (France, for comparison, lost 1.5 per cent). Half the public transport, a third of all industrial installations, 60 per cent of the schools, and 62 per cent of all postal and telephone equipment had gone. (Ascherson, 1981, p. 29)

Moreover, Poland's boundaries were redrawn yet again, shifting the whole state westwards.

Polish history after that, however, is of clever negotiation to keep some autonomy for civil society in the face of the overwhelming threat from the USSR. Although the Communist Party came to power in 1947 only by means of highly dubious elections, its policies did have some support, on the grounds that central planning was probably necessary to rehabilitate the country. Externally, Stalin was not as insistent on dependency as might have been feared, and the bulk of the Polish population acquiesced. Ascherson again puts it well:

> Independence could no longer mean what it had meant to the heroes of the nineteenth-century insurrections, or to Pilsudski . . . But the limited independence which seemed in 1945 to be on offer was still infinitely worth having, and worth defending. (Ascherson, 1981, p. 35)

Until 1948, the regime led by Wladyslaw Gomulka was far more tolerant than that in Czechoslovakia. The church was freer than anywhere else in east-central Europe, private ownership by peasants and small tradespeople was not banned, and some opposition political movements were tolerated. Although this phase lasted less than two years, it created a precedent of relatively open communism in Poland. Indeed, even during the most intensely Stalinist phase of 1948–54, the oppression was not as severe as elsewhere. Thus when Gomulka was reinstated after mass protests in 1956, the Communist Party was full of people who had previously been active in the opposition. The new government was therefore willing to continue to pursue relatively open policies, including an economy that was partly based on market forces. In contrast to Czechoslovakia, the USSR never dominated Poland's economy: in the late 1950s, imports and exports from and to the Soviet Union were in rough balance, and in any case never accounted for more than thirty-eight per cent of the total. The church was not controlled, far less persecuted, and cultural exchanges with the west became largely free in the late 1950s. Gomulka's restoration was therefore greeted with something like genuine popular enthusiasm, especially since he was not the choice of the Soviet leader Khrushchev.

All this was tolerated because Poland never threatened to leave the military alliance with the USSR, and indeed was an ultra-loyal member. Moreover, the strength of the Polish church, and of civil society more generally, would have made interference far more difficult for the Soviet Union than it was in Czechoslovakia. Poland thus arranged a real compromise – not a capitulation, although not independence either. The importance of this should not be lost sight of, despite Gomulka's gradual drift into conservatism in the late 1960s. Dziewanowski argues that his regime did achieve significant gains for Poland, through exploiting the negotiated autonomy skilfully and maintaining that tradition of constructive positivism that had worked in the late nineteenth century. He thus made it available for his successor Edward Gierek, who came to power in 1970 after popular protests against Gomulka. And it bequeathed a fairly autonomous civil society to the opposition movements that eventually overthrew communism between 1981 and 1990.

Poland, in other words, has something of the same tradition of pragmatic adaptation that has allowed Scotland to maintain its somewhat similar degree of partial independence. Certainly, in some respects, a comparison between the two countries in the middle of the twentieth century is absurd. Scotland has never suffered anything like the oppression of those years when the Polish communists lapsed into Stalinism, far less the horrendous persecution of the Nazis. And, on the other hand, Scotland does not have even the trappings of formal statehood. Yet there is something important in common. Scotland, too, in the late 1940s exchanged loyalty in foreign affairs and in macroeconomic policy for substantial control of its domestic affairs. If there was a difference, it was that Poland gave up control of its external environment through force of circumstance, whereas the Scots had come genuinely to accept the same foreign and economic policies as the English. The main conclusion to draw from the Polish example is that even a partly free civil society, and even some limited control over social policy, has seemed to be worth fighting for in parts of Europe where these things are not taken for granted. Scotland, enjoying them more securely and probably more fully, must then be judged to have been in a relatively quite lucky position.

WESTERN EUROPE

Showing that Scotland in the middle of the twentieth century was more autonomous than countries in east-central Europe is not, perhaps, very striking. These places have been widely recognised to have been dependent on the USSR. The surprise might rather be to find that Poland had anything like the same independence as Scotland. But if we turn now to comparisons with small independent states in Western Europe – Ireland, and the nations of Scandinavia – we find that, even here, the Scottish situation cannot be judged to have been straightforwardly more constrained.

IRELAND

The first Western European example is in some obvious ways the most relevant simply because it used to be part of the same state: Ireland. Twenty-six of the thirty-two counties of Ireland became independent in 1922, the partition being the UK government's attempt to solve the problem of nationalist Catholics in the same island as Unionist Protestants in the north. The north gained a home-rule parliament within the UK, which almost no-one wanted; and the Protestants dominated it until 1972, when it was abolished in the face of new violence by the IRA provoked by the discrimination against Catholics which the Unionist government had exercised. The regime which they ran up till then was theocratically conservative. It was also thoroughly dependent on the UK for a level of welfare benefits and public economic investment that the southern republic could never afford. Thus, as far as the economy and welfare were concerned, the northern Protestants with their domestic parliament exploited the Union in something the same way as Scotland, without one, did too.

But the history that concerns us more fully here is of the south (although its relations with the UK continued to be coloured by the partition for many years). The story conveniently divides into three phases: from the Treaty of independence in 1922 until the acceptance of that Treaty by most of the nationalist movement in the early 1930s; from then until the advent of the modernising Sean Lamass as prime minister in 1958; and thereafter until the present day.

For the first decade after independence, the main issue in politics was still nationalism. This was partly because a large minority of nationalists refused to accept the Treaty with the United Kingdom that established the partition. It was not until 1927 that the largest faction of the treaty's opponents finally stopped fighting it, emerging to form the Fianna Fáil party under Eamonn de Valera which then dominated Irish politics for most of the century.

But the treaty was not the only reason why a reductionist nationalism remained so strong an influence. There are good reasons to believe that the more radical ideals of the nineteenth-century nationalists could never have been implemented, even in more favourable circumstances. The first and most important point is that a newly independent country inherits everything from the state it has left. This is obvious, but the difficulties which it raises do not usually figure prominently in nationalist programmes. The Irish economy was stagnant, and the twenty-six counties had only small pockets of industry. All the civil servants continued in their posts; even as late as 1934, forty-five per cent of them had served in the pre-1922 system (R. F. Foster, 1988, p. 522). Local government remained as highly centralised as under the British, and no changes were made to the legal system.

But as well as Britain's legacy was Britain's looming presence. As Brown puts it, 'the gravest problem was the country's proximity to the UK with its advanced industrial economy' (T. Brown, 1985, p. 15). The nationalist leader Oliver MacDonagh compared Ireland's position to the Atlantic provinces in Canada, or to Sicily in Italy: in other words, to the dependent parts of federal or semi-federal states. Thus a massive ninety-eight per cent of Irish exports went to the UK in 1924; this was still ninety-six per cent in 1931, and ninety-one per cent in 1938. With imports, the situation was only slightly better: eighty-one per cent came from the UK in the late 1920s, down to fifty per cent in 1938 (R. F. Foster, 1988, p. 522). Irish agriculture, in particular, was utterly dependent on UK markets, and that mattered a great deal in a country where over half the employed population worked in that sector. Thus the new government failed to achieve even the limited economic freedom which states such as Czechoslovakia had managed to win by the late 1920s.

One effect of this was continuing poverty and emigration: 'the resources of the new state came nowhere near funding social expenditure at the levels set by imperial governments since the Liberal administration of 1906' (R. F. Foster, 1988, p. 519). Severe restrictions on Irish public expenditure in the 1920s thus prevented the socially radical part of the nationalist programme from being implemented. For example, the Dublin slums were not redeveloped, even though they had been frequently cited as a consequence of British rule.

Even in policy areas which could have been reformed at somewhat less expense, the new state achieved little. The education system was almost unchanged: this included schools dominated by the church, a very low status for technical education, and universities that were socially exclusive. In fact, just about the only large-scale reform which the government did introduce was the attempt to impose Gaelic on the national schools. This policy was an example of nationalism at its most naively idealistic, because only if the Gaelic-speaking heartlands had been the beneficiaries of a general policy of social welfare could they have regained the energy that might have indeed guaranteed the language's health. As it was, the situation of Irish Gaelic by the mid-century was parlous: in 1966 probably fewer than 70,000 native speakers remained.

Independence made little difference to general economic and social trends. Agriculture continued to be slowly consolidated into medium-sized farms, the amount of land under cultivation declined, and farms were redistributed from large owners by purchase rather than by state action. Most notable of all was the continuation, even intensification, of emigration, which had been at the heart of nationalist protest since the potato famine of the mid-nineteenth century. The problem was also that no other social or political force was ready to challenge the policies that were pursued. The Labour Party did not even contest the elections of

1918 and 1921, to allow the electorate an unambiguous choice on the national question. Their support in the 1920s and 1930s was weak because they were unable to develop rural roots, and only thirteen per cent of the workforce was in industry. The other potential source of opposition to nationalism in its predominantly clerical form could have been the Protestants, reduced to about seven per cent of the population after the partition. But they were impotent, having given up any political credibility by the distance which most of them had placed between themselves and nationalism in the first two decades of the century.

None of this is to argue that Ireland would have been better off within the Union. The point is simply to note that Scotland was indeed getting a far better deal there, ultimately because of the complex historical differences between its and Ireland's relations to England. Thus the reforming Liberal policies of 1906, which Ireland could no longer afford, were, as we saw in chapter 6, one foundation of the UK welfare state, and therefore of Scotland's new reasons for loyalty. In particular, Scotland could use its own semi-state to extend its education system and to start to rebuild its slums. These actions may not have achieved everything that a socialist or a radical nationalist would have wanted, but they were widely believed to be a reasonable start. Looking to Ireland in the 1920s, it is hardly surprising that some left-wing Scottish supporters of home rule doubted if that policy in its pure form of a Scottish parliament was any longer the best way to solve social problems.

Over the next three decades, little changed in Ireland: throughout this period, according to Brown, 'the 26 counties . . . remained in many ways a social province of the UK', whatever their formal statehood (T. Brown, 1985, p. 216). Occasional tariffs against British goods did not amount to a coherent policy of protection, which would have had to have included state action to develop Irish industry and to eradicate poverty and emigration. Thus 'the structure of economic policy was conditioned by the political relationship with Britain', despite rhetoric to the contrary from the Fianna Fáil government (R. F. Foster, 1988, p. 539).

The social agenda of radical nationalism was still avoided. The recession of the 1930s did provoke attempts to set up a system of social welfare, but more fundamental measures were rejected by the church in 1947. The same fate awaited the attempts to promote planning in Dublin: there was nothing like the concerted Scottish campaign of middle opinion. Brown concludes that the state simply lacked the political self-confidence to deal with the growing social and economic crisis of the 1950s. What did continue was fundamentalist nationalism, partly provoked by the continuing partition, which in turn rested on the Protestants' suspicion of precisely that southern cultural intransigence.

And yet the society remained culturally dependent on England. The mass movement of people from rural areas to the cities indicated a choice against the policy of an 'Irish Ireland'. English newspapers and books were bought widely (unless prohibited by the church censors). English styles dominated domestic architecture, home furnishings, styles of dress and literature. Success in England was praised above achievements at home, and this in turn encouraged mass emigration to England (in place of the USA or Scotland, for example).

In this middle period of the twentieth century, then, it is difficult to avoid concluding that Ireland had all the disadvantages of independence with few of the benefits. Scotland, by contrast, was able to share in the relative wealth of the UK welfare state, and was able to start to use public resources to compensate for the loss of traditional industries. This indigenous action, as we have seen, was also underpinned by a cultural revival, which – ironically inspired by nationalist resentment at England – self-confidently took charge of the country's fate. The respects in which Scotland suffered were common to most of Europe – recession, war, or the internationalisation of popular culture. Ireland did avoid war (if we ignore the occasional IRA campaigns), although it also therefore evaded any official role in the defeat of fascism.

But this phase of dependency did at last begin to come to an end in the early 1960s. The symbolic event was the election of Sean Lamass as prime minister, although this in turn was merely a symptom that a new society was emerging in the generations that had no memory of gaining independence or of the civil war. He abandoned the symbolic nationalism of his predecessors in favour of the technocracy that was by then the dominant mode of European welfare-state thinking. In Ireland, that meant above all an attempt to use the state to modernise the economy and society. The goal became efficiency, and control was put in the hands of professional civil servants. Significant powers moved from the parliament to professional and advisory committees. For example, government economic policy was mediated through a National Economic and Social Council; and health provision was controlled by unelected regional boards. All this looks very Scottish: distinctive bureaucratic agencies to implement policies that were held in common across Europe.

The whole programme was based on a new self-confidence that was able to accept the inevitability of links with Britain. Politicians began to appreciate that modernisation did not mean anglicisation. Ireland might move closer to England, it is true, but that was because both were part of a modernising Europe. Thus foreign investment was welcome, and a free-trade area was established with the UK in 1965. The European Economic Community was seen as an opportunity to participate in a wider international forum than the British context only, although Ireland could not join until the United Kingdom did (in the mid-1970s).

Culturally, therefore, the old nationalism began to die. Models from Europe and Britain were welcomed, for example in education. Secondary education was provided for everyone up to the age of fifteen. A new public examination was introduced, along with a new curriculum that was based on European norms, relegating Gaelic to a less important role than hitherto. Efforts were made to tackle social inequalities in access to education. And the universities and the technical colleges expanded. All of these changes were similar to contemporary developments in England, and many of them were explicitly influenced by English ideas. For example, the programme to use educational institutions to overcome some of the effects of social deprivation was based on the Plowden report in England, and the expansion of higher education was influenced by the parallel expansion in the U K. British vocational examinations were used in schools and colleges. Thus Ireland's cultural relation to England became much more like Scotland's: broad principles were borrowed willingly, but the style of implementation was adjusted to suit the indigenous context and traditions.

As in Britain too, there was growing consumerism, and increasing popular preference for foreign culture:

> much of the material broadcast on RTE [the state television service] is of British and American origin. The advertisements are sometimes British-made on behalf of British products, sometimes Irish-made on behalf of British products, while Irish-made advertisements on behalf of Irish goods and services, where a company can afford it, are created for an audience accustomed to British advertising techniques. (T. Brown, 1985, p. 260)

Brown sums up the effect as 'a sense of Ireland firmly within the British commercial sphere of influence'.

As in Scotland, of course, there were vociferous nationalist complaints that the essence of the nation was being betrayed. An example from the poet and playwright Seán ó Tuama in 1972 could have been written by nationalists about Scotland at any time in the post-1945 period:

> There is very little sign yet of the new or creative Irish milieu that [the late-nineteenth-century nationalist intellectual] Douglas Hyde and his followers envisaged . . . One has only to think for a brief moment of the various aspects of Irish life today to realise that, as a people, we have few ideas of our own, that our model, in most cases, is still the English (or sometimes American) model. In business, science, engineering, architecture, medicine, industry, law, home-making, agriculture, education, politics, and administration . . . the vast bulk of our thinking is derivative. (T. Brown, 1985, p. 278)

But whether choosing to share in these common technocratic concerns was dependency must be doubted. The point was that the Irish electorate, led by a modernised political class, was now behaving as its Scottish counterparts had been doing since the 1930s. They were choosing to take part in an international movement of ideas that favoured state provision of social welfare. Ireland, in fact, was experiencing what Scotland had been able to achieve in the middle of the century as a result of its much more fortunate experience of Union with England, although of course national cultural differences between Scotland and Ireland shaped the experience in different ways:

> In many ways, what had emerged was the kind of Ireland that intelligent conservatives on both sides of the Irish Sea had drafted in the late nineteenth century [that is, constructive Unionism]: embodying a strong Catholic middle class, powerfully entrenched rights of landed property (including small property), an educational system firmly controlled by the Church, and a stable political system built on an English model but adapted to Irish preoccupations. (R. F. Foster, 1988, p. 593)

The apparent paradox was thus that this voluntary choice moved Ireland (like Scotland) towards a European norm. But it is not the source or effect of an idea that determines whether it has been imposed. The earlier Ireland of the 1940s and 1950s was also participating – whether it liked it or not – in a wider movement of European society, and the fundamental difference by the 1970s was that the participation was now voluntary to a much greater extent. And if that does indicate that Ireland was, for the first time, achieving a real independence, then we have to conclude that the similarly self-confident Scotland of the 1950s and 1960s was doing so too.

SCANDINAVIA

If Ireland lies at the one pole of highly constrained autonomy, the other can be found in Scandinavia. And yet in an important sense the outcome was much the same – assimilation to common European movements of political thought. In the introduction to his history of Scandinavian integration in the twentieth century, Solem argues that

> technological development has been so rapid and complex . . . that national goals . . . are often best attained by cooperation and coordination among states. In fact, the problems facing the world require not merely consultation and inter-governmental negotiations, but often organised cooperation that is binding on the participating states. (Solem, 1977, p. 1)

These comments fit very well with the main general theme of this chapter and the previous one: the societies of Europe and North America had become so interdependent by the middle of the twentieth century that the scope for autonomy lay in the ways in which shared goals were put into practice. Thus Scandinavia epitomises the constraints which the techno-cratic welfare state has placed on genuinely independent countries. The decision to construct that kind of state was voluntary; but, having taken it, the need for close cooperation was unavoidable.

There has been a long history of close cooperation in Scandinavia, dating in some cases – as we saw in chapter 5 – from the late nineteenth century. Right from the start, however, the chosen route was technical cooperation rather than a project of political unification. Scandinavian union in the sense of creating a single state was never close to being a political reality. The one Union that did exist – between Norway and Sweden – fell apart in 1905, with so little acrimony, however, that it did not disturb the growing cooperation at the levels of individuals and interest groups.

As elsewhere, pressure for coordination came from social-democratic politics and the labour movements, which had Scandinavian cooperation as an explicit policy. They wanted common standards of welfare, and universal access to such benefits as education and pensions. The Scandin-avian social-democratic parties held regular joint congresses from 1889 onwards, as did the trade unions and the peace movement.

The first phase of welfare-state development was in the 1920s and 1930s. In Denmark, for example, the liberals introduced extensive welfare legislation which was extended by the social democrats after 1924. This continued into the recession of the 1930s: a broad coalition of liberals, radicals and social democrats inaugurated a programme of state interven-tion in industry and agricultural marketing, and of extensive social insurance and welfare. Similar policies were being pursued at that time in Norway and Sweden. The outcome after 1945 throughout Scandinavia was the most thorough system of welfare in the democratic part of Europe.

The common political experience produced formal means of coordina-tion. The main vehicle for official cooperation since 1952 has been the Nordic council, grouping Denmark, Finland, Iceland, Norway, Sweden and the autonomous communities of Åland, Faroe and Greenland. It is a purely consultative body, consisting of delegates from the governments and from all the parties represented in the national parliaments. It meets at least once a year, and its meetings last for about one week. It has no authority to make decisions that are binding, but it deals with a very wide range of issues. It discusses the economy, legal questions, communications, social issues and cultural affairs. For most of its recommendations there is a lobby of support in each country, and so the states are under strong pressure domestically to adopt the recommendations.

However, the Nordic council is not the only forum of governmental cooperation. There is direct contact as well, mostly in order to harmonise legislation. Shadowing this are many permanent committees of civil ser-vants. Regular meetings take place of the national heads of postal services, railways, departments of health, customs offices and trade departments. Local government also has an important role in harmonisation, because it is the main agency by which social policy is implemented in all the Scandinavian countries. There have thus grown up extensive direct contacts between local government, bypassing the diplomatic service.

One effect of all this is – yet again – to intensify the tendency for legislation to be controlled by bureaucrats. The permanent committees which prepare for meetings of the Nordic council have a great deal of influence on its agenda. Some experts participate in the council itself, and the committees of parliamentarians often delegate work to them. There is, as a result, hardly any political dissent in the committees. The officials continue to have tight control over common policies when they are being implemented. The emphasis on finding technical solutions to political problems has produced an expectation that the civil servants who work with the council should eschew national allegiances. An adjunct to cooperation among civil servants is the emergence of interest groups which are organised across the whole of Scandinavia. There are examples in education, among the Lutheran churches, and between business people in similar sectors.

These tendencies towards professional control of legislation are equally evident in the parliaments of each state separately. Thus in Denmark we find a system that is similar to the one we have seen in Scotland. New legislation comes from civil servants, or specialist commissions, and occasionally the parties; it is prepared by the civil servants. This all works because of consensus between the parties. The main political divisions are among interest groups, which therefore have to be consulted by civil servants. People's expectation of politics is that their own interest groups should be consulted. The formal difference in Scotland – that these bureaucratic activities had to be sanctioned, ultimately, by a parliamentary majority at the UK level – was less important than it could have been in theory, again because the broad principles of politics in this welfare-state era were so fundamentally shared between parties. The way in which legislation affected people's lives was shaped more by the activities of the bureaucracy and interest groups than by the legislature.

So Scandinavia has produced a network of cooperative structures precisely because politics has been about implementation rather than fundamental goals. The result has been close convergence of results in many detailed areas of policy. In law, for example, there has been cooperation since 1872, but initially this was through direct contact among lawyers and civil servants, not by means of the legislatures. The first joint law was passed in 1880 by the parliaments of Norway, Sweden and Denmark, significantly to unify commercial law on bills of exchange. The first joint governmental law commission was in 1901, and it proposed uniform legislation in further commercial topics. After 1952, legal cooperation was thorough, and in a sense underlay all the other channels. One of the main functions of the Nordic council is to recommend ways in which separate legislation can be brought into harmony, by means of its permanent committee for legislative cooperation.

In communications, cooperation has lasted since 1874, when the first postal union was established and when railways started coordinating time-tables and fares. Roads have been coordinated since 1930, telecommunications since 1937, and airlines since 1946. The Nordic council has been instrumental in a lot of this, and from 1973 it has been promoting joint research, legislation and regulations.

For social policy, Solem has commented that there is now 'nearly complete equality of treatment' across the whole of Scandinavia (Solem, 1977, p. 29). The first cooperation was, again, at administrative levels. Common funds for health and accident insurance were started in 1907, and common health regulations in 1909. Since the early 1950s, the Nordic committee on social policy has harmonised social security, social care and child welfare. There has been a single labour market since 1954.

There has also been close cooperation on cultural matters, because there is a widespread popular feeling of belonging to different branches of a common culture. This continues to impinge also on legislation: the common traditions in law, government and social values help to achieve common policies.

There are, of course, substantial areas in which harmony has not been reached, although there are no deep conflicts either. The economies are not integrated, because the trading patterns of the different states diverge: for most of the twentieth century, Denmark was heavily dependent on the UK, and Finland on Russia. This has not, however, discouraged the Nordic council's attempts to achieve harmony in commercial laws, and the wider European Free Trade Area induced some cooperation from 1959. Similarly, the Nordic council has not usually discussed defence policy, because the states have had quite markedly different orientations: Finland had to remain friendly with the USSR, Sweden was neutral, and Iceland, Norway and Denmark were in NATO. Nevertheless, on most foreign-policy issues a common policy has been reached, and frequently one of the states speaks for all the others in international forums. In particular, all of Scandinavia has strongly supported efforts to achieve global peace and cooperation, notably through the League of Nations and then the United Nations.

In an important sense, though, the areas where policies are not tightly coordinated prove how voluntary the large area of cooperation is. It is chosen in the sense that it is a recognition of the common social forces affecting all the states in Scandinavia (and beyond). It is thus an explicit recognition of the theme we took from Poggi. In countries which set up a welfare state, the ends of politics were agreed. The Scandinavians seem

to have concluded, therefore, that it makes sense to formalise this agreement into international cooperation. Over significant areas of social policy,
the system seems confederal, or even federal. That this degree of cooperation has been possible shows that foreign and defence policies do not
have to be aligned for domestic policies to be pursued in common.

Scotland did not have that foreign-policy scope for deviating from England, and in that sense has been more constrained. But the main lesson
from the Scandinavian countries for our understanding of Scotland is that
convergence of social policy has been chosen by these formally independent
states for the whole of the twentieth century. They chose it because, like
England, Scotland and Wales, they mostly shared the goals of social
policy. Scandinavia thus illustrates that we cannot deduce that a country
is dependent on another just because their social policies have ended up
looking very similar.

CONCLUSION

As with the nineteenth century, this comparison of small countries or
regions shows how complex the reality of autonomy is. For all the constraints that it faces, Scotland is by no means among the least independent
of the places we have looked at.

In comparison with the component parts of federations, first of all,
Scotland in the middle of the twentieth century enjoyed substantial autonomy. To some extent this could be exercised even over legislation: in
areas such as housing, education or social work, Scotland pursued far
more distinctive social policies than the German Länder. But the main
lesson from the discussion of Germany, the USA and Canada is that
federalism has applied more to administrative matters than to legislation.
In the highly technocratic states of this period, the control of the processes
by which legislation affects people's everyday lives has been important for
shaping the character of a society. The federal centres have been generally
willing to devolve that kind of activity to their provinces, where politics
has become a question of bargaining among interest groups coordinated
by the bureaucracy.

The advantage for the provinces, as for Scotland, is that they have
gained access to the resources of the state as a whole. The pressures for
legislative centralisation and administrative devolution have come from
the welfare-state parties which dominated politics in the middle of the
century. Equalising resources across wide and rich territories would benefit
everyone, they believed. The sacrifice of legislative independence seemed
to be a small price to pay, especially because, in this era of consensus, it
was unlikely that radically divergent policies would have been pursued in
any case.

Whether this system would maintain provincial distinctiveness therefore
depended on whether the society as a whole was truly federal, in

Livingston's terms. In the UK and Canada it undoubtedly was, and so legislation was implemented according to distinctive traditions. In the USA and Germany, the interest groups were mostly national (and there was little dispute as to what the nation was), and so the effects of legislation were more uniform. The main difference between the UK and Canada was the absence in the UK of a clear mechanism for renegotiating the settlement. Thus there was no national body to express the Scottish mood, and so nationalism had to have its effect almost in secret, inside the bureaucracy. It is not surprising, then, that Scottish nationalists have been reluctant to claim the various bureaucratic victories as successes: they usually cannot, like the provincial premiers of Canada, come back from the centre brandishing the results of hard bargaining. Whether the secret or the open route to negotiating gives more actual sovereignty to the provinces is problematic, and perhaps will be finally answered only once a fairly permanent new settlement has been reached in both Canada and the UK. That might, of course, be never.

In any case, at least until the 1980s, Scotland has firmly accepted that its semi-federal situation was preferable to full statehood, believing that formal sovereignty was less safe than continuing to share in the relative wealth and influence of a large state. That this decision was not obviously wrong is seen by comparing Scotland's situation with those of other small nations. The states of east-central Europe have undergone a far more constrained history in the twentieth century, at best achieving through skilled manoeuvring only some temporary and constrained control of domestic policy. These experiences may seem remote from Scotland's, but they do have important lessons for our understanding of autonomy in general, and therefore that of Scotland in particular. The fact that Scotland inherits a fortunate external situation is inseparable from all its other inherited ties with England, just as the tragedies of Poland or Czechoslovakia in the twentieth century have to be traced back to the problems which these peoples have had with Russia or Germany for many centuries. If we ask how independent Scotland has been, we have to answer by referring not just to an ideal, but also to the large number of small nations whose position has been much worse. Scotland, if independent, might have been fortunate enough to have become a Czechoslovakia in the 1920s; but there are plenty of other less attractive examples – such as Poland or Ireland – to suggest that the risk might not have been worth taking. If Scotland within the UK seems to have inherited a fairly liberal and tolerant international situation in contrast to countries in east-central Europe, then perhaps that is something of which the Scots should be modestly proud, because their predecessors have contributed to choosing and constructing it.

In any case, even in Western Europe, the scope for independent action by small nations has been small, especially once more because of the technical complexity of the era of the welfare state. Ireland did not achieve the self-confident independence of which its radical nationalists had dreamed; until the 1960s, for the reasons we have outlined in this and the previous chapter, Scotland in the Union was more fortunate than Ireland outside it. That Scotland had access to a privileged position in the UK was again a legacy of its long partnership with England. The growing independence which Ireland did attain from the 1960s onwards would probably have been impossible without its statehood, but we cannot deduce from the necessity of Ireland's secession that Scotland ought to have done so too.

By choosing to stay in its Union in the twentieth century, Scotland chose a welfare state, and was no less free in doing that than the Scandinavian countries were in their evolving cooperation for similar ends. At the end of the twentieth century, a similar theme is emerging in the European Union. Free states are choosing to share sovereignty. Scotland – or Scandinavia – ought to be better able to handle this cooperation than those large nations such as England which are having to learn how to give up power. Whether that new international framework will make a difference to the nature of Scotland's autonomy is discussed in the final chapter. But the point to take from the Scandinavian experience is that, contrary to what is claimed by some nationalists, there is nothing abject about choosing to cooperate. Scandinavian Union has taken a constitutional form that is different from the British one; but that does not make Scotland's twentieth-century experience any less the outcome of free choices.

8

The End of the Bureaucratic State?

There have always been tensions in the welfare state between efficiency and democracy, but these did not become acute until quite recently, as its capacity to ensure the welfare of its citizens became problematic. This final chapter first sets out these trends in Europe and North America, and then discusses how they have been manifest in Scotland. In all these places, rule by experts now attracts more searching criticism than it did when the priority seemed to be to solve the poverty and social deprivation left over from the nineteenth century. Technocracy has come to be seen as morally inadequate, by radical politicians on both the left and the right. Choices are unavoidable: administration cannot replace the resolution of political conflict. In the European Union, in particular, the argument is evolving into a dispute between one model of development that centralises power in Brussels in the interests of efficiency and homogeneous social welfare, and a challenge to that which insists that small nations and communities have to have guaranteed rights to influence the broad goals by which the bureaucracies operate.

In Scotland, the critique of technocracy has become a questioning of the legitimacy of the Scottish Office, a claim that administrative devolution is not enough. But, despite the rhetoric of the proponents of a Scottish parliament, the central issue in Scottish constitutional politics is not between self-government and dependency, but rather between two types of autonomy. The conflict is between the administrative autonomy that was established earlier this century, and a more participatory form of independence that would have an elected parliament at its heart. The main sections of the chapter assess this debate, placing it in the wider context of the general decay of the post-1945 settlement across Europe.

Constitutional change is not inevitable, especially because most people in Scotland (as elsewhere) continue to judge constitutional arrangements by the same criteria that led to the emergence of a bureaucratic welfare state in the first place: can it ensure security and prosperity? But some change is highly likely, if only because even the defenders of the constitutional status quo conduct the debate in essentially nationalist terms: what structures can best secure Scotland's interests? The debate has this nationalist character precisely because Scotland already has a degree of autonomy: in that sense, what we can imagine for the future is shaped by the outcomes of the centuries of constitutional conflict and settlement that this book has been discussing. The final point, however, is that any outcome will be constrained, because Scotland remains a small country dependent on the world for its well-being.

THE DECAY OF TECHNOCRACY

The most spectacular challenge to technocracy in Europe and North America – to rule by experts – came with the rebellions of young people in the 1960s. It is easy to mock the naivety of that now: power to the imagination seems a naively absurd declaration in the light of what has happened since. It assumed that material problems had been so thoroughly solved that society could henceforth enjoy the luxury of thinking about more important things, love or art for example.

And yet that decade bequeathed an unavoidable suspicion of professionals. It reminded us, in Bell's words, that conflict over values is inevitable: no 'social decision' can satisfy everyone (Bell, 1976, p. 365). What Kumar calls the 'managerialist consensus' had irrevocably broken down, in the sense that henceforth there would always be a questioning of where the whole enterprise was going (Kumar, 1978, p. 185). The revolt against technocracy fed into political movements such as feminism, environmentalism and anti-racism, which have become at least as influential now as social democracy. The technocratic professionals were mostly men with white skins and college degrees; and the resources that they allocated, ostensibly unpolitically, were available to people in some parts of the globe only because they were denied to the vast majority. The consumption of these resources, moreover, was threatening to pollute the planet so thoroughly that there would soon be nothing left to allocate, politically or otherwise.

Bell sums up this revolt, optimistically, as a 'participation revolution'. Society, he wrote in 1973, was engaged in

> an uprising against bureaucracy and a desire for participation, a theme summed up in the statement that 'people ought to be able to affect the decisions that control their lives'. To a considerable extent, the participation revolution is one of the forms of reaction against the 'professionalisation' of society and the emergent technocratic decision-making of a post-industrial society. (Bell, 1976, p. 365)

This was, he continued, a very old political problem being reasserted in modern guise: 'who should make, and at what levels of government, what kinds of decisions, for how large a social unit?' (p. 365). Because this question cannot be avoided, political problems are never 'solved' (despite the rhetoric that dominates politics and the bureaucracy). The difficulty then is to have institutions that are flexible enough to change. The radical critics argue that only popular participation can provide the fresh ideas which will guarantee renewal. Because the bureaucracy and the political class are selected from a narrow social range, even representative democracy might not be pluralistic enough to do that.

Rather ironically, the main energy behind these pressures has been segments of the middle class itself: professional organisations spawned radical critics within their ranks, questioning the values that professional practices took for granted. In the 1960s it was the children of the rich who rejected affluence; in the 1980s, it was the middle class who constituted the main social basis of environmentalism. But other critiques have emerged too. The most significant, because the most effective in practice, is the revival of a faith in laissez-faire markets as a way of challenging the bureaucracy. This underpinned the conservative reformism of Margaret Thatcher and Ronald Reagan. There has also been a reassertion of a radical nationalism based on leftist social politics. And there has been the mirror image of that, the recent resurgence of fascism in Europe. In the 1990s, the welfare state seems to be under attack everywhere, and this has induced fears as well as optimism. Scotland is not the only place where a claim for independence reawakens angst: only the secure middle class can easily afford to weaken the safety which an efficient bureaucracy has seemed to offer.

CONSTITUTIONAL TENSIONS IN EUROPE AND NORTH AMERICA

These debates have provoked unprecedented questioning of the constitutional arrangements that have accompanied the welfare state.

In Germany, the consensus which held until the end of the 1960s has been decaying ever since. This was most notable between 1969 and 1982, when the coalition of the Social Democrats and the liberal Free Democrats in the Bundestag faced a hostile right-wing majority in the Bundesrat. Inevitably, the conflict became an assertion of the rights of the Länder, via the Bundesrat, against the federation as a whole. The opposite happened in the late 1980s, when a right-wing majority had to deal with a Bundesrat dominated by the Social Democrats. In other words, the whole German system can work only if there are no fundamental political tensions between the Bundestag and the Länder. In the aftermath of German reunification in 1990, that consensus seems to be much more difficult to find.

The strengthening of the Christian Democrats in the 1980s was, in fact, something of a popular response to these constitutional tensions. The new government in 1982 asserted that power should be returned to the Länder wherever possible (a policy which echoed the 'new federalism' of Ronald Reagan, who had similarly tried to return powers to the states of the

USA). German Chancellor Helmut Kohl's reform reversed cuts which the Social Democrats had made in programmes that were the joint responsibility of the Bund and the Länder, and the Länder were allocated a share of the sales tax. Later, there was greater Länder involvement in European Union decision-making, as we saw in chapter 7.

But there are reasons to doubt that these relatively minor administrative changes are enough to cope with the political tensions. New disputes have emerged as the Länder have moved to Social Democratic control: the electorates seem to want to politicise the conflicts, rather than leave them to be solved by administrative means. The role of the Bund has continued to increase, partly to finance new capital investment and educational development in response to recession, but partly also to meet the demands of the European Union for uniform legislation. The Christian Democratic policy of privatising public services – for example, hospitals – has encroached on areas that have traditionally been joint responsibilities, and so what had previously been an administrative arrangement has become politicised. This reminds us that one strand of right-wing opposition to technocracy has been a suspicion of any type of government, whether central or local. Thus the previous constitutional arrangements have been challenged from both below and above.

Canadian federalism has undergone even greater tensions, exacerbated by the continuing conflict over Quebec. Smiley notes that because cooperative federalism is based on executive committees of bureaucrats, it 'requires a degree of secrecy in decision-making which is believed to be incompatible with the requirements of democracy' (Smiley, 1977b, p. 266). The value of the federal government is being called into question as it fails to maintain the role which it acquired after 1945 of integrating the Canadian economy. That this failure is partly a consequence of global recessions does not make it go away: the rich provinces of the west might prefer to deal with these international economic pressures on their own.

The proposals that have been made for dealing with these problems are not obviously able to work. It has been suggested, for example, that the judiciary could play a greater role in resolving disputes. But it has been claimed against this that judges would tend to place too much emphasis on the letter of the constitution; they would therefore promote not cooperation but separation of functions between the federal level and the provinces. The proposal of a permanent independent commission for resolving conflicts has not been widely acceptable either: the problems of government by experts are hardly likely to be resolvable by a group of super-experts. The underlying difficulties are political: for example, provincial resentment at federal desires to restrict welfare spending is not only about the most efficient way of dividing up resources to achieve shared goals; the tensions also reflect differences over the goals themselves, over how much public spending is desirable. Similarly, politics is unavoidable in decisions over the rate at which natural resources should be extracted. And there continues to be the cultural schism between Quebec and the rest.

In the end, the Canadian federation might even fall apart. Provincial pressure might so weaken the federal government that it would be unable to carry out its integrating responsibilities at all. The main motor for this change is Quebec, which would seem to prefer direct relationships with the other provinces than coordination through the centre; and whether such semi-diplomatic arrangements could any longer be called a federation is doubtful.

These federal states provide the most graphic instances of the problems of technocracy, because the constitution asserts a democratic right to participate, and so can always be invoked to challenge domination by bureaucrats. That is ultimately also, perhaps, the main strength of federations: they institutionalise the possibilities of reform. Analogous tensions arise between states. Denmark, for instance, remained highly suspicious of European centralisation even in its second referendum on the Maastricht treaty in May 1993, as did France in September 1992. The Maastricht process has inspired the German Länder to assert their rights too. The new and incipiently federal Spanish constitution has allowed Catalonia and the Basque country to develop their autonomy more rapidly than other Spanish regions, thus possibly preventing the disintegration of the Spanish state. Everywhere, political protests against uniformity show that there is a genuinely popular suspicion of centralisation. People are not convinced that there is sufficient agreement over ultimate ends to place all the important decisions in the hands of bureaucrats: one of the reasons for Denmark's doubts was a fear that its high level of welfare would be eroded by a European Union majority which did not share such thoroughly social-democratic goals.

The difficulties over European convergence have probably ensured that any constitution which emerges for the European Union will have the same forums for renewal as federations have always had, and which the UK has conspicuously lacked. In the most optimistic prognosis, the EU may be evolving a new level of genuinely political involvement, perhaps based on the shared values of the rule of law, representative democracy and respect for pluralism. If these are embodied in its institutions, then they are bound to be able to change relatively smoothly over time, because new social pressures will find ready means of articulation.

SCOTLAND

The Scottish situation is merely one instance of these much broader developments. The administrative autonomy which was established in the middle of the twentieth century is in decay, for three reasons. First, power has been drifting away from those institutions in which Scottish autonomy lay in the middle of the century. Second, political tensions between Scotland

and England have in any case undermined the compromises which allowed these institutions to be autonomous. These two reasons are discussed in the present section. The third reason is that the European Union has provided a wholly new context in which limited autonomy can be imagined; that will be dealt with later.

The drift of power away from old institutions is a result mainly of slow social change, just as happened at the beginning of the nineteenth century or in the 1920s. The economy no longer has even the limited degree of Scottish control that it had in the 1930s, and so the various corporatist committees operate in something of a vacuum: the economy cannot be planned from the Scottish Office if the main sources of power are global. The Scottish middle class is not as homogeneous as it was until the 1960s: upward social mobility from the working class has created a more diverse cultural and political inheritance. This diversity of the Scottish elite has reduced the influence of the universities, which moreover have ceased to have a common outlook as they have expanded. The churches have become even more marginalised than the universities, as society has become much more secular: they now have only a very limited role in the administration of welfare and in the formation of social mores.

Nevertheless, the main reason for loss of power by Scottish governing institutions is not social change but political conflict with England, the second way in which the foundations of the twentieth-century constitution are decaying. The signs of this started appearing in the 1960s and 1970s, when the Scottish National Party began to attract significant levels of support. The protests took a nationalist form because – as we saw in chapter 6 – the Scottish semi-state had encouraged the development of a sense of a Scottish national interest. When that state then seemed to be failing to deliver the material well-being that it had promised, new ways of organising the state were proposed more insistently. At the same time, there emerged a critique of the Scottish Office as being insufficiently democratic. Both of these strands are recognisable as specifically Scottish versions of the general trends we have been noting. As elsewhere, the welfare state was no longer able to guarantee the security that had given it legitimacy in the first place. And the technocratic nature of decision-making had raised questions about the unavoidability of political conflict.

The immediate response to this new nationalism came from the Labour government of the 1970s, which proposed to set up a weak Scottish parliament whose powers would largely have been limited to overseeing the work which the Scottish Office had been doing anyway. In a referendum in 1979, this scheme was only narrowly accepted, and the Conservative government that was elected a few months later did not implement it. The weakness of support can best be interpreted as a continuing preference by the Scottish electorate for the type of technocratic autonomy that had worked fairly well between 1945 and the late 1960s: even a limited parliament was believed to place these gains at risk.

But what then became clear was that the old autonomy was not in fact available at all. After the referendum, Scotland retained a broadly social-democratic consensus. But the new government of Margaret Thatcher was radically right-wing, and was less willing than its predecessors to tolerate territorial diversity. Thatcher represented a new Toryism, one that had forgotten a sense of the Union as a partnership. Her government took the absolute sovereignty of parliament literally, neglecting a tradition that it should limit its own power in the interests of tolerable rule; and she was able to do this because the erstwhile constitution had been built on conventions and understandings, rather than on formal documents. Thus she largely ignored Scottish protests against privatisation of public utilities, or the introduction of a more commercial style of management to the health service, or the erosion of the powers of elected local government. She was also crass enough to try to reform that citadel of Scottish middle-class sensitivities, the legal system, which is still seen as a symbol of the entire semi-independence of Scotland within the Union.

This legal example points to an irony in the Scottish reaction to Thatcherism: for all the electoral importance of Scottish working-class alienation from the Conservative government, the most striking protests often came from vested interests. This could happen precisely because Scotland does possess a sort of state and therefore has ruling elites who resent the erosion of their power. The middle class saw themselves as the guardians of the welfare state; any threat to their hegemony was interpreted as a threat to Scotland itself. Thus Thatcher did not have to be deliberately anti-Scottish for her policies to be received as such. Her reforms impinged on specifically Scottish institutions because she wanted to end what she saw as the suffocatingly consensual way in which Britain had been governed since 1945. So she abolished many of the committees and agencies of corporatism, or else she packed them with her ideological supporters. In Scotland, this laid the government open to the accusation of politicising the devolved administration, especially health and education; and that charge is the gravest that can be levelled in the lexicon of technocracy.

And yet, in a sense, her government was merely laying bare a political tension that had always been there, and which had been concealed by the rhetoric of consensual administration. The people whom she was excluding from influence could protest at politicisation, and yet were in fact asserting merely another political point of view, that of social democracy or corporatism. They were the large segments of the professional middle class who did not support the Conservative Party. Their position can therefore be interpreted as defending a class or a sectional interest: they were objecting to the loss of their power and their opportunities for advancement. The same account can be given of the 1980s and 1990s obsession with anglicisation of

Scottish culture: this, too, was a perception that influence was being denied to a class which assumed that it was their own birthright. They resented also the reduction in opportunities to migrate to public-sector jobs in other parts of the United Kingdom, a consequence of the same restriction on the welfare state. And it should be added that the Scottish middle class had a greater personal stake in the welfare state than did their English counterparts: more of them worked in it, and they preferred to use public medicine and public education.

Thatcher's supreme blunder was not to exploit the class nature of this resentment – to fail to mobilise a countervailing sectional interest that would be just as Scottish but on her side ideologically. Her greatest Scottish misfortune was the loss of the only real populist in Scottish Tory ranks in 1979, Teddy Taylor, whose seat fell to Labour: he might have been able to build up a working-class Toryism that could have undermined the nationalist case being made by the middle class. In fact, however, the working class shifted decisively towards Labour and later the SNP: the decline in Protestantism helped the old working-class Toryism to collapse, and so – unlike in England – the Conservatives were never able to capture the allegiance of any more than one fifth of skilled workers.

Nevertheless, the analysis in terms of class interests, although important, is not enough, because it does not explain why the middle-class rebellion did take a nationalist rather than an overtly class form. The only way to understand that is to continue to remind ourselves again that, in crucial respects, what was being attacked was indeed a separate state, not merely the field agencies of a unitary power. It was a state that had remoulded civil society since 1945: in particular, the new middle class that had emerged from working-class origins had reached that position through the reformed and thoroughly Scottish education system. There was some evidence also that the middle class was seeing its territory as Scotland, rather than as a region within the country: university students became much more reluctant to attend the local university (as had been the practice for centuries), and yet ninety per cent of them continued to attend a university in Scotland, in preference to emigrating. University students are now the main source of recruits to the middle class, as credentials became essential for professional employment. Thus this nationalising of the students might have replaced a local identity for the emerging middle class by a more firmly Scottish one.

In the 1970s and 1980s, therefore, there was a shift in middle-class allegiance and social philosophy. This can be detected in surveys of social attitudes: for example, all classes in Scottish society were more favourably disposed to the public sector than were their counterparts in the south of England. Likewise, there was greater scepticism in Scotland about the symbolic trappings of Britain: for example, the monarchy, parliament, the central civil service. The middle class therefore found themselves in some surprisingly nationalist rebellions: for example, the members of the Institute of Chartered Accountants of Scotland rejected a proposal in 1989 to amalgamate the body with its English counterpart. The usual form for the nationalism was a reassertion of consensus, and with it the unavoidably nationalist dimension that had accompanied the welfare state all along. In response to industrial decline, for example, the Scottish Council Development and Industry and several professional organisations came together in 1986 with the Scottish Trades Union Congress to establish a Standing Commission on the Scottish Economy. Local government was involved in this too, having acquired from 1975 significant new powers over planning and economic development; this ensured that it, too, would attract the professional middle class onto its staff, bringing them into alliance with the Labour Party which dominated the local councils electorally.

Most striking of all, however, was the drift of middle-class votes against the Conservative Party: by the late 1980s, only about one third of them supported the Tories, much the same as were for Labour; in the English middle class, by contrast, the Conservatives' proportion was about two thirds (and the Labour proportion about one fifth). Associated with this political change was a growth of middle-class support for self-government, notably for independence. These dissenting beliefs have been held also by elites, not only by the middle class in general. The Labour and Liberal political parties followed this opinion rather than creating it. It gave an intellectual respectability to the schemes for parliamentary self-government; in particular, the Labour Party swung right round to enthusiastic support, replacing the grudging acquiescence which they had shown in response to the SNP rise a decade before. As socialism fell out of fashion, nationalist rhetoric became easier for Labour politicians: even people who were at best lukewarm in their support for a parliament started talking about the national interests of the Scottish people.

In an odd way, too, the Thatcher reforms were encouraging this strengthening of Scottish civil society and undermining the technocracy, even though also undermining some of its old institutions. Her government did centralise some functions in London, but she believed sufficiently in her ideology to create new bodies which did not simply depend on the Scottish Office for their legitimacy. In these respects, she was drawing on an analysis from the right-wing Adam Smith Institute, which revived the old nineteenth-century belief that the essence of the nation lay in its people's autonomous and private activities, and which drew the inference that the best way of defending Scottish interests was to make the Scottish people less dependent on the state.

For example, the government transferred many of the industrial-development powers of the old Scottish Development Agency to new Local Enterprise Companies (LECs), which, although not elected, were required to have on their board the representatives of local industry. Whatever policies these might pursue, they are almost bound to be more embedded in local Scottish society than the single centralised board of the SDA in Glasgow. And their professional personnel have emerged from the decade of debate about new directions for Scottish corporatism. Moreover, when the LECs fail to achieve the technical aims that they have set themselves, the complaints are in terms of their lack of democratic legitimacy in the local community: again, a technocratic matter has been politicised.

A similar point can be made about the new boards which have overseen the running of schools since 1989, with a majority of members to be elected by parents of current pupils. Initially this was seen as anglicisation: Scottish educational professionals have tended not to trust lay people to interfere in their practice, whereas boards of governors have been established in England for a long time. But, being elected, the Scottish boards quickly acquired a democratic legitimacy which the government can hardly have expected. Indeed, they led a popular rebellion against government proposals to require primary schools to test all their pupils annually.

Behind all this overtly political activity has been a great deal of cultural activism. Novels, poetry, theatre, history and music of all sorts have flourished in a way that they had not done at least since the 1930s, and in some respects much longer. A lot of this was vaguely political, in a loosely socialist and nationalist way: it thus helped to create a new account of Scotland as an essentially democratic place which was opposed to an incorrigibly hierarchical Tory England. A new morality was thus being developed to replace the declining Presbyterian Calvinism; and the emphasis on democracy can be interpreted as version of Poggi's and others' general doubts about technocracy.

This kind of process has been described by A. D. Smith (1991) as the invention of a new 'ethnie' – a new ethnic identity – which has tremendous mobilising power for nationalist ends. A tradition of popular sovereignty has been invented. Some words from Cohen characterise the process well:

> the past is being used as a resource, . . . a selective construction . . . which resonates with contemporary influences. Myth confers 'rightness' on a course of action by extending to it the sanctity which enshrouds tradition and lore. (Cohen, 1985, p. 99)

To call this 'myth' is to point to its selectivity. But the tenuous basis of a belief does not affect its power to mobilise people politically: the notion that Scotland had a long tradition of democracy is no less true than the earlier Presbyterian belief that the Scots were a chosen Protestant people, and yet that belief had enormous political and social effect in the activities of the nineteenth-century bourgeoisie. Cohen even argues that 'the finer the differences between people, the stronger is the commitment people have to them' (p. 110); consequently, 'the community can make almost anything grist to the symbolic mill of cultural distance' (p. 117). For example, the assertion of Scottish democracy allowed feminists to raise women's rights in the debates about Scotland's future to an extent that had never happened before: they, and also campaigners against racism, now had a semi-official national ideology of Scottish democracy with which they could challenge anyone who was advocating constitutional or political change.

Although some of this cultural change had an impact on a very wide audience – for example, a few of the rock and folk groups – the main consumers were middle-class. The cultural activity gave to the political resentment a framework that was firmly Scottish. The effect on the middle class was greater than any impact on working-class votes precisely because they already had access to power – to the media, to education, to the resources for setting up alternative political forums. It was only because of this middle-class dissaffection that a nationalist case could be plausibly argued: all classes could seem to be united. That is, indeed, how Scotland's fate has always been decided, as is clear from chapters 3, 4 and 6. Neverthe-less, there have been important working-class versions: for example, there have been groups of tenants in public-sector housing who have questioned the paternalistic traditions of local-authority administration. Many indi-vidual working-class people have exercised this frustration by buying their council house, but they have not thereby acquired the political views that the Conservative proponents of this right to buy originally hoped.

Thus what we have seen in Scotland in the last thirty years has been a local instance of very wide disaffection with the political systems that had been established by social and Christian democracy. The working class has remained supportive of the public provision of welfare, and has trans-lated this in nationalist terms because welfare was threatened by the right-wing hold on the UK state, relying on Conservative votes in England. The middle class has shared this view, both as users of the welfare state and also as providers through their role in governing its autonomous Scottish structures. Along with this argument there has been a questioning of the democratic legitimacy of the Scottish state, made more graphic by the electoral divergence from England in the 1980s, but ultimately merely the Scottish instance of the general moral decay of technocracy that has been identified in many other places.

REVIVING MANAGED AUTONOMY

Nevertheless, the outcome of these processes is no more certain in Scotland than elsewhere. It is even possible that a slightly modified version of administrative autonomy will convince enough people that Scotland's inter-ests can continue to be protected in that way.

After Margaret Thatcher was deposed in 1990, the Conservatives woke up to their mistakes and started to reassert the virtues of a constitutional settlement that would be barely altered, but in which Scottish distinctiveness would be allowed the scope that it had had in the 1950s. The ephemeral details of these proposals are less important than the broad themes; and the memories of that safe type of semi-independence were sufficiently strong to save the party from further Scottish losses in the general election of 1992. The government was doing, in fact, what it should have done immediately after 1979: appreciating that the Scots have frequently been happy to accept limited autonomy in preference to the risks that might flow from pressing more radical demands.

The new prime minister, John Major, and his Scottish Secretary, Ian Lang, started asserting again that Scotland was a partner in the Union. They declared an intention to stop appointing only Tory supporters to the network of Scottish boards, a proposal that provoked outrage from some members of their party. They also borrowed some of the rhetoric of the democratic case for self-government: they proposed new parliamentary methods of monitoring the Scottish Office, thus attempting to expose the bureaucracy to greater scrutiny. Lang has even revived the nineteenth-century unionist nationalism, claiming that the Union is the 'real legacy' of the medieval wars of independence (Lang, 1993).

They could also reasonably assert that the Scottish Office retained considerable autonomy, even after the Thatcher years. That autonomy, as always, lay in the technical details of implementation, not in the broad principles of policy. For example, the curriculum in primary and secondary schools was being developed in a distinctively Scottish way, largely under the control of professional educationalists. New powers over the arts, the environment, the universities and vocational training were transferred to the Scottish Office from London departments.

This Conservative strategy may well succeed. Decades of merely administrative autonomy may have induced a caution among Scots that could be shaken only by a cataclysm of the type that provoked the rebellions in east-central Europe in 1989 and 1990. The Scottish middle class, in particular, have frequently been castigated for their craven dependency. This might be only an abusive way of describing their pragmatic adaptation to circumstances, but it does not suggest that radical rebellion is in the offing. It was the continuing real autonomy of the Scottish Office, after all, that allowed the opposition parties to lapse into inaction when the Conservatives were not wiped out in 1992. Labour especially, with its control of local government, had to choose between outright rebellion and continuing to cooperate at the technocratic level – on committees governing school curricula, for instance, or even over the government's proposed reform of local government itself. As the heirs to the inventors of the cautious administrative autonomy, it is hardly surprising that they chose safety.

These arguments for caution could be strengthened if the UK economy recovered. Most people, according to opinion polls, usually attach more importance to material interests than to the constitution, and so the UK state is likely to lose legitimacy only if it irrevocably fails to deliver prosperity to the electoral majority. That could leave only a few civil-rights activists caring about the moral decay of technocracy.

Moreover, although the European dimension is usually cited as a reason to expect a Scottish parliament to be set up (more on which below), the case could equally well be put the other way. The European Union as presently constituted is essentially a much grander version of the type of interest-group bargaining that has lain at the heart of all welfare states. Old Scottish practices could find a new scope there, as the successful lobbying by some local authorities for European funds has already shown.

But if the new Unionism of Major and Lang is a belated appreciation of what the referendum vote in 1979 indicated about Scottish caution, there are also good reasons to believe that it is, in fact, too late. The world has changed, and it could be that the expectations that the Scottish people have of autonomy are now much greater. Ian Lang's proposals have a dated feel, reminiscent of the 1950s or 1960s. For example, a Conservative party committee chaired by the former prime minister Alec Douglas-Home, set up in response to the SNP's success of the 1960s, argued that nationalism was in effect merely a desire for 'doing more of Scotland's business in public and in Scotland' (G. E. Edwards, 1972, p. 325). Ian Lang would find that phrase congenial.

This approach might not now be enough because recent opposition campaigns in Scotland have been making political demands that go beyond the areas that are supposed to be dealt with by the bureaucracy. For example, the opposition to the local-government poll tax was for complete abolition, not merely for control of how it was implemented. The same can be said about the campaign over franchising of the water-supply industry. The government itself seems to be intent on politicising the bureaucracy: by refusing to set up an independent commission to investigate local-government reform, it was bound to attract criticism that it – like Thatcher – was confusing constitutional issues with party-political ones.

More fundamental, however, are trends which owe little to the details of Lang's constitutional proposals. The UK economy probably will not revive sufficiently to avoid recurrent crisis. Thus the Union may indeed seem not to be delivering the economic security which was the main reason for compromising on autonomy in 1945. The government's minor constitutional reforms do not address this; and that is highly ironic, given the readiness with which the Unionists argue that material issues matter more than constitutional ones.

At the same time, there has been a decline in cultural Britishness, as the Empire has gone, as the monarchy has crumbled into trivial scandal, and as a European allegiance has provided new opportunities for careers. The old Scottish preference for an assimilationist nationalism now seems to be focused on Europe. In the new Scottish culture of the 1980s and 1990s, to be European has been equated to being progressive and democratic, in almost the same way as being British was in the eighteenth and nineteenth centuries; and to be British has been tantamount to being anachronistic.

PROPOSALS FOR PARLIAMENTARY AUTONOMY

No-one now seriously proposes that the Scottish Office be abolished, although such ideas were current in the 1930s and were mooted by the New Right in the 1980s. It is conceivable that they could be revived, especially if a radically right-wing politician such as Michael Forsyth were to become Scottish Secretary. But the broad nationalist reaction would probably be so intense as to make the attempt too risky for the supporters of the Union. Therefore the only other realistic constitutional futures that are on offer involve a Scottish parliament.

The more cautious version is for a parliament with power to legislate on domestic policy only, as favoured now by both the Labour and the Liberal Parties. This idea has been debated for over a century, as we saw in chapters 4 and 6, and it is often claimed to be the first step towards a federal constitution for the whole of the UK: the Liberal Party asserts that officially, and Labour seems to be moving in that direction. The policy was evolved most recently in the Scottish Constitutional Convention, which was set up in the aftermath of the 1987 general election with the intention of finding a scheme of self-government that would be widely acceptable. The Convention became, in effect, a mechanism for converting the Labour Party to home rule, although it also allowed that party to incorporate into its policy a range of ideas from other sources. The Liberals goaded them towards a stronger position than they had had before, and introduced some fairly new ideas on open government and electoral reform. Various groups – notably the STUC – persuaded the Convention to set targets for much higher levels of women's participation in a Scottish parliament than have been achieved in Scottish representation at Westminster (or in local government). There was an awareness also that Scottish self-government would have to be seen in a European context: there was frequent reference to what is seen as the democratic deficit of the European Union, and a linking of that to the similar deficit at the Scottish Office; this is another version of the general concerns about the democratic inadequacy of technocracy.

In many respects, the appearance of this rhetoric is ironic. The Convention was a supreme instance of the Scottish corporatist process at work, its results based on an inscrutable process of consensual decision-making concealed by the 1980s rhetoric of popular sovereignty. But this gap between rhetoric and reality is familiar from Scottish twentieth-century history: the semi-revolutionary politics of the 1920s had as its end result the bureaucratic welfare state. The ability of the Scottish governing elites to convert radicalism into cautious reform frustrates the fundamentalists; but it also is a reason why the programme for limited self-government might eventually succeed.

In the present context, that might also frustrate the proponents of full Scottish statehood, notably the SNP but also now including some prominent people in the Labour and Liberal Parties. But even they recognise the limits on independence: for all but a tiny fringe, independence is now imagined as being within the European Union, and so is inevitably constrained by that framework. Whatever the prospects might realistically be for that policy, the pressure for it remains an unavoidable point of reference for the weaker versions. If only a limited parliament results, then that would not be the first time this century that radical nationalism had been successful in terms that it would refuse to recognise.

WILL PARLIAMENTARY SELF-GOVERNMENT COME ABOUT?

The reasons why a Scottish parliament might indeed be the outcome of the present debate are not necessarily the same that led us to doubt the effectiveness of Ian Lang's proposals. It is possible, after all, that his reform could fail to achieve anything worthwhile, and yet not provoke rebellion because it merely induced apathy.

But if we return to the reasons why nationalism has become strong in the period from the 1960s, we can find clues to what might happen next. The starting point is not cultural symbols, or even constitutional issues, but material benefit: it is that same instrumentalism that has governed Scottish attitudes to the Union since even before 1707 (and which, I argued, underlay attitudes to national autonomy throughout Europe and North America). The tensions that are driving the Labour Party towards a probably irrevocable commitment to self-government might appear to be party-political: as Tory politicians frequently point out, Labour is campaigning for Scottish home rule because they cannot win elections across Britain as a whole. But that claim of cynicism is actually a perceptive comment about the motivation of the Scottish electorate. Nairn (1989) points out that part of the UK political deal in the twentieth century was that the Scottish working class could use the Labour Party to secure temporary access to guiding the UK state at key moments of social reform. In this respect, it resembles nineteenth-century politics, except that the vehicle was then the Liberals. The decline of Labour in England might therefore be permanently excluding its Scottish supporters from any influence on the centre; and this could create pressures for new constitutional arrangements.

Moreover, the reason why the exclusion of Scottish Labour is now seen in increasingly nationalist terms is, yet again, precisely that Scotland has had, and still has, some autonomy. As Nairn (1989) has argued, the institutions that held the Union together now become reasons for breaking it, if their autonomy is being eroded. Coupled with economic stagnation, this could create a decay of legitimacy, in the sense that most Scottish voters would have stopped believing that their interests could be met through the UK state. There is some opinion-poll evidence that this stage might have already been reached: levels of economic optimism are very low, the state is not trusted to deliver effective welfare, and the importance given to constitutional change rose sharply after the result of the 1992 general election was known, coming to lie second only to unemployment among voters' concerns. Thus Scottish autonomy was an issue when other means to material welfare seemed blocked. Analogous processes could be under way in England too. The difference in Scotland (or perhaps Wales) is simply that constitutional reform appears to be available as a solution.

But if the problem is instrumental in this sense, then the dilemma for Labour (and the Liberals) is how to continue to argue that a merely federal arrangement could work any better. As we have seen, the reality of the autonomy of the units in federal systems has been highly circumscribed. A domestic parliament in a federal UK might offer control of the details of policy, but it could not allow Scotland to diverge as far from England as recent Scottish voting patterns suggest would be wanted. In the event of a Conservative government in Westminster and a non-Conservative majority in Scotland, there could be fundamental conflicts over taxation, public expenditure and the public provision of welfare services. In no federation in the world would a subordinate unit be allowed to deviate significantly from federal policy on such matters.

There are reasons to doubt also whether the UK state could be easily turned into a formal federation of the type that could be envisaged under the Labour and Liberal proposals. The basic political problem is that few people in the south of England seem to want it. If England is treated as a single unit, then it could be so big as to dominate Scotland, Wales and Northern Ireland. But if it were split up into autonomous regions, some of them would have no political identity at all; and so, as in Germany with its similarly artificial regions, there would be strong pressures towards uniformity. This, in turn, could conflict with Scottish pressures for diversity. We return then to our conclusions from studying Germany, the USA and Canada: a federation can work only if there is broad political agreement among its territorial units. When that consensus decays, there are strong tendencies towards disintegration. As in Canada, though, the advantage of a formal federation even in fissiparous conditions may eventually turn out to be that it provides the public forums in which these tensions can be resolved. That cannot be said of the current constitutional structures of the UK, where there is no process by which persistently distinctive Scottish voting patterns can be translated into a constructive discussion about reshaping the constitution.

Thus Labour, like the Conservatives, has made the mistake of taking the cultural-nationalist argument too seriously. A parliament with limited powers might be able to contribute to Scottish cultural developments, and might have some symbolic importance in creating a new political culture. But it could never have the freedom to deal with those material issues which will be far more decisive than cultural politics in determining the fate of the Union. The cultural revival of the 1980s was important in creating a new Scottish framework in which political reform could be imagined; but it was not the reason why a different future had to be imagined in the first place.

But this does not allow the easy conclusion that a radically democratic independence is the only real alternative to the constitutional status quo. No state anywhere in the world has successfully democratised a technocracy, and so the democratic frustrations which underlie the radical critiques of the Union would not necessarily be addressed by independence. Indeed, quite the opposite seems to be happening in the European Union, the framework which the SNP has chosen for its policy. Many commentators expect that the European Union will be federal within a generation; thus the constraints on an independent Scotland would be just as great as they would be within the UK under the schemes proposed by Labour or the Liberals. Only if the European Union evolves in the way that the Nordic Union has done will the individual states retain the freedom of a confederation. An independent Scotland might then have some scope to manoeuvre, although it would still be highly constrained by its economic ties to the rest of Europe (especially England). But it would be more democratic only if independence were accompanied by a social revolution. That might be more likely in Scotland than in the UK as a whole, but it is not guaranteed, and would have to be fought for.

CONCLUSIONS

This book has been the outline of a case rather than a claim to finished truth. Its main premise has been that, in discussing the autonomy which small nations can enjoy, we should pay more attention to events than to constitutional theories – to what happened in practice, rather than to what the rules said should happen. Deciding what happened is itself a matter for debate, involving not only historians and social scientists but also the discussions that inform politics, whether in the past or the present. Thus this essay is an intervention in a current debate. That debate is primarily about Scotland. But it is also about the evolution of the European Union, and Scotland can be taken as a paradigm of the interdependence of nations. Wider still, it is a debate about what kinds of democracy any nation can hope to have when faced also with the demands of external security and technical efficiency. The moment at which this essay appears is one where Scottish autonomy is being renegotiated, not formally through a constitutional conference, but by an opaque process of adjustment to popular pressures. This has happened many times before; and, as then, the Scottish past is being mobilised by all sides in the debate.

From the accounts of the past that have been offered here, there are four broad conclusions about its relevance to current politics, and therefore to the future of Scottish autonomy. The first point is that national independence is always only partial, and restricted to some governing elites. But that does not mean it is not real. It is the outcome of a set of constrained practices – bargaining with a dominant foreign power, or preserving the autonomy of traditional institutions, or exploiting social change to carve out new niches. Scotland has been quite successful at this, certainly far more so than many other small nations in Europe. It is only the condescension of retrospect that can pretend that we are the first generation to anguish about Scottish independence, or to worry about the very survival of the nation that has shaped us. The system that we now see in decay was the successful outcome of earlier nationalist pressure. Like all such settlements, it was provisional, lasting at most a couple of generations; and whatever we now evolve will decay and be reformed in turn. These points would have been equally true had Scotland retained a parliament after 1707, although the subsequent forms would have been different.

The second conclusion is about historiography rather than history. The knowledge that we purport to have about what happened in the past is inevitably partly a product of current concerns. For example, the true nature of Scottish education has been reinterpreted over and over again, often by writers using the same source materials. No writer about such matters can avoid being drawn into current political mobilisation. What is more, the past is available to be mobilised precisely because of the recurrent nationalist rhetoric of lament or loss: the past is a politically powerful weapon if people can be persuaded that things were better then. That rhetoric, in turn, is available only because autonomy is always partial, never as great as it could theoretically be. That is why some Scots of every generation since the Union and before have felt that the nation lacked independence. They were right; but so also were their opponents; and out of that tension has come constitutional change.

In one respect, however, that account of change is too sketchy. The groups which fight over Scotland have not been merely abstract interests, but have usually been competing social classes – the third conclusion. In Nairn's words, making a nation has almost always been making a class within the nation, a civil war as much as a war against an imperial power. Thus it was the professional classes who organised the Union in the first place, later the commercial middle class who forged the nineteenth-century settlement, and then a combination of working class and upwardly-mobile technocrats who created the welfare state. This point is especially relevant to radical politics, which, too, is fond of mobilising the past as utopia. Widespread popular agitation accompanied the 1832 reforms, the Disruption of 1843, the extension of the franchise to working-class men and to women, the reform of land laws in the Highlands, the origins and growth of the Labour Party, and the development of the welfare state. The outcomes of these actions were usually rather dull, thus providing later generations of radicals with a particular version of the rhetoric of loss. But the effect of these outcomes was nearly always a maintenance of the capacity of Scottish civil society to resolve its internal social and political tensions for itself. Thus the victorious elites would respond to the popular protests by producing a reform, though not a revolution. That, too, is probably what has been happening in the 1980s and 1990s.

Nevertheless, although these political tensions allow change, we cannot ever escape from the legacy of previous settlements. That is the fourth conclusion. We are constrained by the institutions which have been bequeathed to us – in our imagination as much as in our political practice. By this I mean that the institutions which were developed in previous settlements of Scottish autonomy shape our very understanding of Scotland, and therefore what we can envisage in the way of new reforms. But these institutions are much more subtle and complex than merely a parliament, and this is as true of Scotland as of nations that are formally independent: they are the schools, universities, media, churches and the myriad daily practices that develop informally and slowly. In that sense, nationalists have been successful: they, whether official or oppositionist, have created a world of dense Scottishness which creates a feeling of natural allegiance in nearly everyone who has been brought up here, or who has lived here for an appreciable length of time.

So the future of Scotland will continue to be constrained in this way. The country will continue to be only partly independent, and there will continue to be debates about whether that autonomy is enough. That may seem a depressing conclusion to romantics. But it does not mean that radical action is pointless. The nature of Scottish autonomy is available for debate as perhaps never before in the last three centuries. This is most obviously because the European Union provides a new framework for external security. But it is also because the current debates have raised issues about radical democratisation that are a challenge not only to the constitutional status quo but also to traditional nationalism. In that sense, the Scottish debate is at the centre of the questioning of technocracy. Scotland has recently produced plenty of aspirations that professional bureaucrats should no longer be allowed to control people's lives. Scotland may even have been especially well placed to see the moral inadequacy of such a rule by technocrats, because the Scottish Office has been a uniquely bureaucratic form of national government.

But, finally, this debate is not about whether Scotland exists, nor even about whether Scottish autonomy is possible. It is a civil conflict between social conservatives and proponents of radical visions, and both sides take the Scottish context for granted. The country contains these political struggles within its own evolving civil society and state institutions. Yet the debates which dominate Scottish politics are not unique; they are instances of very general concerns. Scotland has always shared in the development of the wider world, but to no greater an extent than any other small nation. That sharing is realistic, not abject; and willingly recognising its inevitability is a sign of national maturity.

Bibliographic Essay

CHAPTER 1

The nationalist debates around the Union are described by P. H. Scott (1979, 1992), Mitchison (1983) and Pryde (1950). Attitudes in the later eighteenth century are described by Sher (1985). The nationalist rhetoric of nineteenth-century Scottish historians and politicians is analysed by M. Ash (1980) and Fry (1992a), and the development of that rhetoric which surrounded the setting-up and growth of the Scottish Office is traced by Hanham (1965). Fry also describes the Whig interpretation of history. Edwin Muir's famous lament is in his *Scottish Journey* (reprinted in 1979 with an introduction by T. C. Smout). Walter Elliot's contribution is described by Mitchell (1990). The New Right's rediscovery of a classical liberal approach to national independence is discussed by Massie (1984a, b, c) and Fox et al. (1988). The nationalism of the 1980s is articulated by P. H. Scott (1989). Further discussion of the rhetoric of loss is found in Henderson (1992) for folksong, and Aitken (1984) for language. The parliamentary debates on the self-governing schools bill are in Parliamentary Debates (1989a, cols 624–5, 640, 647–8, 651, 682 and 691; and 1989b, col. 146).

Myths and related matters are debated by R. D. Anderson (1983), Morris (1990a), B. Anderson (1983) and A. Cohen (1985); see also chapter 2. The key texts of the 1970s were Kellas (new edition 1984), Nairn (1977) and Smout (1970). The process by which the radical left came to terms with Thatcherism can be traced in Rowbotham et al. (1979) and Hall (1989).

CHAPTER 2

The legal state is the term used by Poggi (1978, 1990). Civil society is discussed by Keane (1988) on Adam Ferguson, and Bobbio (1988) on Gramsci and Hegel. Kumar (1993) provides a clarification of the complexities of the term. The rule of law is debated at length in the reader by

Held et al. (1983), and for Scotland further points can be found in the *Laws of Scotland* (1987a, paras 627–37). Hall (1984) is a key essay on the development of the state, and Vajda (1988) explains the differences between eastern and western Europe. The developing meanings of sovereignty are described by Hinsley (1966), and its relationship to nationalism by Kedourie (1960). Legitimacy is analysed by Beetham (1991).

The technocratic state is discussed by Poggi (1978), Held (1984), Bell (1976), Keane (1988) and Kumar (1978). Beetham (1985) describes Weber's contribution. The origins of this state in welfarism are described by T. H. Marshall (1950), Rimlinger (1971) and – for Scotland – by Harvie (1981a). The problems of such a state are discussed by these same writers, and also by Marquand (1988), Middlemas (1979), Hayek (1960), Crouch (1979), Miller (1968), McLennan (1984) and T. Johnson (1972), who also outlines the role of professionals.

My preferred accounts of nationalism are by Nairn (1977), Kellas (1991), Keating (1988), A. D. Smith (1991), Duchacek (1986) and D. McCrone (1992a). Hobsbawm (1990) is infuriatingly metropolitan, but – as always – highly insightful. The late date at which separatism became widely popular is described in general by A. D. Smith (1991), and by Bradley (1971) and Garver (1978) for Czechoslovakia, Giner (1980) for Catalonia, and O. D. Edwards (1992) for Ireland. Further references are below, under chapter 5. The nationalism of the welfare state and communism in the twentieth century is analysed by Duchacek (1986). The notion of a federal society was first outlined by Livingston (1952, 1956). It can be found also in Vile (1961) on the USA, Bulpitt (1983) on the UK, Watts (1991) on Germany, and McNaught (1988) on Canada.

Myths – Scottish or otherwise – have been analysed by Durkheim (1961), D. McCrone (1992a) and McPherson (1983). The idea that society itself might be a symbolic construction is explained by Berger and Luckman (1979) and Cohen (1985). The importance in this of symbolic centres is argued by Geertz (1983) and A. D. Smith (1991). Scotland's official nationalism as a state within a state is described by Kellas (1984) and Morris (1990a). The role of civil society is described for Scotland by Nairn (1977), and in general by Hall (1984).

CHAPTERS 3 AND 4

Some general points about eighteenth- and nineteenth-century Scottish society and culture are made by Elias (1978), Nairn (1977), Calder (1985) and Keating (1988). The general political history of Scotland is told by Fry (1987, 1992b), Murdoch (1980), Hutchison (1986), Mitchison (1983), Sydney and Olive Checkland (1984), Campbell (1985), Lenman (1977, 1981) and Lynch (1991). Useful further comments are in Kellas (1984) and Harvie (1977, 1981a). Debates about the Union and dependency are presented by Cowan (1979), Whatley (1989, 1992), G. Marshall (1992),

Smout (1970, 1979, 1980), Wallerstein (1980) and Keith (1913). The social structure of nineteenth-century Scotland is analysed by D. McCrone (1992a). The 1832 Reform Act is analysed in all these works, and by Dyer (1983). The ending of the Liberal hegemony, similarly, is discussed widely, and also by McCaffrey (1971). There are few genuinely British histories, as Crick (1993) points out, but two excellent recent examples are Colley (1992) and Kearney (1989), the latter dealing with Ireland too. Bulpitt (1983), too, takes the diversity of the UK as a central theme. The nineteenth-century British constitution is searched for by Hanham (1969a).

The peculiarities of nineteenth-century Scottish nationalism have been studied recently in a path-breaking thesis by Morton (1994). Further comments are by Morris (1990a), Hutchison (1986), Fry (1987) and Finlay (1994), and the campaign for a Scottish Secretary is summarised by Hanham (1965). Craig (1993) shows the reaction of twentieth-century nationalists to what they saw as the feminine image of Scotland left over from the nineteenth.

Scots law in the eighteenth and nineteenth centuries is discussed by several entries in the *Laws of Scotland* (1987a, paras 627–37; 1987b, paras 711–19), and by Cairns (1992) on the Faculty of Advocates. The assimilation of commercial law is considered by Rodger (1992) and in the *Laws of Scotland* (1987a, paras 643–44; 1991, paras 301–11). Industry is dealt with in all the main histories, but notably by S. and O. Checkland (1984), J. Scott and Hughes (1980), and Campbell (1980). The operation of the Factory Acts can be found in Henriques (1971). Religion has been admirably covered by C. G. Brown (1987, 1988, 1993) and by C. G. Brown and Stephenson (1992), and the Disruption was the subject of a recent anniversary volume of essays (S. J. Brown and Fry, 1993). The story of moderatism in the eighteenth century is told lucidly by Sher (1982, 1985) and Phillipson (1969, 1970). The desire for assimilation is expanded on by Murdoch and Sher (1988), and the rise of the middle class by Nenadic (1988). The resulting images of Scotland are analysed by J. A. Smith (1970), Kidd (1993) and Chitnis (1976). Morris (1990b) discusses the real meaning of Victorian values. The phenomenon of tartanry is debated by a symposium in the *Bulletin of Scottish Politics* (1981), including a splenetic contribution from the present author which now seems greatly exaggerated. More measured accounts are by D. McCrone (1992a) and by Donaldson (1988), who also carried out pioneering work uncovering Scottish popular culture in the nineteenth century (Donaldson, 1986); see also Leonard (1990). The importance of common-sense philosophy is discussed by Davie (1961) and Beveridge and Turnbull (1989). Radical politics is discussed by Fraser (1988), and for the Highlands by Hunter (1976) and MacPhail (1989). Local government is dealt with by Whetstone (1981), and the poor law by Levitt (1988a, b) and A. Paterson (1976). Nineteenth-century philanthropy is discussed also by Checkland (1980), Cree (1993) and Morton (1994). The importance

186 THE AUTONOMY OF MODERN SCOTLAND

of emigration is made clear by M. Anderson and Morse (1990). The position of women is looked at in the essays in Breitenbach and Gordon (1992), by Breitenbach (1993), and by Leneman (1991).

The debate about a system of national schools can be found in Bain (1978), Withrington (1983, 1993), Myers (1972) and Hutchison (1986). The attitude of Catholics to the 1872 Act is described by Skinnider (1967). The universities are discussed by Davie (1961), R. D. Anderson (1983, 1992a, b), Withrington (1992), Forbes (1991) and Smout (1986, pp. 209–30). Domestic science for girls is debated by L. Moore (1992) and Corr (1990a, b).

CHAPTER 5

I relied on general histories for each country. For Ireland, I used R. F. Foster (1988), Lyons (1973) and O. D. Edwards (1992). Wandycz (1992) is a general history of east-central Europe. General accounts of Austria-Hungary are by Kann and David (1984), Breuilly (1982) and Taylor (1964). Czechoslovakia is dealt with by Garver (1978), Bradley (1971), Vajda (1988) and Korbel (1977), and Poland by Wandycz (1974), Davies (1984) and Dziewanowski (1977). The story of Catalonia is told by Brenan (1943), Read (1978), Giner (1980), Carr (1982), Moreno (1988, 1993) and Clegg (1987). Finnish history is in Klinge (1979, 1988), Jutikkala and Pirinen (1979), the essays in Engman and Kirby (1987), Andrén (1964) and Luostarinen (1989). The history of Norway is in Andrén (1964), Lindgren (1959), Derry (1973), Sandvik (1979) and Mykland (1979). Both Finland and Norway are the subject of several essays in the volume edited by Mitchison (1980).

These particular histories were supplemented by some general works: Goldstein (1983) on political oppression, and Breuilly (1982) and Keating (1988) on nationalism.

CHAPTER 6

General accounts of the twentieth-century UK state are given by Held (1984), T. Johnson (1972), McIntosh (1984), Hall (1984), Bell (1976), Bulpitt (1983), Marquand (1993) and Crick (1991). The process by which the welfare-state consensus was established is traced by Addison (1975) and Steward and Wield (1984). Middle opinion is discussed by Marwick (1964) and Harvie (1981b), and the continuing influence of Presbyterian morality by Maxwell (1982). The administration of Tom Johnston is discussed by Campbell (1979a) and Harvie (1981b).

Histories of Scotland in the twentieth century are by Kellas (1984), Fry (1987), Marr (1992), Harvie (1977, 1981a, 1992) and Midwinter et al. (1991). The growth of the Scottish Office and its penumbra of related bodies is described by Hanham (1969b), C. Hood et al. (1985), J. Burns (1960), G. E. Edwards (1972), Nairn (1989) and Keating (1988). Local government reform is described by Levitt (1988b), Pryde (n.d.), Shaw (1942) and Macintyre (1980). The economic effects of middle opinion in the 1930s are analysed by J. Foster and Woolfson (1986), Campbell (1979b, 1985) and Harvie (1981a, b). Post-1945 economic policy in Scotland and the UK is analysed by Saville (1985), C. Moore and Booth (1989), Randall (1985), G. McCrone (1985), Thompson (1984), Buxton (1985), N. Hood and Young (1982), the essays in Maclennan and Parr (1979), and B. Moore et al. (1977). Levitt (1994) provides the Cabinet papers. Post-1945 Scottish education is discussed by Gray et al. (1983), McPherson and Raab (1988), Humes (1986) and Hutchison (1992). The development of certification is traced by Philip (1992), the effects of comprehensive education by McPherson and Willms (1987), and the distinctive system of vocational education by Fairley and L. Paterson (1991). Labour Party education policy is discussed by Barker (1972). Housing is dealt with by Gibb and Maclennan (1985), who see it as, on the whole, a story of success. Bowley (1945) and Robertson (1989, 1992) are more critical. Further comments are by Midwinter et al. (1991) and Carmichael (1993). The radical action on Clydeside is discussed by Melling (1980, 1983); Levitt (1994) again gives the Cabinet papers. Social welfare is described by Cree (1993); see also Asquith (1992). Popular culture is discussed by Smout (1992), and the media by Macinnes (1992, 1993).

CHAPTER 7

As with chapter 5, I relied on general accounts. On Germany, the essays in Jeffrey and Savigear (1991) are wide-ranging and informative, especially that by Watts (1991). See also Leonardy (1991) and R. M. Burns (1977). Useful accounts of federalism in the USA are by Vile (1961), McSweeney (1987), Pritchett (1984), Wilson (1985) and Hodder-Williams (1987), and in Canada by Smiley (1977a, b, c), McNaught (1988), Bothwell et al. (1989), Mallory (1977), Gallant (1977), Cody (1992) and Heard (1991). For east-central Europe in general, see Wandycz (1992) and T. G. Ash (1989). For the former Czechoslovakia, see Bradley (1971), Glenny (1990) and Korbel (1977), and for Poland see Dziewanowski (1977), Ascherson (1981), Stehle (1965), Vajda (1988) and Davies (1984). On Ireland, the key works were R. F. Foster (1988), T. Brown (1985) and Lyons (1973). The works on the Nordic union which I used were Andrén (1964), Wendt (1958) and Solem (1977). On Norway's role in this, the works by Derry (1973) and Lindgren (1959) were useful, and on Denmark's I used W. G. Jones (1986), Miller (1968) and Oakley (1972).

CHAPTER 8

The problems of the technocratic state are traced by the authors mentioned under chapter 2, and also by Schlesinger (1992) on the European Union, Vile (1961) and Pritchett (1984) on the USA, Lawton (1992) and Burgess

(1993) on Canada, and Leonardy (1991) on Germany. The new Spanish constitution is discussed by Moreno (1993). The reaction of the Scottish elites is described by D. McCrone (1992b); see also *Scotland on Sunday* (1992) for a survey of their opinion, and *Scotland on Sunday* (1993) for an analysis of the politicisation of official boards and committees. The widening university experience of Scottish students is analysed by L. Paterson (1993), and the reducing opportunities for middle-class geographical mobility by Savage (1988). The Scottish cultural revival is discussed by Calder (1989). School boards are described by Munn (1992), and Local Enterprise Companies by Danson et al. (1990) and Young (1992). The role of local authorities in economic development is explained by Lloyd and Rowan-Robinson (1988). The origins and workings of the Standing Commission on the Scottish Economy are analysed by P. Smith and M. Burns (1988). Wider changes in the Scottish economy are presented by G. McCrone (1993), Ashcroft (1988), and J. Scott and Hughes (1980). The crisis in UK economic policy is outlined by Hutton (1993a, b).

The scope for a rejuvenated managed autonomy is assessed by Parry (1993), Nairn (1993) and D. McCrone (1992a). The approach of the government after the 1992 general election can be found in Macwhirter (1993), *The Herald* (1992) and P. Jones (1993). In particular, the new and more open attitude to appointing opposition members of administrative agencies is found in *The Scotsman* (1993). The forces that might possibly lead to a Scottish parliament are analysed by Nairn (1989), Kellas (1989, 1990, 1992) and L. Paterson et al. (1992). Diverging political opinions in the UK are examined by Curtice (1988, 1992). Further opinion-poll attitudes are traced by MORI (for example, 1993); attitudes to the monarchy etc. are in L. Paterson (1991), and to self-government in L. Paterson (1990).

Bibliography

Addison, P. (1975), *The Road to 1945,* London: Quartet.

Aitken, A. J. (1984), 'Scots and English in Scotland', in Peter Trudgill (ed.), *Language in the British Isles,* Cambridge: Cambridge University Press.

Anderson, B. (1983), *Imagined Communities: Reflections on the Origins and Spread of Nationalism,* London: Verso.

Anderson, M. and Morse, D. (1990), 'The people', in W. H. Fraser and R. J. Morris (eds), *People and Society in Scotland, vol. II, 1830–1914,* Edinburgh: John Donald, pp. 8–45.

Anderson, R. D. (1983), *Education and Opportunity in Victorian Scotland,* Edinburgh: Edinburgh University Press.

—— (1992a), 'The Scottish university tradition: past and future', in J. Carter and D. Withrington (eds), *Scottish Universities: Distinctiveness and Diversity,* Edinburgh: John Donald, pp. 67–78.

—— (1992b), *Universities and Elites in Britain since 1800,* London: Economic and Social History Society.

Andrén, N. (1964), *Government and Politics in the Nordic Countries,* Stockholm: Almqvist and Wiksell.

Ascherson, N. (1981), *The Polish August,* Harmondsworth: Penguin.

Ash, M. (1980), *The Strange Death of Scottish History,* Edinburgh: Ramsay Head.

Ash, T. G. (1989), *The Uses of Adversity,* Harmondsworth: Granta Books.

Ashcroft, B. (1988), 'Scottish economic performance and the environment', in D. McCrone and A. Brown (eds), *Scottish Government Yearbook 1988,* Edinburgh: Unit for the Study of Government in Scotland, pp. 238–58.

Asquith, S. (1992), 'Coming of age: 21 years of the children's hearings system', in L. Paterson and D. McCrone (eds), *Scottish Government Yearbook 1992,* Edinburgh: Unit for the Study of Government in Scotland, pp. 157–72.

Bain, W. (1978), ' "Attacking the citadel": James Moncrieff's proposals to reform Scottish education, 1851–1869', *Scottish Educational Review,* 10, pp. 5–14.

Barker, R. (1972), *Education and Politics 1900–1959: a Study of the Labour Party,* Oxford: Clarendon.

Beetham, D. (1985), *Max Weber and the Theory of Modern Politics,* London: George Allen and Unwin.

—— (1991), *The Legitimation of Power,* London: Macmillan.

Bell, D. (1976), *The Coming of Post-Industrial Society,* Harmondsworth: Penguin.

Berger, P. and Luckman, T. (1979), *The Social Construction of Reality: a Treatise in the Sociology of Knowledge,* Harmondsworth: Penguin.

Beveridge, C. and Turnbull, R. (1989), *The Eclipse of Scottish Culture: Inferiorism and the Intellectuals*, Edinburgh: Polygon.

Blair, P. (1991), 'Federalism, legalism and political reality: the record of the Federal Constitutional Court', in Jeffrey and Savigear (eds), *German Federalism Today*, Leicester: Leicester University Press, pp. 63–83.

Bobbio, N. (1988), 'Gramsci and the concept of civil society', in Keane (ed.), *Civil Society and the State*, London: Verso, pp. 73–99.

Bothwell, R., Drummond, I. and English, J. (1989), *Canada since 1945: Power, Politics, and Provincialism*, Toronto: University of Toronto Press.

Bowley, M. (1945), *Housing and the State, 1919–1944*, London: George Allen and Unwin.

Bradley, J. F. N. (1971), *Czechoslovakia: a Short History*, Edinburgh: Edinburgh University Press.

Breitenbach, E. (1993), 'Out of sight, out of mind? The history of women in Scottish politics', *Scottish Affairs*, no. 2, pp. 58–70.

Breitenbach, E. and Gordon, E. (1992), *Out of Bounds: Women in Scottish Society, 1800–1945*, Edinburgh: Edinburgh University Press.

Brenan, G. (1943), *The Spanish Labyrinth*, Cambridge: Cambridge University Press.

Breuilly, J. (1982), *Nationalism and the State*, Manchester: Manchester University Press.

Brown, C. G. (1987), *The Social History of Religion in Scotland, 1780–1914*, London: Methuen.

—— (1988), 'Religion and social change', in T. M. Devine and T. Mitchison (eds), *People and Society in Scotland, vol. I, 1760–1830*, Edinburgh: John Donald, pp. 143–62.

—— (1992), 'Religion and secularism', in A. Dickson and J. H. Treble (eds), *People and Society in Scotland, vol. III, 1914–1990*, Edinburgh: John Donald, pp. 48–79.

—— (1993), *The People in the Pews: Religion and Society in Scotland since 1780*, Glasgow: The Economic and Social History Society of Scotland.

Brown, C. G. and Stephenson, J. D. (1992), ' "Sprouting wings"?: women and religion in Scotland, c. 1890–1950', in Breitenbach and Gordon (eds), *Out of Bounds: Women in Scottish Society, 1800–1945*, Edinburgh: Edinburgh University Press, pp. 95–120.

Brown, S. J. and Fry, M. (1993), *Scotland in the Age of the Disruption*, Edinburgh: Edinburgh University Press.

Brown, T. (1985), *Ireland: a Social and Cultural History, 1922–1985*, London: Fontana.

Bulletin of Scottish Politics (1981), 'Ossian and after: the politics of tartanry', Edinburgh: Scottish International Institute, pp. 56–86.

Bulpitt, J. (1983), *Territory and Power in the United Kingdom*, Manchester: Manchester University Press.

Burgess, M. (1993), 'Constitutional reform in Canada and the 1992 referendum', *Parliamentary Affairs*, 46, pp. 363–79.

Burns, J. (1960), 'The Scottish committees of the House of Commons, 1948–1959', *Political Studies*, 8, pp. 272–96.

Burns, R. M. (1977), 'Second chambers: German experience and Canadian needs', in J. P. Meekison (ed.), *Canadian Federalism: Myth or Reality*, Toronto: Methuen, pp. 188–214.

Buxton, N. (1985), 'The Scottish economy, 1945–1979: performance, structure and problems', in Saville (ed.), *The Economic Development of Modern Scotland, 1950–1980*, Edinburgh: John Donald, pp. 47–78.

Cairns, J. (1992), 'A history of the Faculty of Advocates', in *The Laws of Scotland,* vol. 13, Edinburgh: Butterworths, paras 1,239–85.

Calder, A. (1985), 'Missionary Scotland: the Arnold history of Scotland', *Cencrastus,* no. 21, p. 37.

—— (1989), 'Autonomy and Scottish culture', *Cencrastus,* no. 34, Edinburgh, p. 6–10.

Campbell, R. H. (1979a), 'The committee of ex-Secretaries of State for Scotland and industrial policy', *Scottish Industrial History,* 2, pp. 1–10.

——(1979b), 'The Scottish Office and the Special Areas in the 1930s', *The Historical Journal,* 22, pp. 167–83.

—— (1980), *The Rise and Fall of Scottish Industry,* Edinburgh: John Donald.

—— (1985), *Scotland since 1707: the Rise of an Industrial Society,* Edinburgh: John Donald.

Carlyle, T. (1899), 'The portraits of John Knox', in *The Works of Thomas Carlyle, vol. XXX: Critical and Miscellaneous Essays V,* London: Chapman and Hall, pp. 313–67.

Carmichael, P. (1993), 'Municipal finance in Glasgow: strategies and performance since 1980', *Scottish Affairs,* no. 4, pp. 54–66.

Carr, R. (1982), *Spain, 1808–1975,* Oxford: Oxford University Press.

Checkland, O. (1980), *Philanthropy in Victorian Scotland: Social Welfare and the Voluntary Principle,* Edinburgh: John Donald.

Checkland, S. and Checkland, O. (1984), *Industry and Ethos: Scotland, 1832–1914,* London: Edward Arnold.

Chitnis, A. C. (1976), *The Scottish Enlightenment: a Social History,* London: Croom Helm.

Clegg, T. (1987), 'Spain', in E. Page and M. J. Goldsmith (eds), *Central and Local Government Relations,* London: Sage, pp. 130–55.

Cockburn, H. (1988), *Memorials of His Time,* Edinburgh: Mercat Press.

Cody, H. (1992), 'MPs and the peripheral predicament in Canada and Britain', *Political Studies,* 40, pp. 346–55.

Cohen, A. (1985), *The Symbolic Construction of Community,* Chichester: Ellis Horwood.

Colley, L. (1992), *Britons: Forging the Nation, 1707–1837,* New Haven: Yale University Press.

Corr, H. (1990a), ' "Home Rule" in Scotland: the teaching of housework in Scottish schools, 1872–1914', in F. Paterson and J. Fewell (eds), *Girls in their Prime,* Edinburgh: Scottish Academic Press, pp. 38–53.

—— (1990b), 'An exploration into Scottish education', in W. H. Fraser and R. J. Morris (eds), *People and Society in Scotland, vol. II, 1830–1914,* Edinburgh: John Donald, pp. 290–309.

Cowan, E. J. (1979). 'The Union of the Crowns and the crisis of the constitution in seventeenth-century Scotland', in S. Dyrvik, K. Mykland and J. Oldervoll (eds), *The Satellite State in the Seventeenth and Eighteenth Centuries,* Bergen: Universitetforlaget, pp. 121–40.

Craig, C. (1993), Paper presented to a symposium: *Destabilising the Drunk Man,* Edinburgh University, 26 February.

Cree, V. E. (1993), *Social Work's Changing Task: an Analysis of the Changing Task of Social Work as Seen through the History and Development of one Scottish Voluntary Organisation, Family Care,* Ph.D. thesis, Edinburgh University.

Crick, B. (1991), 'The English and the British', in Crick (ed.), *National Identities,* Oxford: Blackwell, pp. 90–104.

—— (1993), 'Essay on Britishness', *Scottish Affairs,* no. 2, pp. 71–83.

Crouch, C. (1979), *State, Economy and Society in Contemporary Capitalism,* London: Croom Helm.

Curtice, J. (1988), 'One nation?', in R. Jowell, S. Witherspoon and L. Brook (eds), *British Social Attitudes: the Fifth Report,* Aldershot: Gower, pp. 127–54.

—— (1992), 'The north-south divide', in R. Jowell, L. Brook, G. Prior and B. Taylor (eds), *British Social Attitudes: the Ninth Report,* Aldershot: Gower, pp. 71–88.

Daiches, D. (1979), *Fletcher of Saltoun: Selected Writings,* Edinburgh: Scottish Academic Press.

Danson, M., Fairley, J., Lloyd, M. G. and Newlands, D. (1990), 'Scottish Enterprise: an evolving approach to integrating economic development in Scotland', in A. Brown and R. Parry (eds), *Scottish Government Yearbook 1990,* Edinburgh: Unit for the Study of Government in Scotland, pp. 168–94.

Davie, G. E. (1961), *The Democratic Intellect: Scotland and her Universities in the Nineteenth Century,* Edinburgh: Edinburgh University Press.

Davies, N. (1984), *Heart of Europe: a Short History of Poland,* Oxford: Oxford University Press.

Derry, T. K. (1973), *A History of Modern Norway, 1814–1972,* Oxford: Oxford University Press.

Donaldson, W. (1986), *Popular Literature in Victorian Scotland,* Aberdeen: Aberdeen University Press.

—— (1988), *The Jacobite Song: Political Myth and National Identity,* Aberdeen: Aberdeen University Press.

Duchacek, I. D. (1986), *The Territorial Dimension of Politics: Within, Among, and Across Nations,* Colombo: Westview.

Durkheim, E. (1961), *The Elementary Forms of the Religious Life,* New York: Collier Books.

Dyer, M. (1983), 'Mere detail and machinery: the Great Reform Act and the effects of redistribution in Scottish representation, 1832–1868', *Scottish Historical Review,* 62, pp. 17–34.

Dziewanowski, M. K. (1977), *Poland in the Twentieth Century,* New York: Columbia University Press.

Edwards, G. E. (1972), 'The Scottish grand committee, 1958–1970', *Parliamentary Affairs,* 25, pp. 303–25.

Edwards, O. D. (1992), 'Who invented devolution?', in L. Paterson and D. McCrone (eds), *The Scottish Government Yearbook 1992,* Edinburgh: Unit for the Study of Government in Scotland, pp. 36–49.

Elias, N. (1978), *The Civilising Process: Vol. I, the History of Manners,* Oxford: Basil Blackwell.

Engman, M. and Kirby, D. (1987), *Finland: People, Nation, State,* London: Hurst.

Fairley, J. and Paterson, L. (1991), 'The reform of vocational education and training in Scotland', *Scottish Educational Review,* 23, pp. 68–77.

Finlay, R. (1994), 'Controlling the past: Scottish historiography in the nineteenth and twentieth centuries', *Scottish Affairs,* to appear.

Forbes, A. (1991), Unpublished paper on the 1876 Scottish Universities Commission (read on her behalf by Donald Withrington), History of Education Society, Edinburgh.

Forsyth, M. (1991), 'Introduction', in Jeffrey and Savigear (eds), *German Federalism Today,* Leicester: Leicester University Press, pp. vii–ix.

Foster, J. and Woolfson, C. (1986), *The Politics of the ucs Work-in,* London: Lawrence and Wishart.

Foster, R. F. (1988), *Modern Ireland, 1600–1972,* Harmondsworth: Penguin.

Fox, L., Mayall, M. and Cooke, A. (1988), *Making Unionism Positive,* London: Centre for Policy Studies.

Fraser, W. H. (1988), 'Patterns of protest', in T. M. Devine and R. Mitchison (eds), *People and Society in Scotland, vol I, 1760–1830,* Edinburgh: John Donald, pp. 268–91.

Fry, M. (1987), *Patronage and Principle: a Political History of Modern Scotland,* Aberdeen: Aberdeen University Press.

—— (1992a), 'The Whig interpretation of Scottish history', in I. Donnachie and C. Whatley (eds), *The Manufacture of Scottish History,* Edinburgh: Polygon, pp. 72–89.

—— (1992b), *The Dundas Despotism,* Edinburgh: Edinburgh University Press.

Gallant, E. (1977), 'The machinery of federal-provincial relations', in J. P. Meekison (ed.), *Canadian Federalism: Myth or Reality,* Toronto: Methuen, pp. 216–28.

Garver, B. M. (1978), *The Young Czech Party, 1874–1901, and the Emergence of a Multi-party System,* New Haven: Yale University Press.

Geertz, C. (1983), 'Centers, kings, and charisma: reflections on the symbolics of power', in Geertz, *Local Knowledge: Further Essays in Interpretative Anthropology,* New York: Basic Books, pp. 121–46.

Gibb, A. and Maclennan, D. (1985), 'Policy and process in Scottish housing, 1950–1980', in Saville (ed.), *The Economic Development of Modern Scotland, 1950–1980,* Edinburgh: John Donald, pp. 270–91.

Giner, S. (1980), *The Social Structure of Catalonia,* Sheffield: Sheffield University.

Glenny, M. (1990), *The Rebirth of History,* Harmondsworth: Penguin.

Goldstein, R. J. (1983), *Political Repression in Nineteenth Century Europe,* London: Croom Helm.

Gray, J., McPherson, A. and Raffe, D. (1983), *Reconstructions of Secondary Education: Theory, Myth and Practice since the War,* London: Routledge.

Hall, S. (1984), 'The state in question', in G. McLennan, D. Held and S. Hall (eds), *The Idea of the Modern State,* Milton Keynes: Open University Press, pp. 1–28.

—— (1989), 'The meaning of New Times', in S. Hall and M. Jacques (eds), *New Times,* London: Lawrence and Wishart, pp. 116–36.

Hanham, H. J. (1965), 'The creation of the Scottish Office', *Juridical Review,* 10, pp. 205–44.

—— (ed.) (1969a), *The Nineteenth Century Constitution, 1815–1914,* Cambridge: Cambridge University Press.

—— (1969b), 'The development of the Scottish Office', in J. N. Wolfe (ed.), *Government and Nationalism in Scotland,* Edinburgh: Edinburgh University Press, pp. 51–70.

Harvie, C. (1977), *Scotland and Nationalism: Scottish Society and Politics, 1707–1977.* London: George Allen and Unwin.

—— (1981a), *No Gods and Precious Few Heroes,* London: Edward Arnold.

—— (1981b), 'Labour and Scottish government: the age of Tom Johnson', *Bulletin of Scottish Politics,* no. 2, pp. 1–20.

—— (1992), 'Scottish politics', in A. Dickson and J. H. Treble (eds), *People and Society in Scotland, vol. III, 1914–1990,* Edinburgh: John Donald, pp. 241–60.

Hayek, F. (1960), *The Constitution of Liberty,* London: Routledge and Kegan Paul.

Heard, A. (1991), *Canadian Constitutional Conventions,* Oxford: Oxford University Press.

Held, D. (1984), 'Central perspectives on the modern state', in G. McLennan, D.

Held and S. Hall (eds), *The Idea of the Modern State,* Milton Keynes: Open University Press, pp. 29–79.

Held, D., Anderson, J., Gieben, B., Hall, S., Harris, L., Lewis, P., Parker, N. and Turok, B. (eds) (1983), *States and Societies,* Oxford: Basil Blackwell.

Henderson, H. (1992), *Alias MacAlias,* Edinburgh: Polygon.

Henriques, U. R. Q. (1971), 'An early factory inspector: James Stuart of Dunearn', *Scottish Historical Review,* 50, pp. 18–46.

The Herald (1992), 'Major faces up to English brand of nationalism', Glasgow, 12 September.

Hinsley, F. H. (1966), *Sovereignty,* London: Watts.

Hobsbawm, E. (1990), *Nations and Nationalism since 1780: Programme, Myth and Reality,* Cambridge: Cambridge University Press.

Hodder-Williams, R. (1987), 'Making the constitution's meaning fit for the 1980s', in J. Smith (ed.), *The American Constitution: the First 200 Years,* Exeter: University of Exeter Press, pp. 97–110.

Hood, C. Huby, M. and Dunsire, A. (1985), 'From growth to retrenchment', in D. McCrone (ed.), *Scottish Government Yearbook 1985,* Edinburgh: Unit for the Study of Government in Scotland, pp. 53–76.

Hood, N. and Young, S. (1982), *Multinationals in Retreat,* Edinburgh: Edinburgh University Press.

Humes, W. (1986), *The Leadership Class in Scottish Education,* Edinburgh: John Donald.

Hunter, J. (1976), *The Making of the Crofting Community,* Edinburgh: John Donald.

Hutchison, I. G. C. (1986), *A Political History of Modern Scotland, 1832–1924,* Edinburgh: John Donald.

—— (1992), 'The Scottish Office and the Scottish universities', in J. Carter and D. Withrington (eds), *Scottish Universities: Distinctiveness and Diversity,* Edinburgh: John Donald, pp. 56–66.

Hutton, W. (1993a), 'The not-spending sickness', *Guardian,* London, 28 January.

—— (1993b), 'Moment of truth for the rentier state', *Guardian,* London, 5 April.

Jeffrey, C. and Savigear, P. (eds) (1991), *German Federalism Today,* Leicester: Leicester University Press.

Johnson, N. (1991), 'Territory and power: some historical developments', in Jeffrey and Savigear (eds) (1991), *German Federalism Today,* Leicester: Leicester University Press, pp. 8–22.

Johnson, T. (1972), *Professions and Power,* London: Macmillan.

Jones, P. (1993), 'Green shoots of constitutional recovery', *The Scotsman,* Edinburgh, 16 January.

Jones, W. G. (1986), *Denmark – a Modern History,* London: Croom Helm.

Jutikkala, E. and Pirinen, K. (1979), *A History of Finland,* London: Heinemann.

Kann, R. A. and David, Z. V. (1984), *The Peoples of the Eastern Habsburg Lands, 1526–1918,* Seattle: University of Washington Press.

Keane, J. (1988), 'Despotism and democracy', in Keane (ed.), *Civil Society and the State,* London: Verso, pp. 35–71.

Kearney, H. (1989), *The British Isles: a History of Four Nations,* Cambridge: Cambridge University Press.

Keating, M. (1988), *State and Regional Nationalism,* Brighton: Wheatsheaf.

Kedourie, E. (1960), *Nationalism,* London: Hutchinson.

Keith, T. (1913), 'The influence of the Convention of Royal Burghs of Scotland on the economic development of Scotland before 1707', *Scottish Historical Review,* 10, pp. 250–71.

Kellas, J. (1984), *The Scottish Political System,* Cambridge: Cambridge University Press.
—— (1989), 'Prospects for a new Scottish political system', *Parliamentary Affairs,* 42, pp. 519–32.
—— (1990), 'Constitutional options for Scotland', *Parliamentary Affairs,* 43, pp. 426–34.
—— (1991), *The Politics of Nationalism and Ethnicity,* London: Macmillan.
—— (1992), 'The Scottish Constitutional Convention', in L. Paterson and D. McCrone (eds), *Scottish Government Yearbook 1992,* Edinburgh: Unit for the Study of Government in Scotland, pp. 50–8.
Kidd, C. (1993), *Subverting Scotland's Past: Scottish Whig Historians and the Creation of an Anglo-Scottish Identity, 1689–c. 1830,* Cambridge: Cambridge University Press.
Klatt, H. (1991), 'Centralising trends in the Federal Republic: the record of the Kohl Chancellorship', in Jeffrey and Savigear (eds), *German Federalism Today,* Leicester: Leicester University Press, pp. 120–37.
Klinge, M. (1979), 'The growth of Finnish national consciousness in the age of the Enlightenment – the economic, social and cultural factors', in S. Dyrvik, K. Mykland and J. Oldervoll (eds), *The Satellite State in the Seventeenth and Eighteenth Centuries,* Bergen: Universitetforlaget, pp. 174–84.
—— (1988), *A Brief History of Finland,* Helsinki: Otava.
Korbel, J. (1977), *Twentieth Century Czechoslovakia,* New York: Columbia University Press.
Kumar, K. (1978), *Prophecy and Progress: the Sociology of Industrial and Post-Industrial Society,* Harmondsworth: Penguin.
—— (1993), 'Civil society: an inquiry into the usefulness of an historical term', *British Journal of Sociology,* 44, pp. 375–401.
Lang, I. (1993), 'Fly on the wall', *The Weekend Scotsman,* 27 November, p. 3.
Laws of Scotland (1987a), 'Sources of law (general and historical)', Edinburgh: Butterworths, vol. 22.
—— (1987b), 'Constitutional law', Edinburgh: Butterworths, vol. 5.
—— (1991), 'Companies', Edinburgh: Butterworths, vol. 4.
Lawton, W. (1992), 'The crisis of the nation-state: a post-modernist Canada?', *Acadiensis,* 22, pp. 134–45.
Leneman, L. (1991), *A Guid Cause: the Women's Suffrage Movement in Scotland,* Aberdeen: Aberdeen University Press.
Lenman, B. (1977), *An Economic History of Modern Scotland,* London: Batsford.
—— (1981), *Integration, Enlightenment and Industrialisation: Scotland 1746–1832,* London: Edward Arnold.
Leonard, T. (1990), *Radical Renfrew,* Edinburgh: Polygon.
Leonardy, U. (1991), 'The three-levels-system: working structures of German federalism', Paper presented to the International Political Science Association, Buenos Aires, 21–25 July.
Levitt, I. (1988a), *Government and Social Conditions in Scotland, 1845–1919,* Edinburgh: Scottish History Society.
—— (1988b), *Poverty and Welfare in Scotland, 1890–1948,* Edinburgh: Edinburgh University Press.
—— (1994), *The Scottish Office: Depression and Reconstruction, 1919–1959,* Edinburgh: Scottish History Society.
Lindgren, R. E. (1959), *Norway-Sweden: Union, Disunion, and Scandinavian Integration,* Princeton: Princeton University Press.

Livingston, W. S. (1952), 'A note on the nature of federalism', *Political Science Quarterly*, 67, pp. 81–95.
—— (1956), *Federalism and Constitutional Change,* Oxford: Clarendon Press.
Lloyd, M. G. and Rowan-Robinson, J. (1988), 'Local authority responses to economic uncertainty in Scotland', in D. McCrone and A. Brown (eds), *Scottish Government Yearbook 1988,* Edinburgh: Unit for the Study of Government in Scotland, pp. 289–346.
Luostarinen, H. (1989), 'Finnish Russophobia: the story of an enemy image', *Journal of Peace Research,* 26, pp. 123–37.
Lynch, M. (1991), *Scotland: a New History,* London: Century.
Lyons, F. S. L. (1973), *Ireland since the Famine,* London: Fontana.
McCaffrey, J. F. (1971), 'The origins of Liberal Unionism in the west of Scotland', *Scottish Historical Review,* 50, pp. 47–71.
McCrone, D. (1992a), *Understanding Scotland: the Sociology of a Stateless Nation,* London: Routledge.
—— (1992b), 'Towards a principled elite: Scottish elites in the twentieth century', in A. Dickson and J. H. Treble (eds), *People and Society in Scotland, vol. III, 1914–1990,* Edinburgh: John Donald, pp. 174–200.
McCrone, G. (1985), 'The role of government', in Saville (ed.), *The Economic Development of Modern Scotland, 1950–1980,* Edinburgh: John Donald, pp. 195–213.
—— (1993), 'The Scottish economy and European integration', *Scottish Affairs,* no. 4, pp. 5–22.
Macinnes, J. (1992), 'The press in Scotland', *Scottish Affairs,* no. 1, pp. 137–49.
—— (1993), 'The broadcast media in Scotland', *Scottish Affairs,* no. 2, pp. 84–98.
McIntosh, M. (1984), 'The family, regulation, and the public sphere', in G. McLennan, D. Held and S. Hall (eds), *The Idea of the Modern State,* Milton Keynes: Open University Press, pp. 204–40.
Macintyre, S. (1980), *Little Moscows,* London: Croom Helm.
Maclennan, D. and Parr, J. B. (1979), *Regional Policy: Past Experience and New Directions,* Oxford: Martin Robertson.
McLennan, G. (1984), 'The contours of British politics: representative democracy and social class', in G. McLennan, D. Held and S. Hall (eds), *State and Society in Contemporary Britain,* Cambridge: Polity, pp. 241–77.
McNaught, K. (1988), *The Penguin History of Canada,* Harmondsworth: Penguin.
MacPhail, I. M. M. (1989), *The Crofters' War,* Stornoway: Acair.
McPherson, A. (1983), 'An angle on the geist: persistence and change in the Scottish educational tradition', in W. M. Humes and H. M. Paterson (eds), *Scottish Culture and Scottish Education, 1800–1980,* Edinburgh: John Donald, pp. 216–43.
—— (1990), 'How good is Scottish education, and how good is the case for change?', in A. Brown and R. Parry (eds), *Scottish Government Yearbook 1990,* Edinburgh: Unit for the Study of Government in Scotland, pp. 153–67.
McPherson, A. and Raab, C. D. (1988), *Governing Education,* Edinburgh: Edinburgh University Press.
McPherson, A. and Willms, J. D. (1987), 'Equalisation and improvement: some effects of comprehensive reorganisation in Scotland', *Sociology,* 21, pp. 509–39.
McSweeney, D. (1987), 'Political parties and the constitution in the twentieth century', in J. Smith (ed.), *The American Constitution: the First 200 Years,* Exeter: University of Exeter Press, pp. 83–96.
Macwhirter, I. (1993), 'Scottish politics at Westminster', *Scottish Affairs,* no. 4, pp. 111–21.

Mallory, J. R. (1977), 'The five faces of federalism', in J. P. Meekison (ed.), *Canadian Federalism: Myth or Reality,* Toronto: Methuen, pp. 19–30.

Marquand, D. (1988), *The Unprincipled Society: New Demands and Old Politics,* London: Fontana.

—— (1993), 'The twilight of the British state? Henry Dubb versus sceptred awe', *Political Quarterly,* 64, pp 210–21.

Marr, A. (1992), *The Battle for Scotland,* Harmondsworth: Penguin.

Marshall. G. (1992), *Presbyteries and Profits,* Edinburgh: Edinburgh University Press.

Marshall, T. H. (1950), *Citizenship and Social Class, and Other Essays,* Cambridge: Cambridge University Press.

Marwick, A. (1964), 'Middle opinion in the thirties: planning, progress, and political "agreement"', *English Historical Review,* 79, pp. 285–98.

Massie, A. (1984a). 'Scotland – Omega One', *The Spectator,* 14 January, pp. 8–10.

—— (1984b), 'Towards economic self-rule', *The Spectator,* 21 January, pp. 14–15.

—— (1984c), 'A curriculum for Scotland', *The Spectator,* 4 February, pp. 14–15

Maxwell, S. (1982), 'The secular pulpit: Presbyterian democracy in the twentieth century', in H. M. Drucker and N. L. Drucker (eds), *Scottish Government Yearbook 1982,* Edinburgh: Unit for the Study of Government in Scotland, pp. 181–98.

Melling, J. (1980), 'Clydeside housing, and the evolution of state rent control, 1900–1939', in Melling (ed.), *Housing, Social Policy, and the State,* London: Croom Helm, pp. 139–67.

—— (1983), *Rent Strikes,* Edinburgh: Polygon.

Middlemas, K. (1979), *Politics in Industrial Society,* London: Andre Deutsch.

Midwinter, A., Keating, M. and Mitchell, J. (1991), *Politics and Public Policy in Scotland,* Edinburgh: Mainstream.

Miller, K. E. (1968), *Government and Politics in Denmark,* Boston: Houghton-Mifflin.

Mitchell, J. (1990), *Conservatives and the Union,* Edinburgh: Edinburgh University Press.

Mitchison, R. (ed.) (1980), *The Roots of Nationalism: Studies in Northern Europe,* Edinburgh: John Donald.

—— (1983), *Lordship to Patronage: Scotland 1603–1745,* London: Edward Arnold.

Moore, B., Rhodes, J. and Tyler, P. (1977), 'The impact of regional policy in the 1970s', *CES Review,* 1, pp. 67–77.

Moore, C. and Booth, S. (1989), *Managing Competition: Meso-Corporatism, Pluralism, and the Negotiated Order in Scotland,* Oxford: Oxford University Press.

Moore, L. (1992), 'Educating for the "women's sphere": domestic training versus intellectual discipline', in Breitenbach and Gordon (eds), *Out of Bounds: Women in Scottish Society, 1800–1945,* Edinburgh: Edinburgh University Press, pp. 10–41.

Moreno, L. (1988), 'Scotland and Catalonia: the path to home rule', in D. McCrone and A. Brown (eds), *Scottish Government Yearbook 1988,* Edinburgh: Unit for the Study of Government in Scotland, pp. 166–82.

—— (1993), 'Ethnoterritorial concurrence and imperfect federalism in Spain', paper presented at the Joint Conference of the International Association of Centres for Federal Studies and the International Political Science Association on *Federalism: a Contemporary Perspective,* Centre for Constitutional Analysis, Kwae Maritane, South African Republic, 1–6 August.

MORI (1993), *British Public Opinion,* London: MORI.

Morris, R. J. (1990a), 'Scotland: 1830–1914: the making of a nation within a nation', in W. H. Fraser and R. J. Morris (eds), *People and Society in Scotland, vol. II, 1830–1914*, Edinburgh: John Donald, pp. 1–7.

—— (1990b), 'Victorian values in Scotland and England', paper to Royal Society of Edinburgh/British Academy symposium on Victorian Values, 14 December 1990.

Morton, G. (1994), *Unionist Nationalism: The Historical Construction of Scottish National Identity, Edinburgh, 1830–1860*, Ph.D. thesis, Edinburgh University.

Mosher, F. C. (1985), 'The professional state', in F. E. Rourke (ed.), *Bureaucratic Power in National Policy Making*, Boston: Little, Brown, pp. 74–86.

Muir, E. (1979), *Scottish Journey*, Edinburgh: Mainstream.

Munn, P. (1992), 'Devolved management of schools and FE colleges: a victory for the producer over the consumer?', in L. Paterson and D. McCrone (eds), *Scottish Government Yearbook 1992*, Edinburgh: Unit for the Study of Government in Scotland, pp. 142–56.

Murdoch, A. (1980), *'The People Above': Politics and Administration in Mid-Eighteenth Century Scotland*, Edinburgh: John Donald.

Murdoch, A. and Sher, R. B. (1988), 'Literary and learned culture', in T. M. Devine and R. Mitchison (eds), *People and Society in Scotland, vol. I, 1760–1830*, Edinburgh: John Donald, pp. 127–42.

Myers, J. D. (1972), 'Scottish nationalism and the antecedents of the 1872 Education Act', *Scottish Educational Studies*, 4, pp. 73–92.

Mykland, K. (1979), 'The growth of Norwegian national consciousness in the age of the Enlightenment – the economic, social and cultural factors', in S. Dyrvik, K. Mykland and J. Oldervoll (eds), *The Satellite State in the Seventeenth and Eighteenth Centuries*, Bergen: Universitetforlaget, pp. 185–98.

Nairn, T. (1977), *The Break-Up of Britain*, London: Verso.

—— (1989), 'Tartan power', in S. Hall and M. Jacques (eds), *New Times*, London: Lawrence and Wishart, pp. 243–53.

—— (1993), 'Short-lived era on way out', *The Scotsman*, Edinburgh, 8 February.

Nenadic, S. (1988), 'The rise of the urban middle classes', in T. M. Devine and R. Mitchison (eds), *People and Society in Scotland, vol. I, 1760–1830*, Edinburgh: John Donald, pp. 109–26.

Oakley, S. (1972), *The Story of Denmark*, London: Faber and Faber.

Parliamentary Debates (1989a), *House of Commons Official Report*, 6 March, London: HMSO.

—— (1989b), *House of Commons Official Report*, 21 March, London: HMSO.

Parry, R. (1993), 'Towards a democratised Scottish Office?', *Scottish Affairs*, no. 5, pp. 41–57.

Paterson, A. (1976), 'The new poor law in Scotland after 1845', in D. Fraser (ed.), *The New Poor Law in the Nineteenth Century, 1780–1918*, London: Macmillan.

Paterson, L. (1990), 'Are the Scottish middle class going native?', *Radical Scotland*, no. 45, pp. 10–11.

—— (1991), 'Ane end of ane auld sang: sovereignty and the renegotiation of the Union', in A. Brown and D. McCrone (eds), *Scottish Government Yearbook 1991*, Edinburgh: Unit for the Study of Government in Scotland, pp. 104–22.

—— (1993), 'Regionalism among entrants to higher education from Scottish schools', *Oxford Review of Education*, 19, pp. 231–55.

Paterson, L., Brown, A. and McCrone, D. (1992), 'Constitutional crisis: the causes and consequences of the 1992 Scottish general election result', *Parliamentary Affairs*, 45, pp. 627–39.

Philip, H. L. (1992), *The Higher Tradition: a History of Public Examinations in Scottish Schools and how they Influenced the Development of Secondary Schooling*, Dalkeith: Scottish Examination Board.

Phillipson, N. T. (1969), 'Nationalism and ideology', in J. N. Wolfe (ed.), *Government and Nationalism in Scotland*, Edinburgh: Edinburgh University Press, pp. 167–88.

—— (1970), 'Scottish public opinion and the Union in the Age of the Association', in N. T. Phillipson and R. Mitchison (eds), *Scotland in the Age of Improvement*, Edinburgh: Edinburgh University Press, pp. 125–47.

Poggi, G. (1978), *The Development of the Modern State*, London: Hutchinson.

—— (1990), *The State: its Nature, Development and Prospects*, Cambridge: Polity.

Pritchett, C. H. (1984), *Constitutional Law of the Federal System*, Englewood Cliffs: Prentice-Hall.

Pryde, G. S. (1950), *The Treaty of Union of Scotland and England*, London: Nelson.

—— (n.d.), 'The period of reform', in *Local Government in Scotland*, Dunfermline.

Raab, C. D. (1992), 'Taking networks seriously: education policy in Britain', *European Journal of Political Research*, 21, pp. 69–90.

Randall, J. N. (1985), 'New towns and new industries', in Saville (ed.), *The Economic Development of Modern Scotland, 1950–1980*, Edinburgh: John Donald, pp. 245–69.

Read, J. (1978), *The Catalans*, London: Faber.

Rimlinger, G. V. (1971), *Welfare Policy and Industrialisation in Europe, America, and Russia*, New York: Wiley.

Robertson, D. S. (1989), 'The regeneration of Glasgow: the contribution of community-based housing associations to Glasgow's tenement improvement programme, 1964–1984', *Scottish Geographical Magazine*, 105, pp. 67–75.

—— (1992), 'Scottish home improvement policy, 1945–1975', *Urban Studies*, 29, pp. 1,115–36.

Rodger, A. (1992), 'The codification of commercial law in Victorian Britain', *The Law Quarterly Review*, 109, pp. 570–90.

Rowbotham, S., Segal, L. and Wainwright, H. (1979), *Beyond the Fragments*, London: Merlin.

Said, E. (1993), *Culture and Imperialism*, London: Chatto and Windus.

Sandvik, G. (1979), 'The Norwegian economy in the eighteenth century: a satellite of Denmark?', in S. Dyrvik, K. Mykland and J. Oldervoll (eds), *The Satellite State in the Seventeenth and Eighteenth Centuries*, Bergen: Universitetforlaget, pp. 36–48.

Savage, M. (1988), 'The missing link? The relationship between spatial mobility and social mobility', *British Journal of Sociology*, 39, pp. 554–77.

Saville, R. (1985), 'The industrial background to the post-war Scottish economy', in Saville (ed.), *The Economic Development of Modern Scotland, 1950–1980*, Edinburgh: John Donald, pp. 1–46.

Schlesinger, P. (1992), ' "Europeanness" – a new cultural battlefield?', *Innovation*, 5, pp. 11–23.

Scotland on Sunday (1992), 'Who's who in Scotland poll', 29 March, pp. 33–4.

—— (1993), 'Someone to watch over you', 5 December, pp. 4–5.

The Scotsman (1993), 'Labour and s n p backers get seats on health trusts', 14 January.

Scott, J. and Hughes, M. (1980), *The Anatomy of Scottish Capital*, London: Croom Helm.

Scott, P. H. (1979), *1707: the Union of Scotland and England*, Edinburgh: Chambers.

200   THE AUTONOMY OF MODERN SCOTLAND

—— (1989), *Cultural Independence,* Edinburgh: Scottish Centre for Economic and Social Research.

—— (1992), 'Why did the Scots accept the Treaty of Union?', *Scottish Affairs,* no. 1, pp. 121–6.

Shaw, J. (1942), *Local Government in Scotland,* Edinburgh: Oliver and Boyd.

Sher, R. B. (1982), 'Moderates, managers and popular politics in mid-eighteenth century Edinburgh', in J. Dwyer, R. A. Mason and A. Murdoch (eds), *New Perspectives on the Politics and Culture of Early Modern Scotland,* Edinburgh: John Donald.

—— (1985), *Church and University in the Scottish Enlightenment,* Edinburgh: Edinburgh University Press.

Skinnider, M. (1967), 'Catholic elementary education, 1818–1918', in T. R. Bone (ed.), *Studies in the History of Scottish Education, 1872–1939,* London: University of London Press, pp. 13–70.

Smiley, D. V. (1977a), 'Federal-provincial conflict in Canada', in J. P. Meekison (ed.), *Canadian Federalism: Myth or Reality,* Toronto: Methuen, pp. 2–18.

—— (1977b), 'Cooperative federalism: an evaluation', in J. P. Meekison (ed.), *Canadian Federalism: Myth or Reality,* Toronto: Methuen, pp. 259–77.

—— (1977c), 'Federalism and the public policy process', in J. P. Meekison (ed.), *Canadian Federalism: Myth or Reality,* Toronto: Methuen, pp. 366–74.

Smith, A. D. (1991), *National Identity,* Harmondsworth: Penguin.

Smith, J. A. (1970), 'Some eighteenth century ideas of Scotland', in N. T. Phillipson and R. Mitchison (eds), *Scotland in the Age of Improvement,* Edinburgh: Edinburgh University Press, pp. 107–24.

Smith, P. and Burns, M. (1988), 'The Scottish economy: decline and response', in D. McCrone and A. Brown (eds), *Scottish Government Yearbook 1988,* Edinburgh: Unit for the Study of Government in Scotland, pp. 259–88.

Smout, T. C. (1970), *A History of the Scottish People, 1560–1830,* Glasgow: Collins.

—— (1979), 'Scotland in the seventeenth and eighteenth centuries: a satellite economy?', in S. Dyrvik, K. Mykland and J. Oldervoll (eds), *The Satellite State in the Seventeenth and Eighteenth Centuries,* Bergen: Universitetforlaget, pp. 9–35.

—— (1980), 'Scotland and England: is dependency a symptom or a cause of underdevelopment?', *Review,* 3, pp. 601–30.

—— (1986), *A Century of the Scottish People, 1830–1950,* London: Collins.

—— (1992), 'Patterns of culture', in A. Dickson and J. H. Treble (eds), *People and Society in Scotland, vol. III, 1914–1990,* Edinburgh: John Donald, pp. 261–81.

Solem, E. (1977), *The Nordic Council and Scandinavian Integration,* New York: Praeger.

Stehle, H. (1965), *The Independent Satellite: Society and Politics in Poland since 1945,* London: Pall Mall Press.

Steward, F. and Wield, D. (1984), 'Science, planning and the state', in G. McLennan, D. Held and S. Hall (eds), *State and Society in Contemporary Britain,* Cambridge: Polity, pp. 176–203.

Taylor, A. J. P. (1964), *The Habsburg Monarchy,* Harmondsworth: Peregrine.

Thompson, G. (1984), 'Economic intervention in the post-war economy', in G. McLennan, D. Held and S. Hall (eds), *State and Society in Contemporary Britain,* Cambridge: Polity, pp. 77–118.

Vajda, M. (1988), 'East-central European perspectives', in Keane (ed.), *Civil Society and the State,* London: Verso, pp. 333–60.

Vile, M. J. C. (1961), *The Structure of American Federalism,* Oxford: Oxford University Press.

Wallerstein, I. (1980), 'One man's meat: the Scottish Great Leap Forward', *Review,* 3, pp. 631–40.

Wandycz, P. S. (1974), *The Lands of Partitioned Poland, 1795–1918,* Seattle: University of Washington Press.

—— (1992), *The Price of Freedom: a History of East-Central Europe from the Middle Ages to the Present,* London: Routledge.

Watts, R. L. (1991), 'West German federalism: comparative perspectives', in Jeffrey and Savigear (eds), *German Federalism Today,* Leicester: Leicester University Press, pp. 23–39.

Wendt, F. W. (1958), 'Nordic cooperation – past and present', in J. A. Lauwerys (ed.), *Scandinavian Democracy,* Copenhagen: Danish Institute, pp. 370–87.

Whatley, C. A. (1989), 'Economic causes and consequences of the Union of 1707: a survey', *Scottish Historical Review,* 68, pp. 150–81.

—— (1992), 'An uninflammable people?', in I. Donnachie and C. Whatley (eds), *The Manufacture of Scottish History,* Edinburgh: Polygon, pp. 51–71.

Whetstone, A. E. (1981), *Scottish County Government in the Eighteenth and Nineteenth Centuries,* Edinburgh: John Donald.

Wilson, J. Q. (1985), 'The rise of the bureaucratic state', in F. E. Rourke (ed.), *Bureaucratic Power in National Policy Making,* Boston: Little, Brown, pp. 125–48.

Withrington, D. (1983), '*Scotland a half educated nation in 1834*: reliable critique or persuasive polemic?', in W. M. Humes and H. M. Paterson (eds), *Scottish Culture and Scottish Education,* Edinburgh: John Donald, pp. 55–74.

—— (1992), 'The Scottish universities: living traditions? Old problems renewed?', in L. Paterson and D. McCrone (eds), *The Scottish Government 1992,* Edinburgh: Unit for the Study of Government in Scotland, pp. 131–41.

—— (1993), 'Adrift among the reefs of conflicting ideals? Education and the Free Church, 1843–1855', in Brown and Fry (eds), *Scotland in the Age of the Disruption,* Edinburgh: Edinburgh University Press, pp. 79–97.

Young, A. (1992), 'Scottish Enterprise: a change too far?', *The Herald,* Glasgow, 21 December.

INDEX